D1349683

The Science of
GEOLOGY

D. A. Robson

BLANDFORD PRESS
London

© *Blandford Press* 1968
First published 1968

ERRATA

Page 47. Captions for figs. 55 and 56 are transposed.

Page 52. In fig. 63, 'cole alkali' should read 'calc alkali'.

Page 160. In fig. 206, certain contour lines (in green) are shown inaccurately in that they do not always cross geological boundaries at the intersection of the latter with the strike lines (in red).

Page 233. Fig. 277 should be labelled PLEISTOCENE.

Page 240. Fig. 280 should read '. . . salt on the right and folded Eocene limestone on the left'.

Printed and bound in Great Britain by Jarrold and Sons Ltd, Norwich

Acknowledgements

In producing this book, much help and advice has been received from the author's colleagues in the Department of Geology at the University of Newcastle upon Tyne. Among them, the following should be especially thanked: Dr. Jack Shirley, who, with his expert knowledge has been of great assistance over the chapters on Fossils and Historical Geology; Mr. John Lee, who constructed all the crystal drawings and offered constructive criticism for that part of the text falling under the heading of the Geometry of Crystals; Dr. M. H. Battey, who gave valuable advice on the section dealing with the Internal Structure of Crystals, and Professor J. E. Hemingway for his helpful comments on Chapter V. From the Department of Soil Science, Mr. G. P. Askew offered helpful guidance on the short section on Soils. The author, nevertheless, accepts responsibility for any errors of fact.

The author is indebted to Mr. Eric Lawson for most of the black-and-white drawings, to the Department of Photography in the University for the colour photographs of specimens of rocks and minerals (the latter belonging to the Wallington Collection), and to Dr. Battey for the four colour photographs of rocks in this section. Thanks are also due to Mr. N. L. Falcon, F.R.S., for his colour photograph of diapiric salt, to Mr. J. W. Pallister, O.B.E., for the colour photographs from Somalia, to Mr. Peter G. Robson for the colour view of an Auvergne volcano, to Dr. C. E. Thiébaud for the colour view of the Arabian sands and to Mr. H. S. Thorne, A.R.P.S., for the two colour photographs of the whin sill and dyke in Northumberland. He is also glad to able to include a number of sketches by Mr. Paul Geraghty which appeared in a recent number of the *Transactions of the Natural History Society of Northumberland, Durham and Newcastle Upon Tyne*. Finally, most grateful thanks are due to Mrs. Mary B. McArd, who wrestled for many hours with the draft of the text, and produced the final, typed manuscript.

Blandford Press express their thanks to the following for supplying photographs which illustrate this book.

Almquist & Wiksell Figs. 15, 25
BP Fig. 153
Canadian National Railways Fig. 230
A. Costa Fig. 279
The Explorer's Club Fig. 195
Iceland Tourist Information Bureau Fig. 40
Jarrold & Sons Ltd. Figs. 26, 41, 53, 152, 158, 169, 224, 244, 250
L. F. Johnstone Fig. 22
National Publicity Studios, New Zealand Fig. 168
Photo Survey Inc. Fig. 166
Kenneth Scowen Fig. 247
Shell Fig. 210
Swissair Fig. 170
Dr. J. Wellard Fig. 156

Contents

IN GRATEFUL ACKNOWLEDGEMENT

OF

THE ENTHUSIASTIC AND IMAGINATIVE TEACHING

OF

PROFESSOR GEORGE HICKLING, F.R.S.

1883–1954

Introduction

Diseasèd nature oftentimes breaks forth
In strange eruptions; oft the teeming earth
Is with a kind of cholic pinch'd and vex'd
By the imprisoning of unruly wind
Within her womb; which, for enlargement striving,
Shakes the old beldame earth, and topples down
Steeples and moss-grown towers.

Glendower, in Shakespeare's *King Henry IV*, Part I, Act III,

Scene 1.

Before the days of the earliest civilisations—of Sumeria, Babylon and Ancient Egypt—man was exclusively preoccupied in the quest for food and in the protection of himself and his family against the forces of nature and against his fellow men. He possessed a brain capable of speculation and deduction, but he had little opportunity for exercising it in that way. He was fully engaged in the struggle for survival. If he stopped to think, he ran a considerable risk of stopping altogether. Yet with all the technological advances of the twentieth century this is still true, to our discredit, for over half of the world's population. Even today these people wrest a meagre living from the soil, still restricted to Stone-Age methods.

Pre-historic man, in the countries around the eastern Mediterranean, at length wrenched himself free from the shackles of food-gathering and discovered the technique of food-growing. In cities like Ur, Tell-el-Amarna (the capital of the progressive Egyptian pharaoh, Akhnaton) and Jerusalem, at least some citizens found themselves with time and with the physical security in which to meditate upon the world around them. But even in the most highly developed of these ancient centres of thought—Athens and Alexandria—natural phenomena like volcanic eruptions and earthquakes were still regarded with superstitious awe.

As the influence of the Christian Church grew in Europe, the word of the theologian became law in the most literal sense. It was considered wrong to speculate about the nature of the universe, the age of the earth, the development of life. The final word had been given, and was to be found within the pages of the Bible. Those whose writings sought to amend that law suffered in varying ways—Galileo in the seventeenth century, Darwin in the nineteenth and even Teilhard in our own day.

Thus, though the spirit of enquiry blossomed for a while in Ancient Greece, it was soon smothered and only began to emerge during the sixteenth century, in the days of the Italian Renaissance. The Greeks had excelled in mathematics

7

and philosophy, yet they never grasped the twin essentials of experimental science —those of observation and deduction. Without painstaking observation, deduction can degenerate into superstition. Adams has recalled how Pliny the Elder believed the report that a diamond could be dissolved in goat's blood; he obviously did not test this out for himself. Herodotus observed the minute shells of the Foraminifera which, weathering out from the limestone blocks of the Great Pyramid, litter the adjacent desert surface. He described them as the remains of food left by the pyramid builders, though had he examined them critically he would surely have seen their similarity to the modern shells of the Mediterranean shore.

The giants among the scientific pioneers were those who, in the first place, undertook the arduous discipline of observation and then, in the end, made the deductions upon which depended (as we now know) the future growth of their science. Behind the discoveries of Newton and Faraday lay years of observation and experiment. Darwin's investigations spanned a whole generation before he felt sure enough to announce his theory of evolution.

In the development of the science of geology, there was an early and exhausting struggle during the latter half of the eighteenth century between those (the Neptunists) who believed that basalt was precipitated from the oceans, and those (the Vulcanists) who maintained that it had been derived, in a molten condition, from the depths of the earth. The German, Werner, clung with the utmost tenacity to his precipitation theory against his rival the Scotsman, Hutton, and was only finally discredited through the detailed observations of Desmarest, and later, von Buch, among the extinct volcanoes of the Auvergne. In every branch of science there are similar instances of erroneous conclusions drawn from inadequate evidence.

It seems, however, that what sets apart the greatest scientists of each generation from their fellows is the imagination to draw the correct deductions from their observations. Perhaps every research scientist develops this in some degree. Indeed, Professor Polanyi has argued that what is needed most in the graduate newly embarking on research is the training in 'creative guesswork'. More than a generation ago Sir Arthur Eddington likened this faculty to intuition, to the same kind of inspiration which in some may produce great music or great poetry, and in others the mystical experience.

The word 'geology' comes from the Greek and simply means 'the science of the earth'. The geologist studies the way in which the two fundamental groups of rocks have been formed—the sedimentary strata derived from surface processes and the igneous rocks, the once-molten material, which have been thrust up from the depths of the earth. A third group, the metamorphics, including all those rocks which have, subsequent to their formation, undergone change by means of heat or pressure, also claims the geologist's attention.

By studying the composition and pattern of the sedimentary rocks, the fossils which they contain and the dislocations to which they and the igneous rocks have from time to time been subjected, the geologist can reconstruct the catalogue of changes which have taken place in the distribution of land and sea throughout the ages. As the remoter regions of the earth are explored, so does this catalogue become expanded and modified.

During the greater part of last century, geology remained an interest exclusive to the amateur. But as the science grew and as the demand for the earth's raw materials increased, the professional geologist emerged. Today he, and to a lesser extent she, are to be found working in collaboration with applied scientists in many different fields.

Geology is a wide discipline. With mathematics and physics it shares the study of crystals and minerals; with chemistry the constitution of the rocks; with biology the study of the structure and function of living organisms past and present; with the engineer the problems of water-supply, of the search for oil, coal and mineral deposits; with the geophysicist the evidence about the unseen movements beneath the surface of the earth; with the astronomer the problems concerning the origin of the universe. Above all, the trained geologist should be a field man, sharing with the naturalist the eye which discerns in every feature of the ground—be it desert, jungle or ice-bound mountain chain—the pattern of the underlying rock.

The student in geology, or in any other branch of science, must become familiar, in the first instance, with the great body of knowledge accumulated over the years by research workers in his subject. He will soon find that he may grasp, in an evening, some particular geological principle with which the pioneers wrestled for decades. As a field naturalist—and it is better that every embryo geologist should approach the subject along this path—a few hours in the lecture room and a few days' guidance across the countryside will equip him to make elementary discoveries on his own.

Nevertheless, it is not less arduous to absorb the whole background of the knowledge of earth sciences for examination purposes than it is in other disciplines. This book affords an introduction to this task. It covers the ground for the Advanced Level of the General Certificate of Education, for students in the university year preliminary to the honours course in geology and for those many students reading geology as a subsidiary subject towards a degree in either pure or applied science. For pupils preparing for the Ordinary Level of the G.C.E., certain chapters could be selected.

In planning this book, the author has sought to introduce the reader at once to the field aspects of the subject, by describing the great groups of rocks with their various sub-divisions. This is followed by Chapter IV, a chapter on crystals and minerals—mainly a laboratory study. The reader is next asked to view, in Chapter V, the modern processes of degradation on the earth's surface, processes which afford the key to past geological events. With this general background the study, in Chapter VI, of earth-movements as they have affected the surface of the globe, including the interpretation of geological maps, should naturally follow: while Chapter VII summarises some of the chief lines of evidence concerning the nature of the interior of the earth. Chapter VIII introduces the reader to the study of fossils, while Chapter IX seeks to demonstrate how, by using the evidence described in the previous chapters, the geological history of a region can be reconstructed. The final chapter considers some of the more important aspects of applied geology.

Eras	Periods	Millions of Years *	Earth Movements
QUATERNARY	Holocene (Recent) Pleistocene (Glacial)	0 — 0.025 2	
TERTIARY	Pliocene Miocene Oligocene Eocene	67 65 —	ALPINE
MESOZOIC	Cretaceous	70 135 —	
	Jurassic	55 190 —	
	Triassic ⎫ New Red ⎬ Sandstone Permian ⎭	35 225 — 55 280 —	HERCYNIAN
PALAEOZOIC UPPER ⎰	Carboniferous	65 345 —	
	Devonian Old Red Sandstone	50 395 —	CALEDONIAN
LOWER ⎰	Silurian	45 440 —	
	Ordovician	60 500 —	
	Cambrian	70 570 —	
PRE-CAMBRIAN			

* Approximating to : "The Phanerozoic Time Scale", Geol. Soc. London, 1964

1 Table showing the chief divisions of the sedimentary rocks of the earth's crust, their relationship to the geological time-scale and to the principal mountain-building movements.

I. The Sedimentary Rocks

GENERAL PRINCIPLES

The science of geology includes the study of the most ancient rocks of the earth's surface—those which were first to solidify from the molten state. During the early stages in the slow process of cooling, clouds of sulphurous vapours no doubt enshrouded the globe, but as the temperature of the surface gradually decreased, the time came when a thin skin of solid rock enveloped the earth, forming the CRUST.*

At first, it is assumed that this skin was ruptured and torn by the violent, indiscriminate movements of the liquid rock within, but in time it must have become sufficiently thick and firm to contain all but the more violent eruptions of the interior forces. Meanwhile, conditions had grown cool enough to allow the steam in the atmosphere to condense, to occupy the great depressions and to form the seas and oceans of the world.

The distribution of the continental plateaus and the great ocean trenches, as well as the disposition of the mountain chains with their associated volcanoes and earthquake zones, are matters which still, even after 100 years of geological speculation, await explanation. Nevertheless, especially during the past two decades, instruments like the gravimeter, the magnetometer, the seismograph and the geophone have provided much new information about the interior structure of the earth, and modern geophysical research is contributing extensively to the geologist's knowledge within these fields.

The foundations of modern geological knowledge were firmly laid by the naturalists of last century. Their equipment was limited to the hammer, the clinometer (a simple instrument to measure the inclination of the rock) and the hand-lens (fig. 281). Their laboratory was the countryside itself, a fact which needs to be emphasised in these days when students, and even teachers, may sometimes be tempted to believe that a shiny laboratory instrument is a substitute for field observations and mapping, rather than supplementary to them.

Probably the most important principle in the science of geology was that established by Hutton in the eighteenth century, in the phrase 'the present is the key to the past'; that materials deposited by the action of water, wind or ice are laid down in precisely the same pattern today as at the dawn of geological history. This is the PRINCIPLE OF UNIFORMITARIANISM.

---

* When technical terms appear for the first time in the text, they are written THUS and they are accompanied by an explanation of their meaning. An index of these terms has also been compiled (page 265) so that the reader can refer back to them. Colour figures are referred to in the text in **bold**.

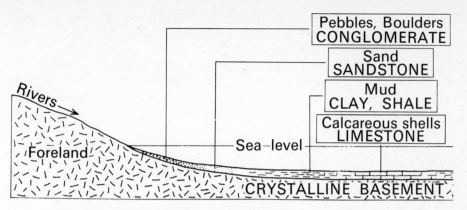

2 Diagrammatic cross-section of a part of the earth's crust, showing the mode of formation of some of the chief sedimentary rocks.

The accompanying diagram (fig. 2) represents a profile of a part of the earth's surface as it might be today, or indeed as it might have been at any time since the formation of the solid crust. In the diagram, crystalline rocks outcrop both across the mountain slopes and on the sea-bed. Rainfall over the mountain summit gathers into streams and rivers which, dislodging loose fragments of rock along their downward paths, carry the material towards the sea. During transport, some of the material is reduced to a fine mud; some is reduced to sand, while the large fragments of more strongly indurated rock are broken into smaller pebbles. Of the material which is carried away by water, the heavy fragments which are rolled or bounced along the river-bed become highly rounded, while the finer fractions, carried in suspension, are cushioned by the water itself and retain their original angular character.

The gradient of a river slackens as it enters the lower reaches, its velocity is reduced as also is its power to transport pebbles and boulders. The latter, together with some sand, are strewn along the river-bed, while the main load of sand and mud is swept on towards the sea. As the river enters the sea, its velocity undergoes a further abrupt reduction and its load of sand is at once deposited, leaving only the fine silt and mud, held in suspension, to be wafted seawards by the much weakened river current.

MECHANICAL DEPOSITS

This process accounts for the formation of one of the main groups of SEDI-MENTARY ROCKS—the MECHANICAL or CLASTIC deposits. The pebbles and boulders, abandoned along the river-bed, become indurated as CONGLO-MERATES (fig. 4); the sands become SANDSTONES (figs. 6, 7), while the muds, their water-content progressively reduced by the weight or OVERBURDEN of the accumulating deposits, are transformed into CLAYS and eventually SHALES.

Conglomerates are also formed from pebble-beds thrown up along the shore by heavy seas. Sandstones as well as conglomerates may be derived from the induration of ancient beach deposits.

In the deposits just described there is always a marginal mingling of pebble-beds with sand and of sand with mud, due to slight variations in the velocity of flow—a process which can readily be demonstrated in the laboratory. When indurated, each particular layer is described as a BED, and adjoining beds of sedimentary rock are said to be separated from one another by BEDDING-PLANES. When a number of beds, say of sandstone, lie one on top of the other, having accumulated under similar conditions, they constitute a FORMATION. A particular bed, traceable laterally for some distance because of a recognisable feature such as colour, grain-size or fossil content, is termed a HORIZON. A number of formations, one succeeding the other may, because of their related characters, be classified as a distinctive GROUP or SERIES of rocks, while any assemblage of beds, either within a formation or a group, is described as a SUCCESSION. The character or 'make-up' of a rock, whether it be sandy, shaly or calcareous, is described as its FACIES. The term LITHOLOGY, confined strictly to sedimentary rocks, has a similar meaning.

Sands laid down in shallow water at a river's mouth usually preserve the pattern which the depositing currents imposed upon them. This pattern is known as CURRENT-BEDDING; it is also referred to as CROSS-BEDDING, CROSS-LAMINATION, CROSS-STRATIFICATION or FALSE-BEDDING. As the diagram shows (fig. 3), in each complete UNIT of current-bedding the BOTTOM-SET, the FORE-SET and the TOP-SET beds can be recognised. However, the top-set beds are generally eroded by the current which lays down the next unit, so that the new bottom-sets are deposited on the tops of the underlying fore-set beds. Thus, units of current-bedding generally succeed one another in a distinctive pattern; ASYMPTOTIC at the base but TRUNCATED at the top. Units of current-bedding seldom exceed four feet in thickness; they may be no more than three inches. Sometimes, in fine-grained sandstones, units only a fraction of an inch thick are developed, constituting RIPPLE-DRIFTING (fig. 9).

If a river should pour its deposits of sand and mud into deep water off-shore, then the material gradually settles. Pebbles sink first, followed successively by increasingly fine grains of sand and mud. Therefore a series of beds is built up which shows a gradation upwards from coarse to fine material. This type of deposit, which is characteristic of deeper water sedimentation, is described as GRADED-BEDDING. Both current-bedding and graded-bedding can be produced under laboratory conditions.

Though conglomerates are always deposited by water action, certain equally coarse deposits may be formed on land. These are the BRECCIAS, or indurated screes consisting of highly angular material; they are formed from the fragmentation of nearby cliffs (fig. 5). Both conglomerates and breccias are described as the RUDACEOUS rocks. Sandstones may also be derived from the land in the

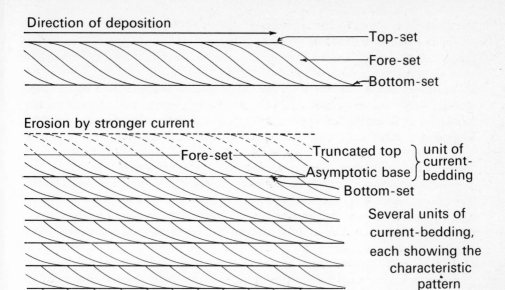

3 Diagrammatic sections showing the formation of current-bedding.

form of wind deposits; ancient sand-dunes, now become rock, can be recognised by the roundness of their individual grains, by the worn surfaces of each grain and by the characteristic DUNE-BEDDING (fig. **8**) in units which, in marked contrast to current-bedding, may sometimes exceed 30 feet in thickness.

A quartz sand (most sandstones consist of at least 90% quartz grains) is light grey or even white, but it may undergo post-depositional or DIAGENETIC changes which transform it into red, purple, yellow, brown or green sandstone. This is the result of CEMENTATION, a process in which solutions precipitate iron oxide, calcium carbonate or even silica round each grain. Often this 'staining' is evenly distributed; sometimes it is irregular and produces intricate patterns in the rock. A sandstone is described according to the cementing material as, for example, FERRUGINOUS, CALCAREOUS, SILICEOUS, etc. (fig. **13**). A ferruginous sandstone, in which the cementing material is limonite, has a yellow or brown shade; when hematite, the colour is red or purple. Glauconite cement, a silicate of iron and potassium, is a green colour. The effectiveness of cementing material in binding grains together varies in different sandstones.

Of the other substances present in a sandstone, one of the commonest is muscovite or white mica. Mica is composed of tiny white plates which are deposited in layers which may be only one plate thick. The frequency of these layers depends upon the availability of mica in the source rock. Sandstones readily split along these micaceous layers which, if only a fraction of an inch apart, form a LAMINATED sandstone. When these parallel layers occur at intervals of one or two inches, the rock is termed a FLAGSTONE. When mica is absent, or when it only occurs at vertical intervals of several feet, the sandstone is described as THICK-BEDDED.

Another common constituent of sandstone is feldspar (fig. **130**). The feldspars are chemically and physically much less stable than quartz, and they commonly undergo chemical change accompanied by physical breakdown, during transport. However, if conditions favour the survival of the feldspars (such as a granite source with rapid transport and chemically neutral waters) an ARKOSE is formed, in which the proportion of feldspars may exceed that of quartz.

Sandstones can be roughly classified in the field, and more accurately in the laboratory, into coarse, medium and fine-grained. GRITS (a term less used now than hitherto) are extremely coarse sandstones, while SILTSTONES—an indurated silt—are very fine-grained sandstones. These rocks are classified under the term ARENACEOUS.

Mud, because of its extraordinary fineness of grain, is deposited by weak currents on the seaward side of the arenaceous material (fig. 2), but it may also be laid down along with the finest grades of sand and silt; such a mixture becomes indurated as a SANDY SHALE. Mud differs from silt not only in grain-size but also in composition. Whereas siltstone is composed largely of minute quartz grains, mud consists of even smaller particles of the 'CLAY MINERALS'. These powdery fragments are derived from the breakdown of decomposition products, mainly of the feldspars, and are dominantly silicates of aluminium; they include illite, montmorillonite and chlorite. A newly deposited mud may contain about 80% by volume of water. In clay, the weight of overburden has reduced the water content to 50%, while in a MUDSTONE it may become as low as 5%. A shale is a laminated mudstone. These rocks are classified as ARGILLA-CEOUS and the process by which water is removed is described as COMPACTION.

The chief clastic deposits are thus:
- Rudaceous—conglomerate, breccia
- Arenaceous—grit, sandstone, siltstone
- Argillaceous—clay, mudstone, shale

Deposits like breccias, dune-sand and till (see page 143), which are formed on land, are described as TERRESTRIAL or SUB-AERIAL. Material which is laid down along the course of a river is termed FLUVIATILE and that deposited in lakes is LACUSTRINE. All material derived from the land but laid down in the sea is called TERRIGENOUS. Terrigenous deposits, therefore, include those in marine estuaries (PARALIC), those laid down at a river's mouth (DELTAIC), those along the shore (LITTORAL) and they may contribute to those spread out over the continental shelf (NERITIC). Terrigenous material may also contribute to the formation of deposits on the floors of the open oceans (PELAGIC), of the moderately deep parts of the oceans (BATHYAL) and of the great depths (ABYSSAL). There is confusion over the term 'terrigenous', since some authorities confine its meaning to describe the neritic deposits of only the continental shelf. Its original definition was established by the H.M.S. *Challenger* Expedition (1872–76), and is used here.

RED CLAY, an extremely fine-grained assemblage of quartz, mica and clay minerals, is terrigenous material which occurs as a pelagic, bathyal and abyssal deposit. Part of this material is derived from volcanic dust, but it is considered that much of it is simply the most finely disseminated of the muds brought down from the land; that because of its very slow rate of settling, it may be swept by ocean currents for many thousands of miles before coming to rest on the ocean floor.

Some clastic rocks show no sign of bedding because their material has been laid down rapidly in one swift event; such rocks are described as MASSIVE. The rock known as GREYWACKE is of this type. Greywacke is a very compact rock consisting of angular fragments of quartz, feldspar and other substances together with rock fragments, all set in a muddy base or MATRIX. It is associated with shales. Deposits of greywacke are found on the edges of the continental shelves.

Controversy still surrounds the origin of greywacke because it is against the normal laws of sedimentation that sand and mud should be laid down together. Some authorities maintain that greywacke is formed by submarine avalanches or TURBIDITY CURRENTS of sand plunging forward and intermingling with deposits of mud; others, that under certain conditions, mud particles will tuft together or FLOCCULATE, and that these tufts form units sufficiently dense to be deposited along with grains of sand; yet others maintain that the original material of a greywacke was of equal grain-size throughout, but that chemical alteration has broken down the less stable substances to produce the fine matrix.

ORGANIC DEPOSITS

The deposits which have accumulated through the death and decay of living organisms form an important group. Of these, by far the most abundant and widespread are the calcareous deposits formed by the shells of sea-living creatures. In the following paragraphs, organic deposits are described.

Calcareous. Many of the marine creatures secrete protective shells. They flourish in shallow waters where there is abundant light and a paucity of terrigenous deposits. When these creatures die, their soft bodies undergo rapid chemical decay and dispersion, but their hard shells accumulate on the sea-floor. Eventually, these shelly layers become indurated to form a limestone. During the course of the process of induration, the substance of the shells may be dissolved and the lime reprecipitated; in such cases the visible pattern of the shelly material is destroyed.

As is to be expected from a deposit laid down over the open sea-floor, deposits of limestone are fairly persistent, in contrast to the markedly local nature of

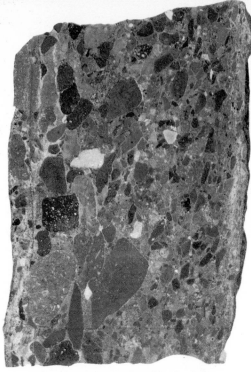

4 Old Red Sandstone conglomerate, Stonehaven.

5 Permian breccia (brockram), Eden Valley.

6 Permian yellow sandstone, Culler-coats, Northumberland.

7 Red sandstone, Berwickshire, from the Old Red Sandstone.

8 The hammer shank lies across the truncated top of a unit of dune-bedding in the Permian sandstones of Corrie, Isle of Arran. The depositional dip is steep, as is often the case with wind-borne sand.

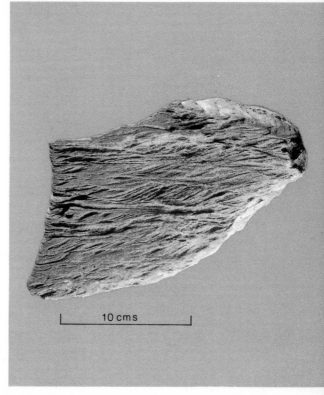

9 Ripple-drifting in sandstone, from the Cementstones, Lower Carboniferous, Northumberland.

10 cms

10 Jurassic oolitic limestone, Gloucestershire.

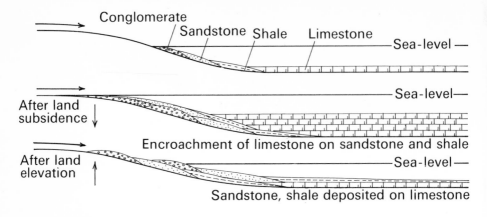

11 Diagrammatic cross-sections showing encroachment of arenaceous and argillaceous deposits upon organic limestones and vice versa.

most sandstones. The thickness of a limestone will depend upon the stability of the earth's crust and upon the influence of the land. For example, conditions once favourable to the formation of a limestone may, by elevation of the sea-bed, be rapidly superseded by a muddy environment, restricting a calcareous deposit to a few feet or even only a few inches in thickness (fig. 11). Constant marine conditions, however, may produce a limestone deposit several hundred feet thick. Since limestone is soluble in streams and rivers containing CO_2, the latter gradually dissolve a passage through these rocks, forming the ramifying channels and enormous underground chambers for which limestone country is so well known.

Limestones are classified according to the type of organism from whose shells they are derived. Coral, algal and foraminiferal limestones are common varieties which are, of course, identical in chemical composition. Clastic limestones are composed of shell remains broken and worn by wave action. CHALK is a pure form of limestone, composed of the shells of minute marine organisms and ooliths (see below), as well as the shells of larger creatures, which accumulated in shallow seas free from terrigenous deposits.

CALCAREOUS OOZE consists of the tiny shells of Foraminifera and the skeletons of plankton; the latter are floating organisms whose hard skeletons sink to the ocean bed when they die. They are found as pelagic deposits only, for any calcareous material is dissolved by the great water-pressure before it can sink to the bathyal and abyssal depths of the ocean. Where calcareous oozes and red clay occur together, the latter is often hidden by the abundance of the ooze.

The diagram (fig. 2) indicates the conditions in the open sea with material being brought down from the land, as described above; it shows that while sand and mud is being laid down near the shore, lime is accumulating in the shallow waters away from the land. There is, of course, a zone in which both mud and lime are being laid down together, and the rock which is the product of this admixture is described as an IMPURE LIMESTONE. This is a flexible term, and impure limestones grade, on the one hand, into dark, almost black CALCAREOUS SHALES or MARLS, and, on the other, into pure light grey or white limestone.

If the earth's crust is stable, without upward or downward movement, the shallow waters will gradually become filled with sediment. This will lead to the extension of the argillaceous and arenaceous deposits at the expense of the calcareous. However, any shift in the relative elevation of land and sea will cause a redistribution of deposits. Thus, while elevation of the sea-bed will be followed by encroachment of arenaceous upon calcareous deposits, subsidence of the sea-bed will cause lime to be laid down over argillaceous and perhaps even over arenaceous deposits (fig. 11).

Carbonaceous. Deposits rich in carbon are derived from the decay of plant remains; therefore while limestones are mainly neritic and pelagic, carbonaceous deposits are terrestrial. The great carbonaceous deposits of the past have arisen from the accumulation of vegetation growing on swampy land at or near sea-level.

The first stage in the transformation of vegetable matter into coal is marked by the formation of PEAT, a brown, crumbly substance when dry, and containing still-recognisable twigs and branches of the parent material. LIGNITE, also known as BROWN COAL, represents the next stage, in which compaction has occurred over a long period of time; the plant remains from the Tertiary era occur in the form of lignite.

BITUMINOUS COAL is the product of a very long process in the compaction of lignite and peat. It is black in colour and consists of numerous layers which are recognisable in the hand specimen. The dull-black, powdery layers contain mineral matter and are described as FUSAIN; fusain-rich coals leave much ash on burning and are therefore of poor quality. The woody material which, in bituminous coal, has resisted complete decay and which includes spore-cases, forms a dull, hard layer known as DURAIN. The completely decomposed plant remains form a structureless coaly layer which is hard and bright, termed VITRAIN. CLARAIN is a mixture of vitrain and durain.

The final stage in the compaction of vegetable matter occurs with the formation of ANTHRACITE, a hard, bright substance without recognisable banding. In anthracite, almost all the volatiles of the original plant material—oxygen, hydrogen, nitrogen—have been driven off and it is described as a substance of high RANK. Peat and lignite are materials of low rank. The transformation of bituminous coal into anthracite may be effected by enormously increased pressure produced by crustal compression in regions of strong folding.

Many coal deposits have accumulated on the very ground where vegetation grew and decayed; these are known as IN SITU deposits. On the other hand,

12 Units of current-bedding in the glacial sands which form a moraine across the Tyne Valley near Riding Mill, Northumberland. The depositional dip is gentle, as is characteristic for water-deposited sands. The succession, being of Pleistocene age, is unconsolidated, yet shows a fault (having a throw of a few inches) passing on the right of the hammer.

13 Calcareous cementing in a bed of Jurassic sandstone, Isle of Eigg, Inner Hebrides. Calcareous solutions have percolated down from an overlying limestone, and have precipitated their contents to form an irregular, firmly cemented 'horse'. The horizontal stratification of the sandstone can be seen running through the 'horse'.

14 Shaly sandstone, showing symmetrical ripples. (Natural size)

15 Sandstone showing asymmetrical ripples.

16 A flow of the Hegebo basalt, forming a protective cap over Cretaceous rocks in Somalia.

the decaying remains may have been swept away by rivers and deposited in extremely thick masses. Such conditions account for the thick coal seams characteristic of some coal-fields in the world; they are the DRIFT deposits. In situ deposits are thin, up to 6 or 8 feet thick, and persistent. Drift deposits are very thick, up to 20 feet, but only of local extent. An accumulation of about 10 feet of peat will eventually compress to 1 foot of coal.

The in situ deposits are generally underlain by several feet of light grey clay which often contains fossil roots. This is the compacted soil on which the vegetation grew, and is termed the SEAT-EARTH or SEGGAR CLAY. Deposits associated with in situ coal seams are generally deltaic—shales and sandstones. Limestones, indicative of marine conditions, are often absent from a coal measure succession.

Phosphatic. The hard parts of certain marine creatures—especially the bony skeleton and the scales of fish—are rich in phosphates. The remains of these animals are found scattered among the rocks of the geological succession, but are sometimes concentrated along certain horizons, providing beds rich in phosphates. Of these, the most important are the so-called BONE-BEDS. They may be only a few inches thick, as that at Ludlow (page 227), or several feet thick as in the deposits of North Africa. There is also evidence that some phosphate deposits are of chemical origin.

Siliceous. The deposit known as SILICEOUS OOZE consists mainly of the shells of the Radiolaria, and is in fact often referred to as RADIOLARIAN OOZE. This highly insoluble siliceous material is deposited, in the deepest parts of the oceans along with the red clay, as a bathyal or abyssal accumulation. These shells are of course also deposited in the shallower waters together with the material which forms the calcareous ooze, but the latter is so much more abundant that the siliceous material (and the red clay) is smothered.

CHEMICAL DEPOSITS

These are generally classified under two headings, namely, the PRECIPITATE and the REPLACEMENT deposits.

Precipitates. Limestone is formed not only through the accumulation of animal remains but also by precipitation in the open seas. This process can be observed, for example, in the shallow areas of the Bahama Banks, where the waters have become saturated with calcium carbonate. Tiny spherical or egg-shaped particles of $CaCO_3$ (either in the form of aragonite or of calcite), known as oolites or (preferably) OOLITHS, are formed. These are generally less than 1 mm in diameter, but when larger than 2 mm in cross-section they are described as PISOLITHS. They possess a concentric structure, indicating growth round a central nucleus which may be either calcite or silica. They form extensive deposits which become indurated as OOLITIC LIMESTONES (fig. 10). Aragonite is chemically less stable than calcite and in course of time it changes to the latter; aragonite ooliths which undergo this change lose their concentric pattern and develop a radial arrangement of crystals.

TRAVERTINE or CALC-SINTER is a compact form of limestone which is deposited from solution by waters either emerging at the surface as springs or percolating down through rock fissures. CALICHE is a calcium deposit formed by the evaporation of lime-rich solutions migrating upwards to the land surface in regions of low rainfall. STALACTITES grow like icicles from the roofs of caves as lime-bearing waters drip from them. STALAGMITES grow up from the points where the drops strike the floor. These calcareous deposits are known collectively as DRIPSTONES.

The commonest of the group of precipitates known as the EVAPORITE deposits are HALITE (rock salt, NaCL), with ANHYDRITE ($CaSO_4$) and its hydrous form GYPSUM ($CaSO_4 . H_2O$). Evaporites are so named because they are precipitated by evaporation, under arid conditions, on the beds of shallow, enclosed lakes or of lagoons having restricted access to the sea. The Dead Sea, between Israel and Jordan, is a good example; the River Jordan, in its course from the mountains of Lebanon, accumulates dissolved salts which eventually pass into the Dead Sea. But the latter has no outlet and its level is controlled by evaporation. The Dead Sea has long since become saturated and therefore cannot take up further salts in solution. So the salts contributed by the Jordan are precipitated and accumulate on the sea-bed, producing an ever-thickening deposit of crystalline salts. There are many examples in the arid regions of the world where evaporite deposits are being formed today, and there are many such deposits among the rocks of past geological ages.

Replacements. The most widespread of the deposits due to chemical replacement is DOLOMITE, a grey or yellow-brown rock. Dolomite is a carbonate in which the calcium has been partially replaced by magnesium, having the chemical composition $CaCO_3 . MgCO_3$. There are conflicting opinions about the origin of dolomite: many authorities believe that it is always of secondary occurrence—that is to say, that the rock was laid down as a limestone ($CaCO_3$), but that the introduction of solutions containing magnesium led to replacement of calcium by magnesium. A limestone, for example, may be dolomitised only in the neighbourhood of fissures. Some consider that dolomite may sometimes have its origin as an evaporite, and point to the frequent association of dolomite with the salt and gypsum deposits.

Rocks composed of a mixture of limestone and dolomite are also described as DOLOMITIC LIMESTONE, and where calcium predominates, as MAGNESIAN LIMESTONE. The recrystallisation which a dolomite rock generally appears to have undergone usually destroys fossil remains and oolitic textures. Dolomites, like limestones, generally show SOLUTION FISSURES, or cracks in the rocks, widened by solution as the penetrating fluids made their way downwards.

CHERT is a siliceous deposit formed of extremely minute crystals of quartz. It varies in colour, which is often white or grey; it also may occur in shades of green, blue or red. Broken fragments form a sharp cutting edge. The term FLINT is synonymous with chert, but it is becoming the practice to confine the use of the world 'flint' to archaeological implements.

Chert occurs either in continuous bands within beds of chalk and limestone, or in nodular form. Though most authorities regard it as a replacement deposit (of calcite by silica), there are some who maintain that it was laid down upon the sea-bed as a 'silica gel'. SILICEOUS SINTER, like its calcareous counterpart, calc-sinter, is deposited by spring waters. PORCELANITE is a cherty rock containing calcareous material.

IRONSTONES include a variety of replacement deposits in which, by definition, the iron content forms not less than 20% of the rock. Iron sulphides (marcasite and pyrite) occur either bedded or in the form of nodules, especially in shales (fig. 114). Iron carbonate (siderite) is found associated with chert, while of the oxides, red iron oxide (hematite, fig. 111) is the most important. All these accumulations of iron compounds are considered to be replacement deposits.

The descriptive study of a rock, which may involve the extensive use of the microscope, is known as petrography; the investigation into its origin is known as petrogenesis, while the term petrology embraces the examination of every aspect of the rock. This chapter, for example, might be described as an introduction to sedimentary petrology, while the following chapter would come under the heading of igneous petrology.

17 Baked limestone lying against the vertical wall of the Lindisfarne dyke, beneath the Heugh (see fig. 19), Northumberland.

18 Hexagonal jointing seen in plan in Tertiary plateau basalts, Isle of Eigg, Inner Hebrides.

19 A whin (dolerite) dyke, 100 feet wide, crosses the southern tip of the Isle of Lindisfarne, Northumberland, forming a prominent feature known as the Heugh. It narrows at the point where the sea has eroded a natural harbour, widening again to the east to form the ridge on which the castle stands. Photographed from the west-north-west.

20 A spectacular outcrop of the the Great Whin (dolerite) Sill, above Crag Lough, Northumberland. The sill is tilted southwards to form a long dip slope towards the Tyne Valley. The associated sediments form recognisable, but less distinct features. The Roman Wall stands along the length of the crag.

II. The Igneous Rocks

VOLCANOES

Before the establishment of the science of geology, volcanic eruptions were the only geological processes being witnessed and recorded by man. The birth of a new volcano, like Paracutin in Mexico, can never fail to impress an observer whether he be from the Stone Age or in the twentieth century. In a matter of weeks, or even days, a volcanic eruption can obliterate the character of the countryside for many miles around, by a thick covering of steaming, jagged rock which engulfs what was hitherto quiet woodland or cultivated fields.

The products of volcanic activity belong to one of a number of groups of rocks, all of which have been derived from within the earth in the molten state. They are described as the IGNEOUS rocks. The volcanic products themselves are collectively termed EXTRUSIVE. The groups other than the volcanoes will be considered later in this chapter.

The Composite Volcanoes. Paracutin began as a wisp of GAS in a farmer's field in 1943. Gas is present in all volcanic eruptions, often as a dominant product, sometimes only subsidiary. The commonest volcanic gases are steam and compounds of sulphur, carbon and chlorine. Paracutin's initial emission was followed, within a few hours, by an eruption of stones and blocks of rock torn by the enormously increased gas pressure from the sides of the VENT; this is the vertical, circular duct through which the exploding gases find their way to the surface.

Within 24 hours of Paracutin's birth a CONE of loose rubble, over 100 feet high, had been built up round the central depression, or CRATER, with the vent at its centre. At this stage, the molten rock within the earth (MAGMA) began to well up and, under the pressure of the associated gases, was hurled into the air in white-hot liquid lumps, rising to a height of 10,000 feet. As they descended they cooled and became consolidated as VOLCANIC BOMBS. These bombs, a foot or more in diameter, together with the blocks of country rock torn from the walls of the vent, constitute AGGLOMERATE or VOLCANIC BRECCIA. The finer material, including LAPILLI or fragments of lava the size of small pebbles, is termed TUFF, while the dust-like, glowing particles are known as ASH. This term is misleading; it was described as such at a time when it was thought to be burning, combustible material, like the products of a coal fire. All this volcanic ejectamenta is collectively described as PYROCLAST.

Magma, on reaching the surface through volcanic activity, is described as LAVA. In explosive volcanoes, lava seldom emerges from the central crater, but

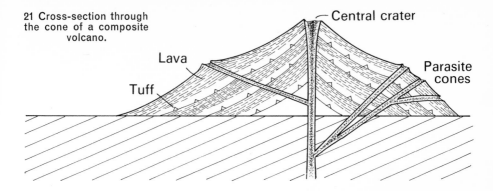

21 Cross-section through the cone of a composite volcano.

Central crater

Lava

Tuff

Parasite cones

rather forces its way out through circular conduits in the loose ashy slopes of the cone. In the case of Paracutin, flow upon flow issued from the flanks of the volcano, spreading for several miles over country which had already been buried under pyroclast. By the time Paracutin had exhausted itself, after a decade of unbroken activity, the summit of the cone stood over 1,300 feet above the fields and villages which lay buried beneath it.

Volcanoes of the Paracutin type, in which pyroclast and lava alternate, are described as COMPOSITE (fig. 21). Most of the world's volcanoes are of this type, and include the perfectly symmetrical cones of Fujiyama in Japan, Cotopaxi in Ecuador and Ngauruhoe in New Zealand (fig. 22). However, within the group there is considerable variation in behaviour, depending upon the viscosity of the lava and presumably upon the conditions within the subterranean magma chamber. Stromboli, in the Mediterranean, erupts explosively at intervals of several minutes. The eruptive product is mainly incandescent lava. Occasionally the lava solidifies within the vent, when gas pressures build up below it and eventually produce an explosion of greatly increased violence. The nearby volcano, known as Vulcano, exudes lava which is more viscous than that of Stromboli and which therefore more readily congeals. In intervals between eruptions, a long column of lava solidifies in the vent, pressures build up over a longer period of time and the climax is reached in a shattering explosion. Vesuvius is similar, though the interval of time between periods of eruption is measured in decades rather than in years or months. During early historical times, Vesuvius was thought to be extinct, but activity was suddenly renewed in A.D. 79. The eruption has been described in a vivid account by the nephew of Pliny the Elder, who told how the latter died at the very foot of Vesuvius, poisoned by the fumes.

In modern times, the most violent of all recorded eruptions was that of Krakatoa, which lies in the Sunda Strait between the Indonesian islands of Java and Sumatra. Krakatoa had been quiescent for some 200 years when in 1883, after three months of moderately explosive eruptions, the cone was rent and dispersed by a catastrophic explosion. Ash blackened the sky and fell widely over

22 Mount Ngauruhoe, one of New Zealand's active volcanoes. Like Fujiyama in Japan and Cotopaxi in Ecuador, it has a perfectly symmetrical cone.

23 A village in the Auvergne district of France, built on the slopes of an extinct late Tertiary volcano.

24 Vesicular basalt (Kenya) with vesicles drawn out in direction of flow.

25 Vesicular basalt (Sweden) with infilled vesicles (amygdales).

26 Cliffs of Tertiary plateau basalts forming the coast of Antrim, Northern Ireland. The junction between individual lava flows can be seen. The castle is that of Dunluce.

27 St. Pierre, after its destruction by the nuée ardente which erupted from Mt. Pelée. The latter, with its spine, can be seen in the background.

the surrounding islands. The volcanic dust remained in suspension in the air and gradually encircled the globe. The displacement of enormous volumes of water created tidal waves 100 feet high, and thousands of people, living in the coastal districts of the neighbouring islands, were drowned. When the pall around Krakatoa had settled, it was found that the volcanic island had almost entirely disappeared.

Equally destructive of human life, but more restricted in the circle of its destruction, was the eruption of Mont Pélée on the island of Martinique. In the spring of 1902, after 50 years of quiescence, Mont Pélée began to erupt with a series of Vesuvian-like outbursts. These were followed, within a few months, by a gigantic detonation which hurled a cloud of exploding gas and lava high into the air. It descended on the flanks of the volcano, rolled down its slopes and enveloped the city of St. Pierre, which stood directly in its path. In this catastrophe 30,000 people suffered an instantaneous death. The lava, which had blocked the path of the growing forces within the vent up to the moment of the explosion, was highly viscous, and in the autumn of the same year a spine of this lava, now consolidated, was forced upwards. It came to rest as its top towered several hundred feet above the summit of the cone (fig. 27).

These avalanches of exploding pyroclast, such as that which burst out of Mont Pélée, are by no means an uncommon occurrence in association with violent volcanic explosions. They are described as NUÉES ARDENTES. This finely disseminated material settles round the flanks of the volcano and often contains sufficient heat within itself to cause individual particles to adhere together, giving the appearance of a lava flow. Such deposits are known as WELDED TUFFS. IGNIMBRITE, a more general term, may contain fragments of varying sizes within the welded tuff; that is, fragments already cooled before the nuée ardente is actually deposited.

The Pyroclast Volcanoes. Some volcanoes are short-lived and their products are confined to pyroclastic material and gas. A cone of ash, tuff and agglomerate may be built up in a matter of hours or days and eruption may then cease. Paracutin, in its earlier stages, produced only pyroclast and gas; Barcena, off the coast of Mexico, which erupted in 1952, is an ash cone which rises to a height of 1,000 feet. The last phase in the activity of this volcano occurred within a year of its inception, when lava flowed from its base. Another example of an ash cone is that of Monte Nuovo adjacent to Vesuvius, which, over 400 years ago, in a single eruption attained a height of several hundred feet and then ceased all activity. Small PARASITIC CONES composed entirely of ash, may also form on the flanks of a volcano. Such cones, when in a late stage of activity, emit only gas; they are then described as FUMAROLES. Another example of the late phase of volcanic activity is the GEYSER, a hot spring from which steam and hot water is explosively discharged at intervals (fig. **40**).

The Lava Volcanoes. There are many volcanoes whose eruptive products are dominantly lava with only subsidiary phases of pyroclastic activity. The lava in these volcanoes is generally highly fluid and spreads out widely from the central vent. The slope of the cone is extremely low, generally not exceeding 3 or 4 degrees, in contrast to the ash cone with its slope of 35 degrees. Moreover, the lava emerges not only from the central vent but also from fissures on the flanks of the volcano. On account of the shape of the cone, it is described as a SHIELD VOLCANO (fig. 28). Mauna Loa, in Hawaii, is the text-book example of a shield volcano; but others occur in Samoa, for example, and in Iceland. Mauna Loa rises to a height of 30,000 feet above the ocean-bed, having a base about 70 miles in diameter.

The fluidity of a lava flow depends upon its chemical composition. Magma contains oxides of silicon, aluminium, potassium, sodium, calcium, iron and magnesium in varying proportions. A magma rich in silica (and with it, alumina,

28 Diagrammatic cross-section through a shield volcano.

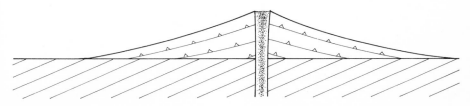

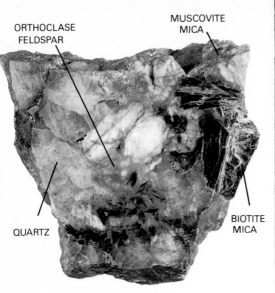

ORTHOCLASE FELDSPAR

MUSCOVITE MICA

QUARTZ

BIOTITE MICA

FELDSPAR PHENOCRYSTS

29 Pegmatite with quartz (white), orthoclase feldspar (pink), muscovite (grey). (Natural size)

30 Granite (Shap) with large phenocrysts of orthoclase feldspar (pink) in ground of quartz (white), orthoclase feldspar (pink) and biotite (black). (Natural size)

31 Granite (Rubislaw, Aberdeen) with quartz, orthoclase (grey) and biotite. (Natural size)

32 Granite (Peterhead) with quartz, orthoclase (pink) and biotite. (Natural size)

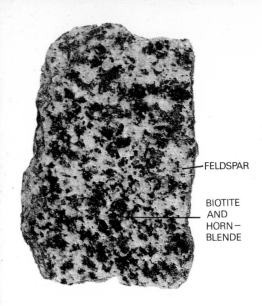

FELDSPAR

BIOTITE
AND
HORN-
BLENDE

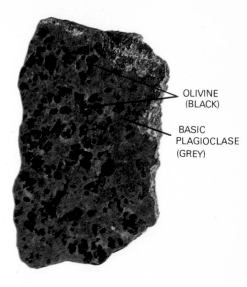

OLIVINE
(BLACK)

BASIC
PLAGIOCLASE
(GREY)

33 Diorite with plagioclase feldspar (grey), hornblende (black) and biotite (black). (Natural size)

34 Gabbro (Belhelvie, Aberdeen) with plagioclase (dark grey) and olivine (black). (Natural size)

35 Peridotite (Belhelvie, Aberdeen) with augite (black) and oliving (black). (Natural size)

36 Dolerite (Cullernose Point, Northumberland) with laths of plagioclase feldspar. (Natural size)

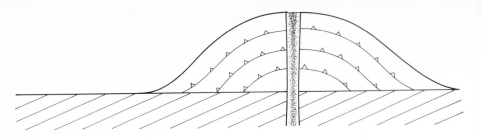

37 Diagrammatic cross-section through a puy volcano.

potash and soda) is described as ACID; a magma in which iron and magnesium is high at the expense of silica and its associated oxides, is BASIC or ULTRA-BASIC. Between the acid and the basic groups lie the rocks INTERMEDIATE in composition. Figure 63 indicates the limiting percentages of silica for these groups. Basalt is a typical basic lava; because of its high fluidity, entrapped gases can easily emerge without explosive violence.

Acid lavas are highly viscous and it is because of this that they are generally associated with violent eruptions. In an eruption where acid lava rather than pyroclast is dominant, the shape of the cone is bulbous in contrast to the shield form of the basalt volcano. The bulbous cone is described as a PUY, after the characteristic shape of the extinct volcanoes of the Auvergne in central France (figs. **23** and 37).

Plateau Basalts. Without exception, the volcanoes which are active at the present time emit their products from a central, more or less circular vent. Yet in the past this has not always been the case. There are many examples across the world in which highly fluid lavas have been erupted from long vertical cracks in the earth. These are classed as FISSURE ERUPTIONS (in contrast to the CENTRAL ERUPTIONS) and their products form the PLATEAU BASALTS, so-called because they provide a cover of lava of even thickness over a wide area of ground. The plateau basalts of Antrim, Northern Ireland (fig. **26**), attain a thickness approaching 1,000 feet and must, at the time of eruption, have covered well over 100,000 square miles of the earth's surface. In Antrim, the fissures (filled with basalt)

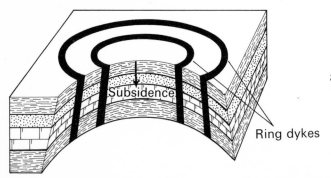

38 Diagram showing ring-dykes.

Subsidence

Ring dykes

36

39 Crater Lake, Oregon, with its caldera and subsidiary cone.

through which the material passed on its way to the surface, can today be seen penetrating the older flows. Plateau basalts also form much of the Isles of Skye, Mull and Eigg, Inner Hebrides, as well as the whole of Canna and Muck.

The Laki fissure in Iceland affords the only known example of fissure eruption in historical times. This occurred about 200 years ago when a 20-mile length of fissure opened and disgorged a series of basalt flows. This lava buried an area 10 miles across and extended in tongues over a much wider zone. The eruption ended in a pyroclastic phase, with the development of numerous conelets along the length of the fissure. Today, the Laki fissure stands as a unique reminder of the way in which the material of the plateau basalts reached the surface in past geological ages.

Calderas. In many volcanoes, both ancient and modern, the long slope up to the summit of the cone is abruptly broken by a precipitous, inward-facing circular cliff of volcanic material. This cliff encloses a depression varying in diameter in different volcanoes from half a mile to more than a dozen miles. Within the depression, which may lie 1,000 feet below the rim of the cliff, one or more volcanic cones may be developed; or, as in the case of Mauna Loa, a lava lake may occupy the entire depression.

These depressions are known as CALDERAS. It used to be thought that calderas owed their origin to the shattering of the top of the volcano by explosive force. This, indeed, may be so in the case of the smaller volcanoes, with calderas approaching half a mile in diameter. But it is now generally believed that the majority are formed through subsidence. During the course of a prolonged eruption, the evidence suggests that the magma reservoir beneath the cone became exhausted, and that therefore the support for the central part of the volcano was removed; it is a matter of observation that concentric fissures have developed as the volcano subsided and that lava welled up into these fissures, forming the well-known RING DYKES (fig. 38). The evidence for the mechanism has been established not only by observation of modern volcanoes but also by close study of deeply eroded ancient volcanoes—like those at Slieve Gullion, Northern Ireland, and Glencoe, Scotland. A classic example of a recently extinct volcano of this type is Crater Lake, Oregon, U.S.A. (fig. 39). The process is described as CAULDRON SUBSIDENCE.

40 An Icelandic geyser, a late phase of Tertiary volcanic activity.

41 The regular hexagonal jointing of Tertiary basalts, the Giant's Causeway, on the coast of Antrim, Northern Ireland.

Volcanic Plugs. Many of the geologically ancient volcanoes and lava-fields have been eroded down to or below the old surface on which the erupted materials accumulated. In such cases, only the lava-filled vent, known as the PLUG, is preserved as evidence of former volcanic activity. These plugs, roughly circular, vary from under 100 feet to a mile in diameter. The material of the plug is generally much more resistant to erosion than the country-rock into which it has been emplaced, and therefore volcanic plugs form very prominent and recognisable features of the countryside.

The detailed structure of the plug itself has been the subject of much investigation in recent years. It includes not only volcanic material but also blocks of the country-rock which had become loosened and torn away by the violence of the uprush of fragment-charged gases. In some cases, where the eruptive products have been dominantly tuffaceous, it can be shown that great blocks of country-rock have been wedged off from the walls of the vent and have come to rest, surrounded by pyroclast, only slightly below their original position. This consolidated pyroclast is described as TUFFISITE.

Lava Structures. It is characteristic of basic lava that it flows extensively from the source of eruption. However, its viscosity varies with the volume of dissolved gas. A basalt which has lost much of its contained gas becomes viscous and breaks into irregular, rugged fragments or SCORIA, described as BLOCK LAVA. It is more widely known by its Hawaiian term AA (pronounced ah-ah, and ascribed by a wit to the ejaculations of the Hawaiians as they walk barefoot across its sharp surfaces!). Basalts which retain their dissolved gas remain fluid and advance in coherent flows; on cooling, they form wrinkled surfaces described as ROPY LAVA (Hawaiian: PAHOEHOE, pronounced 'pa-ho-e-ho-e').

When basalt is erupted into shallow water, it tends to subdivide into blocks a foot or so in diameter. By rapid cooling each block gains a thin skin; the interior lava remains liquid and the whole block rolls forward like a caterpillar tractor. These individual fragments eventually come to rest, piled up against each other, forming PILLOW LAVAS. Another form of submarine lava, usually showing pillow structure, but erupted in deep water, is SPILITE. A spilite differs from a normal basalt in composition because the water-pressure has prevented the escape of gas, and also has stimulated a chemical reaction between the sea-water and the basalt itself.

The upper surface of a lava flow often presents an appearance very different from its base. The lower layers are generally uniformly compact but the upper layers become cracked and punctured by cavities left by gas during its explosive release. These cavities are described as VESICLES (fig. 24). At some later date they may become filled with a chemical compound—silica itself is perhaps the commonest—to form AMYGDALES (fig. 25). Of these, the agate stone is the best known. Highly vesicular lava is known as PUMICE.

The ramifying fractures in the uppermost layers of certain ancient lava flows, often a mere fraction of an inch wide, are sometimes filled with a deposit of silt, showing graded-bedding. This is quite common among the lavas of the Old Red Sandstone in Britain (see page 227), which are frequently inter-bedded with shallow-water sandstones. These SANDSTONE DYKES are particularly well preserved in the lavas along the shore south of Montrose, Scotland.

When a mud-surface dries, a polygonal pattern of cracks develops. If the drying occurs evenly throughout the material, the polygons appear as regular hexagons. The same pattern can develop in a basalt flow. As it cools from the molten state, the basalt shrinks, and cracks or JOINTS are initiated. If the cooling is evenly distributed throughout the rock, a highly symmetrical hexagonal system of joints develops, producing sets of columns which run at right angles to the cooling surface. This COLUMNAR JOINTING is perfectly developed in the rare examples of the Giant's Causeway in Northern Ireland (fig. 41) and of Fingal's Cave on the Island of Staffa. It can be seen in other areas where the plateau basalts occur, though the hexagons are usually less symmetrical (fig. 18).

Distribution of Volcanoes. Almost all the active and recently extinct volcanoes of the world are found along recognised zones of weakness across the earth's surface, that is, against the great mountain chains and rift valleys. The map (fig. 42) shows their distribution: a line of volcanoes extends along the western margin of the Americas, extends across Alaska, the Aleutian Islands and down the Japanese archipelago to New Guinea and New Zealand. This is the so-called

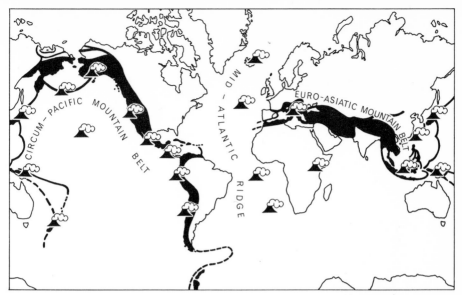

42 World distribution of volcanoes which are still or were recently active. The trend of the Tertiary mountain chains is shown in black.

Circum-Pacific belt. From New Guinea, a branch runs westwards through Indonesia, the Malay Peninsula to Italy and central France, while a third line is developed along the mid-Atlantic ridge. The belt of volcanoes in central Africa is associated with the great depression in the earth's surface known as the African Rift. Finally, there are the group of mid-Pacific volcanoes, including Hawaii, which lie within the Circum-Pacific belt.

A similar disposition of volcanoes can be traced in past geological times. To take one example: in central and South Scotland there were many centres of volcanic eruption associated with the old Caledonian mountain chain which extended across what is now the Scottish Highlands (see page 224). The eruptive products of the Scottish volcanoes, now often deeply eroded, may be examined in Forfarshire, Argyll, Ayrshire and in the Cheviot Hills (fig. 214). These ancient volcanic deposits, like those of widely differing ages all over the world, reveal characters identical with the modern eruptions—yet another example of the principle that 'the present is the key to the past'.

INTRUSIONS

The previous pages recorded some of the information obtained from the detailed study of present-day volcanic processes, and showed how such information can provide the key to the origin of ancient eruptive deposits. The other great group of igneous material is formed by the INTRUSIVE ROCKS and must now be considered. By definition, the members of this group are those which are formed

41

43 Dolerite (Cullernose Point, Northumberland), showing spheroidal weathering. (Natural size)

44 Rhyolite with phenocrysts of quartz (white) and biotite (black) in a ground of feldspar (pink). (Natural size)

45 Rhyolite (Threlkeld, Cumberland) with phenocrysts of feldspar (grey) in a ground of feldspar. (Natural size)

FELDSPAR
PHENOCRYSTS

GROUND
MASS

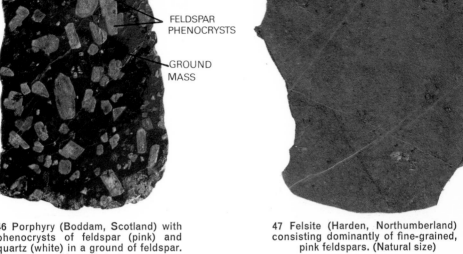

46 Porphyry (Boddam, Scotland) with phenocrysts of feldspar (pink) and quartz (white) in a ground of feldspar. (Natural size)

47 Felsite (Harden, Northumberland) consisting dominantly of fine-grained, pink feldspars. (Natural size)

48 Basalt (Eycott Hill, Cumberland) with phenocrysts of feldspar (grey) in ground of feldspar mainly. (Natural size)

49 Pitchstone (Isle of Arran) showing glassy texture.

from the molten magma as it comes to rest within the earth's crust. Therefore the process of intrusion is hidden from the observer.

However, many of these intrusive bodies eventually become exposed at the surface through removal, by denudation, of the overlying rock. Their relationship to the surrounding country-rock, their texture (see pages 49–54) and chemical composition can then be studied. This has enabled geologists to establish a classification which is based upon both field and laboratory evidence. Furthermore, advances in the development of modern instruments often enable the shape, extent and depth of igneous bodies to be predicted, even though they still lie, entombed, beneath hundreds of feet of overburden.

Major Intrusions. Just as, during certain phases of the earth's history, widespread volcanic eruptions have occurred, so there have been periods when intrusive igneous activity has been dominant. This can take place on a very large scale indeed, with the intrusion of the BATHOLITH. A batholith is the largest of the PLUTONS (or PLUTONIC ROCKS, large bodies of magma intruded into the crustal rocks) ranging in diameter or in length to well over 100 miles. Bodies of this size are found in many different parts of the world, and are particularly associated with mountain chains. Smaller plutons, known as STOCKS and BOSSES (the latter term is reserved for those which are circular in cross-section) and having a diameter of under 20 miles, are very widespread (figs. 50a

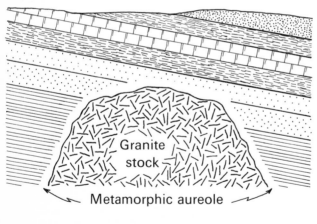

50a Cross-section through a buried stock.

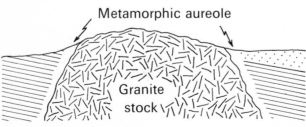

50b Cross-section through a stock exposed by denudation.

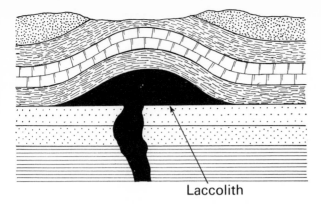

Laccolith

and b). The geological map of the British Isles (fig. **214**) shows a few examples of granite plutons in South-west England (fig. **53**), and many in Scotland.

These igneous bodies can be recognised in the field by the size of their outcrop and by the fact that, because of the enormous amount of heat involved at the time of their intrusion, the materials in the adjacent country-rock have become altered. This change in the character of the surrounding rock is described in Chapter III.

Another form of major intrusion is the LACCOLITH (fig. 51), produced when the magma forces up the overlying strata, the underlying rocks meanwhile remaining flat. If the overlying rock should be penetrated rather then merely thrown up, the structure becomes a DIAPIR. The LOPOLITH is an enormous sagging sheet of magma forming a basin-like structure, of which the Bushveld Complex in South Africa, having a diameter of over 200 miles, is the largest known example. A PHACOLITH, the reverse of a lopolith, is a dome-like structure with an arched base (fig. 52).

Minor Intrusions. Whereas major intrusions owe their emplacement to forceful intrusion from the depth, often with absorption of the country rock, MINOR INTRUSIONS are permissive in the sense that the magma occupies a zone of

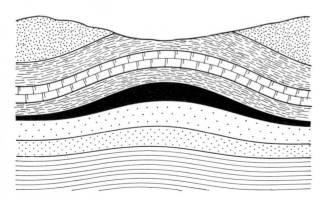

53 Jointing well developed in the stock of granite which forms the cliffs at Land's End, Cornwall.

54 Granite (Rubislaw, Aberdeen) in plane polarised light. Showing pleochroic, elongated crystals of biotite which appear dark when orientated north–south and light when east–west. Quartz crystals white and clear; feldspars grey and 'smudgy' (due to partial alteration).

56 Gabbro (Belhelvie, Aberdeen) under crossed polaroids. Olivine can be recognised by its numerous cracks filled with opaque iron ores and by its strong polarisation colours of yellow, purple and green. The feldspars show repeated twinning.

55 Granite (Rubislaw, Aberdeen) under crossed polaroids. The same section as fig. 54 showing brown polarisation colours of biotite and bright colours of muscovite (this mineral is almost invisible under plane polarised light). Outlines of anhedral quartz crystals are clearly seen and feldspars show simple twinning.

57 Basalt (Isle of Arran) under crossed polaroids. Olivines appear in shades of red, green and yellow while the feldspars are lath-shaped and show repeated twinning.

58 Basaltic dykes cutting granite in the Sinai desert, Egypt.

weakness which has opened out for it. For example, when the crust of the earth is subjected to horizontal tension, vertical fissures appear, into which magma may be intruded, in the form of a DYKE (figs. **19** and 58). A dyke reaching the surface at the time of intrusion would form a fissure eruption (see page 36). Tension at certain levels up the fissure may be such as to cause the advancing magma to be diverted laterally between the adjacent layered rocks. A body formed in this way is known as a SILL, and the dyke supplying the material is described as a FEEDER DYKE (figs. **20** and 59). A sill which cuts across the strata from time to time is said to be TRANSGRESSIVE. Both dykes and sills may represent a history of repeated intrusions, into the same fissure, of material of similar composition; they are then said to be MULTIPLE. Those in which successive intrusions vary in composition are termed COMPOSITE (fig. 60). Ring

59 Sill (with its feeder-dyke), producing a dominant topographical feature. Compare with **20**.

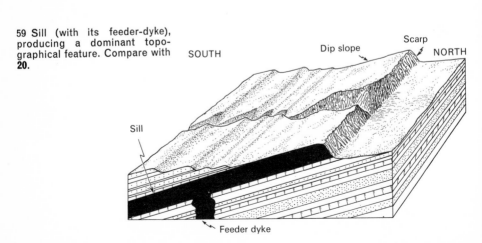

SOUTH

Dip slope

Scarp

NORTH

Sill

Feeder dyke

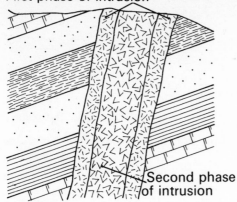

First phase of intrusion

Second phase of intrusion

60 Cross-section through a composite dyke.

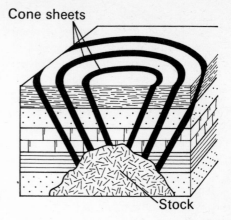

Cone sheets

Stock

61 Diagram showing cone-sheets.

dykes, as described above (see page 37), are found in association with calderas, while CONE-SHEETS are produced by magma being intruded into the outward sloping fissures which may develop above a batholith or stock (fig. 61). Laccoliths, lopoliths and phacoliths may develop through the local swelling of a dyke or a sill; they are then classed as minor rather than as major intrusions.

Jointing (see page 40) occurs in intrusive bodies as well as in lava flows. As in lava flows, the joints develop at right angles to the cooling surfaces—producing in a dyke horizontal, and in a sill, vertical columns. In major intrusions, especially granites, horizontal fissures develop, producing the characteristic MURAL JOINTING, so-called from its wall-like appearance.

THE CHEMISTRY OF IGNEOUS ROCKS

Reference has already been made to the chemical composition of magma and to the importance of its main constituent, silica (see page 33). Silica is present in almost all the so-called ROCK-FORMING MINERALS. Minerals are chemical compounds, usually crystalline, being the constituents of all rocks. Some rocks are monomineralic; most are polymineralic. The chemical composition of a mineral remains constant; that of a rock may vary because it is a mixture of minerals. A list of the chief rock-forming minerals, in the order in which they crystallise, is given below. There is some overlapping within this order; in particular, those plagioclase feldspars rich in calcium begin to crystallise at higher temperatures, along with the components rich in iron and magnesium (i.e. FERROMAGNESIANS like olivine and enstatite). Moreover, as is indicated (below), reaction between crystals and melt frequently eliminates the earlier-formed SPECIES. (Crystals and minerals having the same composition and/or structure are said to belong to the same species. The term is also used in classifying organisms, page 189):

49

Apatite—a phosphate of calcium, with fluorine or chlorine

Sphene (titanite)—a silicate of titanium and calcium

Zircon—a silicate of zirconium

Magnetite—magnetic oxide of iron

Hematite—'kidney' oxide of iron or specular oxide of iron

Limonite—hydrated oxide of iron (rust)

Olivine—a silicate of iron and magnesium

Enstatite—a silicate of magnesium
Hypersthene—a silicate of iron and magnesium } the orthorhombic pyroxenes

Augite—a silicate of aluminium, calcium, iron and magnesium (monoclinic pyroxene)

Hornblende—a silicate of aluminium, sodium, calcium, iron and magnesium (an amphibole)

Biotite—a silicate of hydrogen, aluminium, potassium, iron and magnesium (black mica)

Muscovite—a silicate of hydrogen, aluminium and potassium (white mica)

Plagioclase feldspar—a silicate of sodium and calcium (in varying proportions) and aluminium

Orthoclase feldspar—a silicate of potassium and aluminium

Quartz—silica

Microcline—a silicate of potassium and aluminium (like orthoclase but with a different crystal form)

|
Decreasing
|
temperature
↓

During the process of crystallisation, a cooling magma or MELT undergoes continuous chemical change as the growing crystals abstract material from it. Consider basalt: Olivine will crystallise early, but with falling temperature the composition of the melt may become unstable for olivine, and a reaction will then take place between the olivine and the melt itself. The result is that the olivines are dissolved, partially or wholly, and contribute to the formation of pyroxenes which are stable at the lower temperature. The reaction, however,

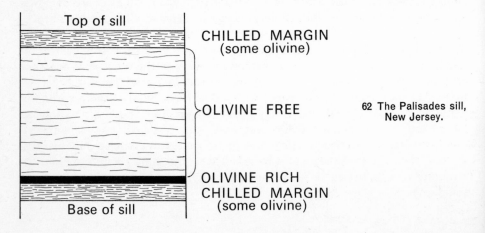

Top of sill

CHILLED MARGIN
(some olivine)

OLIVINE FREE

OLIVINE RICH
CHILLED MARGIN
(some olivine)

Base of sill

62 The Palisades sill, New Jersey.

may not be complete and a crystal having an internal core of olivine may be left with an outer shell of pyroxene known as a REACTION RIM. Alternatively, the olivines may be removed by gravitational sinking, to'be preserved on the floor of the intrusive body. This is precisely what occurred in the thick Palisades sill, New Jersey; the CHILLED MARGINS (where the sill rapidly cooled and consolidated against the country-rock) represent the original composition of the intrusion, and contain a little olivine. As the main part of the interior cooled, olivine was the first to crystallise and sank by gravitation. Therefore the body of the consolidated sill lacks olivine, but contains a concentration of these crystals at the base, immediately above the lower chilled margin. The final mineral distribution in the sill is as shown on the diagram (fig. 62), and is an example of GRAVITATIONAL DIFFERENTIATION.

Differentiation may explain the wide variation in rock types, from those rich in silica to those composed dominantly of ferromagnesians; if it is true that the material below the crust is basic or ultrabasic, then intrusion of a melt having the composition of granite may have occurred after the ferromagnesian minerals had already been filtered away in the depth by gravitation. There is no doubt, too, that digestion of the country-rock by the magma in a stock or batholith can profoundly alter the final composition of the consolidated intrusion. Fragments of only partially digested country-rock, varying from the microscopic to the size of an elephant's head, are described as XENOLITHS. The colour and texture of xenoliths generally distinguish them from the enveloping pluton.

The igneous rocks are classified on the basis of grain-size and chemical composition. Grain-size is considered under 'texture', below. Chemical composition relies upon the ratio of ferromagnesian (dark-coloured or basic and ultrabasic) to silica-rich (light-coloured or acid) materials, and is based upon silica percentage; chemical composition also takes into account the proportion of alkali-feldspar (potash or soda-rich) to calc-alkali feldspar (lime-rich). The accompanying diagram (fig. 63) illustrates this classification and indicates the composition and grain-size of 30 of the common igneous rocks. Of these rocks GRANITE, RHYOLITE, DIORITE, ANDESITE and BASALT are the most widespread.

TEXTURES IN IGNEOUS ROCKS

By TEXTURE is meant the size, shape and arrangement of crystals within a consolidated igneous body. For example, rocks from a batholith or a stock can be recognised in the laboratory by their texture. It is a well-established law that 'slow cooling promotes crystallisation' and that, conversely, if a magma is cooled rapidly it solidifies into an AMORPHOUS mass (having no crystalline form) known as a GLASS. A major intrusion—possessing an enormous volume of heat compared to the area of surface through which, alone, that heat can escape—cools slowly and therefore yields large crystals. Such a rock is said to possess a COARSE-GRAINED texture.

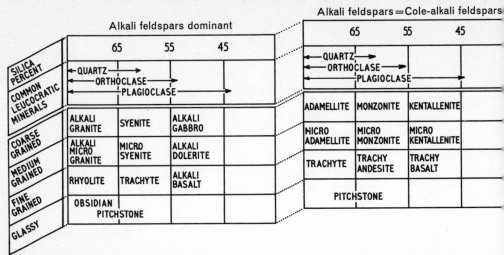

Minor intrusions, being smaller bodies, contain far less heat than the plutons and therefore they cool more rapidly. The rocks of the minor intrusions are MEDIUM-GRAINED, except for their chilled margins, a few inches wide, lying in contact with the country-rock where cooling is rapid. These chilled margins are consequently FINE-GRAINED. There is inevitably some overlap between these definitions; in a sill which is several hundred feet thick or in a dyke several hundred feet wide, the crystal texture of the interior may be as coarse as that of a major intrusion. On the other hand, cooling in a dyke which is only a few inches thick, or in a sill of comparable thickness, may be so rapid as to permit only a fine-grained or even a glassy texture, indistinguishable in the hand specimen from that of a lava flow, which is invariably fine-grained or glassy.

The shape of a mineral in an igneous body depends upon its place in the order of crystallisation. The first crystals to appear are able to grow, unimpeded, in the liquid magma; they can therefore develop their natural crystal faces and are said to be EUHEDRAL or IDIOMORPHIC. Those which begin to form in what has already become a loose framework of crystals, are subjected to some restriction in growth and are unable to develop, fully, their external crystal shape; they are termed SUBHEDRAL or HYPIDIOMORPHIC. Those, like quartz and microcline, which are the last to crystallise, exhibit no external crystal shape but are able only to fill in the gaps between the now close meshwork of crystals; they are described as ANHEDRAL or ALLOTRIOMORPHIC.

An igneous glass may contain extremely fine-grained crystals, too small to be identified even under the microscope; such a texture is termed CRYPTO-CRYSTALLINE. An igneous body consisting partly of glass and partly of crystals is said to be HEMICRYSTALLINE, while a wholly crystalline mass is described as HOLOCRYSTALLINE.

When two sets of crystals of different species grow at the same time, they penetrate one another, and this texture, on a microscopic scale, is described as

Cole-alkali feldspars dominant

	65	55	45	
◄QUARTZ→				
◄—ORTHOCLASE→				
◄————————PLAGIOCLASE————————►				
GRANO-DIORITE	DIORITE	GABBRO	PICRITE PERIDOTITE
MICRO GRANO-DIORITE	MICRO DIORITE	DOLERITE	
DACITE	ANDESITE	BASALT	
	TACHYLYTE		

63 Table showing the classification of igneous rocks in terms of grain-size and chemical composition.

MICROGRAPHIC INTERGROWTH. When individual crystals of an early-formed species become entirely enclosed within those which have crystallised later (i.e. olivine within pyroxene), the texture is described as POIKILITIC. In the special case of feldspar which is often to be found partially or wholly enveloped by augite, the texture is termed OPHITIC. Occasionally, late-forming crystals are able to develop their own form by growing into minute cavities known as DRUSY CAVITIES.

Under certain conditions within the liquid magma, there may be two phases of crystallisation. The first phase takes place before intrusion or eruption, and the early-formed crystals remain floating in the melt. The second phase occurs after the body has been emplaced or extruded so that the earlier and larger crystals are termed PHENOCRYSTS and the texture is described as PORPHY-RITIC (figs. **30, 44–46**). Porphyritic texture is very common in volcanics and minor intrusions; less common in the rocks of major intrusions. In medium and fine-grained rocks there is often an alignment of the lath-shaped feldspars, some-times seen sweeping round the phenocrysts, in the direction along which the body was moving just before final consolidation; this is described as TRACHYTIC- or FLOW-TEXTURE, and is particularly common among the lime-feldspar rocks known as TRACHYTE.

PEGMATITES (fig. **29**) are extremely coarse-grained rocks (containing quartz, feldspar and mica) found in veins generally within the granite parent rock. They represent the final phase in the consolidation of a magma. The intrusive material is made very mobile by the presence of superheated water, and this accounts for the large grains—often several inches across, exceptionally even several feet—which are formed. APLITES, like pegmatites, are also the product of the final stages of consolidation, and consist of quartz with some feldspar. Aplites are much finer in grain than the pegmatites and have probably been formed under conditions in which the volatiles were less active. A MIGMATITE is a rock consisting of a mixture of the pre-existing country-rock and the intruded granite.

Figure 63 combines the chemistry and textures of igneous rocks into a comprehensive classification. The main rock-types are given, though there are many others which, if included, would occupy intermediate positions within the table. Textures are classified, in the vertical columns, according to the description given in the text.

The position in the table of the rock-types according to chemical composition depends upon two factors:

1. The amount of silica—for example, the acid igneous rocks contain over 65% of silica and include quartz and orthoclase feldspar; the intermediate rocks contain 55–65% silica (with or without crystals of quartz—'free quartz'); the basic rocks vary between 45 and 55% in silica content while the ultrabasics show less than 45% silica, together with a very high proportion of ferromagnesian minerals.

2. The proportion of alkali feldspars to calc-alkali feldspars in each rock—for example, the alkali feldspars include orthoclase (rich in potash) and acid plagioclase (rich in soda) while the calc-alkali feldspars are the basic plagioclases (rich in lime). Of the three rectangles comprising the table, that on the left illustrates rocks which have a preponderance of alkali over calc-alkali feldspars, that in the centre has about equal proportions of each, while that on the right lists rocks with a preponderance of calc-alkali over alkali feldspars. This is further demonstrated by the distribution of LEUCOCRATIC or light-coloured minerals, of which quartz and feldspar are the most important.

To illustrate this classification, some of the rocks within the coarse-grained division may be considered: ALKALI GRANITE and ALKALI GABBRO resemble one another in that both contain feldspars having a preponderance of alkalis over lime (though in the gabbro the alkali is represented entirely by soda, since orthoclase feldspar is not present). The two rocks differ from one another in that alkali gabbro is both much richer in ferromagnesians and much poorer in silica than the alkali granite. On the other hand, alkali granite and GRANODIORITE possess the same abundance of silica and the same paucity of ferromagnesian minerals, but differ in that the feldspar in the granodiorite is predominantly calc-alkali, that is lime-bearing.

The ultrabasic rocks, PICRITE and PERIDOTITE, occur only in very deep intrusions and therefore are confined to the division of the major intrusions (coarse-grained). Furthermore, the feldspars which are present in these rocks are exclusively lime-rich silicates. As is also seen from the table, the classification of the glasses is confined to four rock-types. The appearance of the rocks in the coloured illustrations (figs. **29–36** and **44–49**) should be studied by the reader and related to their position in fig. 63.

54

III. The Metamorphic Rocks

METAMORPHISM literally means a change of form. In geology the term is used to refer to certain types of change only. A rock is described as a product of metamorphism if, after being subjected to heat and pressure, it still retains some of its original sedimentary or igneous pattern. The process is distinct from diagenesis. Diagenetic processes include all the varieties of change which a sedimentary rock may undergo, under conditions of normal temperature and pressure of overburden, at any time after its deposition. For example, a limestone may be transformed into a dolomite, a porous sandstone may become firmly cemented by the precipitation of iron oxide between its grains, a clay may be subjected to compaction to form a shale (page 15). Metamorphism is also distinct from migmatisation. This occurs when sedimentary rock is melted and interpenetrated by tongues or lenses from a magmatic intrusion. As described at the end of the previous chapter and as the name implies, it is a mixed rock.

Metamorphism involves recrystallisation but not melting; heat may cause a crystal to react with the surrounding material, and pressure with heat may also produce a change in its shape. Metamorphism is dependent upon the interaction of three variables, namely heat, pressure and the chemical composition of the original rock. Changes in rocks which are brought about by heat from an igneous intrusion are said to be due to CONTACT (also called THERMAL) metamorphism; changes due to pressure but also with considerable increase in heat are ascribed to REGIONAL (also called DYNAMIC) metamorphism.

CONTACT METAMORPHISM

When a minor intrusion like a dyke or sill is injected into a varied sedimentary succession, the changes that occur in the sediments will depend chiefly upon the heat involved and upon the mineral composition of each formation; pressure will play a very minor role. A sandstone becomes affected within a few feet or a few inches of the contact with the intrusion, depending upon the width or thickness of the latter and thus upon the heat contained within it. This process is described as BAKING (fig. 17), and the sandstone is recrystallised as a close-textured and more indurated METAQUARTZITE. A coal seam, being much more sensitive to heat change, is cindered.

However, these changes due to contact metamorphism are more profitably studied in the neighbourhood of a major intrusion, where the influence of heat is much more extensive. These changes occur in a zone around the intrusion, known as the METAMORPHIC AUREOLE (fig. 50). Metaquartzites are again formed, and limestones are changed to MARBLE—a close-textured crystalline rock having the same chemical composition ($CaCO_3$). A pure limestone, heated artificially under atmospheric pressure, evolves carbon dioxide, leaving lime: $CaCO_3 \rightarrow CaO + CO_2 \uparrow$. But this reaction is unknown in nature, presumably because even a low weight of overburden is sufficient to inhibit it. However, at shallow depths, CO_2 may be evolved in the course of the metamorphism of impure limestones, and the following reactions occur, leading to the production of new rock types:

At low temperature, the metamorphism of a limestone containing both silica and magnesium gives FORSTERITE MARBLE:

$$2(CaCO_3 . MgCO_3) + SiO_2 \rightarrow 2CaCO_3 + Mg_2SiO_4 \text{ (forsterite)} + 2CO_2 \uparrow$$

At rather higher temperatures, dolomitic limestone is changed to BRUCITE MARBLE:

$$CaCO_3 . MgCO_3 + H_2O \rightarrow CaCO_3 \text{ (marble)} + Mg(OH)_2 \text{ (brucite)} + CO_2 \uparrow$$

At very high temperatures, a siliceous limestone is converted to WOLLASTONITE MARBLE:

$$CaCO_3 + SiO_2 \rightarrow CaSiO_3 \text{ (wollastonite)} + CO_2 \uparrow$$

At great depths, where the pressures become enormous, these reactions cannot occur. Metaquartzites and marbles, composed of equidimensional grains, are said to possess a GRANULAR texture.

Shales possess a greater sensitivity to heat than either sandstones or limestones and their metamorphic derivatives are more complex. In the neighbourhood of a major intrusion, a shale may have become completely recrystallised, forming a hard, granular rock. This is known as a HORNFELS (fig. **134**). In addition to a fine-grained ground it may contain large crystals, for example of andalusite, called PORPHYROBLASTS. Successive concentric zones in the aureole outside the hornfels ring may show varying degrees of metamorphism, each zone containing minerals which were stable under the temperatures prevailing within that zone at the time of intrusion. Thus, a granite intrusion may have an aureole in which porphyroblasts appear in succession from the contact outwards as follows: silliminite, cordierite, andalusite and finally in the least affected zone, chlorite. It may be that the contact between a hornfels and the igneous intrusion is not abrupt but is blurred by a zone in which the magma has reacted with the country-rock; this zone is then ascribed to migmatisation rather than to meta-

Slaty or flow cleavage in folded strata

64 Development of slaty cleavage in a folded succession.

morphism (see above). Furthermore, within the metamorphic aureole there may be areas in which the influence of circulating gases and liquids from the intrusion has been dominant; such products should be ascribed to pneumatolytic and hydrothermal action respectively (see page 260) rather than to metamorphism. The origin of some rocks is in doubt; they may be in part either metamorphic, metasomatic or migmatic.

REGIONAL METAMORPHISM

In regional metamorphism, stress is the dominant factor, with heat playing a very important part. The so-called index minerals are developed in zones which are related to the distribution of regional pressure and temperature at the time of their formation. Whereas contact metamorphism is confined to areas at most a few square miles in extent, the effects of regional metamorphism may embrace many hundreds of square miles of the earth's crust, most notably in the great mountain chains of the world.

The products of regional metamorphism may be classified in three grades. In the lowest grade, shales under the influence of stress develop minute flakes of mica, chlorite and sericite; these minerals grow with their flat surfaces at right angles to the direction of greatest compression and produce a series of closely set parallel planes along which the rock will readily split. This property is described as SLATY CLEAVAGE or FLOW CLEAVAGE and the rock itself is called a SLATE (fig. 138). Such rocks, in which the mineral FABRIC is related to the stress direction, are described as TECTONITES, possessing a PREFERRED ORIENTATION.

As the diagram (fig. 64) indicates, slaty cleavage may be parallel to, or inclined at any angle to the bedding. It is to be found on the fringes of a folded mountain region, as for example the Southern Uplands of Scotland, where the rocks have been isoclinally folded (see page 226).

PHYLLITES mark the next stage in the process of low-grade metamorphism. They are rather coarser in grain than the slates, but still show the parallel

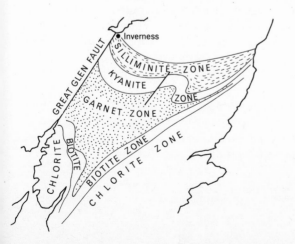

65 The Barrow zones across the Central Highlands of Scotland.

57

development of minerals, including mica. These minerals develop a wavy pattern and obliterate the slaty cleavage. In both slates and phyllites, iron oxides and organic matter react to produce cubes of pyrite (FeS_2). The low-grade regional metamorphism of sandstones and limestones leads again to the formation of metaquartzites and fine-grained marbles respectively, but with little reaction between the parent material and the impurities.

With the development of medium-grade regional metamorphism, slates and phyllites are replaced by quite coarse-grained rocks which are often rich in mica. The micas, which may be developed partly by compression and partly by deformation, lie in beds along with the more equidimensional minerals, including porphyroblasts of garnet (fig. 129), silliminite and kyanite. They impart a fabric to the rock which is much more wavy or FOLIATED than that of the phyllites; it is known as SCHIST. These rocks may be specified as, for example GARNET SCHIST, MUSCOVITE SCHIST, STAUROLITE SCHIST (figs. 135, 136), etc., according to the dominant minerals present.

Sandstones which have undergone medium-grade metamorphism often show micas together with elongated quartz grains, while impure limestones develop diopside, epidote and hornblende. Basic rocks exposed to medium-grade metamorphism often develop plagioclase and hornblende, and are described as AMPHIBOLITES.

GNEISS is a product of high-grade metamorphism in which the schistose character is largely replaced by a granular texture. The rock is coarse-grained and when derived from schists it may contain quartz with mica, garnet, silliminite and kyanite; when derived from quartzite it consists chiefly of quartz and feldspar; when it originates from marble with impurities, the resulting gneiss contains diopside and hornblende. Basic rocks which have been metamorphosed to gneiss form a rock similar to amphibolite. ECLOGITE, consisting of a magnesian-garnet and a soda-rich pyroxene, may possibly be regarded as a gneiss formed under conditions of very high temperature and pressure in the depths of the crust.

A characteristic feature of a gneiss is its banded appearance. Sometimes the deforming pressures cause a concentration of bunches of feldspar porphyroblasts along these bands, giving the appearance of 'eye' structure, known as AUGEN GNEISS. Some gneisses may be produced by the interaction of igneous magma with metamorphic rocks and are thus, strictly speaking, the product of the process of migmatisation.

The result of detailed study of metamorphic areas has led to the establishment of the concept of zones, based upon the species of minerals developed in each zone. Thus in Scotland, the Dalradian and Moine schists, south of the Great Glen, show a decreasing grade of metamorphism from north-east to south-west, with successive mineral facies of silliminite, kyanite, staurolite, garnet, biotite and chlorite (fig. 65). These are known as the BARROW ZONES, named after the geologist by whose researches they became established.

IV. Crystals and Minerals

THE INTERNAL STRUCTURE OF CRYSTALS

The Structure of the Atom. During the nineteenth century, the chemistry of matter was based on Dalton's theory that ATOMS are the fundamental particles and that they combine with one another to form MOLECULES. The atom is almost infinitesimally minute; 30 million atoms could be arranged alongside one another on a pin-head. Atoms of the same kind, linked together, form the simplest of chemical substances, known as ELEMENTS. When atoms of different kinds combine together, CHEMICAL COMPOUNDS are formed. Certain chemical substances including oxygen, mercury, carbon and copper, exist in the natural state as elements, but the vast bulk of the earth's material is composed of compounds—such as combinations of the elements oxygen and hydrogen to form water, oxygen and carbon to form carbon dioxide, oxygen and silicon to form silica.

At the turn of the century, the discovery of X-rays led to a much closer scrutiny of the atom than had hitherto been possible, and the nuclear theory was advanced to supplement that of Dalton. Workers in the nuclear field were able to show that the atom is itself composed of a number of different particles, of which the PROTON, the ELECTRON and the NEUTRON are of chief importance in the processes of chemical reactions. The protons, each bearing a positive unit charge of electricity, lie at the centre of the atom and with the neutrons (which carry no electric charge) constitute the NUCLEUS. The electrons, bearing each a negative unit charge, revolve in orbit round the nucleus (fig. 66).

Each atom of a particular element bears its own constant and specific number of protons, constituting the ATOMIC NUMBER for that element. No two elements contain the same number of protons in their atoms. For each proton there is a corresponding electron and, since unlike charges attract one another,

66 The structure of the hydrogen, helium, neon and argon atoms.

The electron with a negative charge

The proton within the nucleus bearing a positive charge

THE HYDROGEN ATOM THE HELIUM ATOM THE NEON ATOM THE ARGON ATOM

an atom is in a state of electrostatic equilibrium. Hydrogen, for example, possesses one proton and one electron; neon has 10 and uranium has 92 of each.

The sum of the protons and neutrons in the nucleus constitutes what is known as the MASS NUMBER for a particular element. But the atoms in some elements may be of two or more kinds, differing only by the number of neutrons in their nuclei. These varieties, otherwise identical, are described as ISOTOPES. For example, two of the isotopes of uranium, distinguished from one another by their different mass numbers, are U^{235} and U^{238}, with 143 and 146 neutrons respectively. In uranium these neutrons, added to the number of protons in each isotope, which in each atom is constant at 92, give the mass numbers 235 and 238. In geology, the analysis of isotopes plays an important part in calculating the age of the earth (Chapter VII).

In each atom, as mentioned above, the electrons may be pictured as occupying orbits around the nucleus, within which they continuously revolve. As the atomic number in successive elements increases (and hence the number of electrons), the arrangement of the electrons in their orbits becomes more complicated. However, this arrangement remains simple in elements in the Periodic Table bearing low atomic numbers, and is as follows: There are a number of shells within which the electrons may be considered to orbit; the innermost shell, known as K, can contain no more than two electrons, while the second and third shells, L and M respectively, can have up to eight electrons each. But each inner shell must bear its full complement. These facts are illustrated in the following table:

Element:	Shells: K	L	M	Element:	Shells: K	L	M
Hydrogen (H)	1			Neon (Ne)	2	8	
Helium (He)	2			Sodium (Na)	2	8	1
Lithium (Li)	2	1		Magnesium (Mg)	2	8	2
Beryllium (Be)	2	2		Aluminium (Al)	2	8	3
Boron (B)	2	3		Silicon (Si)	2	8	4
Carbon (C)	2	4		Phosphorus (P)	2	8	5
Nitrogen (N)	2	5		Sulphur (S)	2	8	6
Oxygen (O)	2	6		Chlorine (Cl)	2	8	7
Fluorine (F)	2	7		Argon (A)	2	8	8

It can be seen from this table, and the accompanying diagram (fig. 66) that helium has its full complement of two electrons which fills the K shell only, neon's electrons fill both the K and the L shells while in argon the K, L and M shells each have their full complement. These are inert gases and they are stable substances.

Combinations of Atoms. However, elements are unstable if their outermost shells do not possess their full complement of electrons. Those with a small

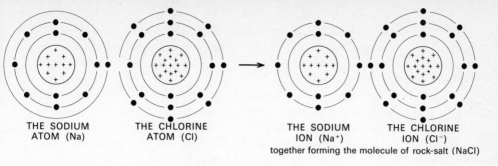

THE SODIUM
ATOM (Na)

THE CHLORINE
ATOM (Cl)

THE SODIUM
ION (Na⁺)

THE CHLORINE
ION (Cl⁻)

together forming the molecule of rock-salt (NaCl)

67 Ionic bonding as illustrated by the sodium
and chlorine atoms.

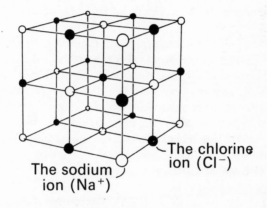

The chlorine
ion (Cl⁻)

The sodium
ion (Na⁺)

68 The crystal lattice of rock-salt.

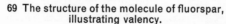

69 The structure of the molecule of fluorspar,
illustrating valency.

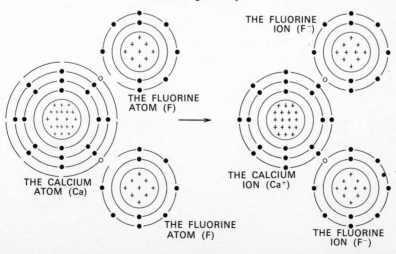

THE FLUORINE
ION (F⁻)

THE FLUORINE
ATOM (F)

THE CALCIUM
ATOM (Ca)

THE FLUORINE
ATOM (F)

THE CALCIUM
ION (Ca⁺)

THE FLUORINE
ION (F⁻)

number of electrons in the outermost shell become ELECTRON DONORS and yield them to other atoms; those with a larger number but less than the full complement act as ELECTRON RECEPTORS and accept electrons from the donor atoms.

Therefore, if two unstable substances, having these conditions within their atoms, are brought into juxtaposition, such an exchange may take place. When this occurs, each pair of involved atoms is thrown out of electrostatic equilibrium; the atoms of the one having lost a balancing negative charge now have a positive charge, while the others will have acquired an extra negative charge. Since unlike electrical charges attract one another, the charged atoms of the two substances are therefore drawn together to form a stable chemical compound. This process, which always involves only the electrons of the outermost shell round the nucleus, is described as IONISATION, and the charged atoms are termed IONS.

The mineral halite, or rock salt, is a compound of the elements sodium (Na) and chlorine (Cl), having the chemical formula NaCl. In the outermost shell of the sodium atom there is only one electron, while in that of the chlorine there are seven. Thus, if the sodium atom acts as a donor to the chlorine atom and loses one electron, its next inner shell will have the stable number of eight electrons while chlorine will have obtained the necessary single electron to make its outermost shell stable. By this means the sodium atoms become positive ions (Na^+) and the chlorine atoms become negative ions (Cl^-); they will be attracted to one another to form a stable chemical compound. The sodium ion is described as electro-positive and is a CATION; the chlorine ion is electro-negative and is an ANION. This process is described as IONIC BONDING (fig. 67).

X-ray analysis of crystals is able to demonstrate that the external form of a crystal reflects its internal ionic structure, and shows that the ions are arranged in a precise pattern, known as the SPACE LATTICE or CRYSTAL LATTICE. The crystal lattice of rock salt, throughout which one ion of sodium is balanced by one ion of chlorine, has a unit of pattern which is a cube. This in turn gives to the crystal its cubic form (fig. 68).

In rock salt, where constituent atoms have gained or lost one electron, each ion is said to have a VALENCY of one and the electrons in the outermost shell are described as VALENCY ELECTRONS. In the same way fluorspar, which has the

70 The structure of the molecule of oxygen, illustrating covalent bonding.

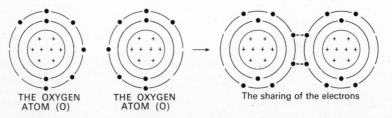

THE OXYGEN ATOM (O)　　　THE OXYGEN ATOM (O)　　　The sharing of the electrons

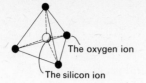

The oxygen ion

The silicon ion

71 The lattice diagram of
the silica tetrahedron.

chemical formula CaF_2, has a pattern of ionic bonding in which two ions of fluorine balance one of calcium. Therefore calcium has a valency of two, whilst fluorine is univalent (fig. 69).

Another type of combination of atoms is known as COVALENT BONDING, as distinct from ionic bonding. In this type of bonding, there is a sharing, not a transference of electrons. For example, the outermost shell of the oxygen atom lacks two electrons, but if pairs of oxygen atoms share, then each atom obtains eight electrons in its outermost shell, forming a stable gas (fig. 70). The combination of oxygen and silicon provides another example. The outermost shell of silicon possesses only four electrons, and when oxygen and silicon atoms are brought together, each of the latter forms reaction pairs with four oxygen atoms. This, however, still leaves four oxygen electrons unbalanced—one electron in the outermost shell of each oxygen atom. Therefore, the resulting complex atom, the SILICA TETRAHEDRON (fig. 71), has four unsatisfied negative charges and must combine with other atoms before it can achieve stability. The commonest and most stable combination is that in which each oxygen atom of the silica tetrahedron shares an electron with an oxygen atom of the neighbouring tetrahedron (fig. 72) forming the mineral, silica. Another pattern of the tetrahedron is developed when atoms of iron or magnesium (each with two electrons in their outermost shells) are introduced; each shares its electrons with two adjacent oxygen atoms of the silica tetrahedron. This example of covalent bonding forms the basis of the olivine series.

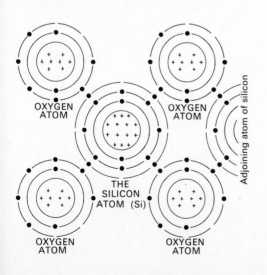

OXYGEN ATOM

OXYGEN ATOM

Adjoining atom of silicon

THE SILICON ATOM (Si)

OXYGEN ATOM

OXYGEN ATOM

72 The structure of the molecule of silica.

63

Atomic Radii. The dimensions of an atom, from its outermost shell to the centre of the nucleus, is described as the ATOMIC RADIUS. Its measurements can be obtained on evidence provided by X-rays; these measurements are expressed in Ångstrom units. One Ångstrom is one ten-millionth part of a millimetre or one ten-thousandth part of a micron. In a positively charged ion, the electrons are drawn somewhat closer to the nucleus than in the uncharged atom, and therefore the ionic radius is less than the atomic radius—in the case of silicon, 0·42 Å as against 1·17 Å. In a negatively charged ion, the shells expand because of the mutual repulsion of the electrons and therefore the ionic radius is greater than the atomic radius—in the case of oxygen 1·40 Å as against 0·60 Å.

The olivine series provides an important example of replacement of one atom by another, in this case between magnesium and iron. This is made possible not only because these elements possess the same valency but also because their atomic radii are similar. Thus, the possible additional atoms in the silica tetrahedron may be entirely iron (forming the mineral fayalite) or entirely magnesium (the mineral forsterite) or they may be any proportion of the two. This forsterite-fayalite series forms what is termed a SOLID SOLUTION, and provides an example of an ISOMORPHOUS SERIES.

In elements whose chemical properties are similar, the formation of solid solutions nevertheless is unlikely to occur if there are considerable differences in the size of their ionic radii. Thus sodium and calcium, with ionic radii of 0·97 Å and 0·99 Å respectively, readily form the plagioclase solid solution, whereas potassium (with ionic radius of 1·35 Å) though with similar chemical properties, will combine in solid solution with either sodium or calcium only under special conditions.

Polymorphism. Certain substances, having precisely the same chemical composition, may yet develop two quite distinct forms of crystal. Graphite and

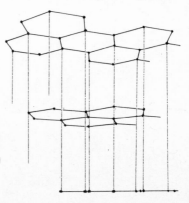

74 The lattice diagram of graphite.

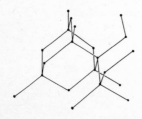

73 The lattice diagram of diamond.

diamond are the best examples of this phenomenon, known as POLYMORPHISM. Both are pure carbon, but whereas diamond is the hardest of all known substances, graphite rubs away between the fingers. The reason is to be found in the nature of the crystal bonding of the two substances. The atom of carbon has only four electrons in its outer shell, but in diamond each atom is linked with its four neighbours (fig. 73). By means of this sharing of electrons (another example of covalent bonding), each outer shell possesses the equivalent of eight electrons. Graphite, on the other hand, has its atoms arranged in sheets. Within every sheet, each carbon atom is securely bound to its three neighbours, while it is only loosely bound to the corresponding atoms in the adjacent sheets (fig. 74). The arrangement of atoms in carbon is the cause of its pronounced property of breaking away in parallel sheets, which is described as CLEAVAGE. Biotite is another example. Other crystal substances may possess two or more planes of cleavage. Calcite has three of such planes. They are invariably a reflection of the atomic structure of a crystal.

THE GEOMETRY OF CRYSTALS

In the last section it has been shown how the space-lattice arrangement of atoms or ions constitutes the internal structure of all crystals. This section introduces the subject of CRYSTALLOGRAPHY, which is the study of crystal geometry. Crystallography demonstrates that the internal structure of a crystal may be reflected in its external shape. This is not always so; a crystal may grow in a confined space or the crystallising solution may not be uniform in concentration, with the result that its external shape can become quite distorted.

Definitions. Rutley described crystals as 'bodies bounded by surfaces, usually flat, arranged on a definite plan which is an expression of the internal arrangement of the atoms'. These surfaces, which only in rare cases are curved, are called FACES. Some crystals, like the simple cube of fluorspar, may be composed entirely of identical faces. These are known as LIKE FACES and constitute a SIMPLE FORM. Other crystals are made up of a set of two or more different kinds of faces and these are termed UNLIKE FACES, constituting a COMBINATION. A simple form, in which the entire crystal is composed of like faces, is said to be CLOSED; a group of like faces which cannot alone enclose space, is described as OPEN. The cube (fig. 75a) is a closed form as also is the octahedron (fig. 85), while the combination shown in figure 75b consists of the two closed forms of cube and octahedron. But the faces of the tetragonal prism (defined below) constitute an open form (fig. 76) because they cannot by themselves enclose space. The characteristic shape into which a crystal normally grows is defined as its HABIT (fig. 78).

The line of intersection between any two faces is described as the EDGE, and the angle between the normals to these two, or indeed to any two faces, is the INTERFACIAL ANGLE (fig. 77). Crystal faces are parallel to planes within the

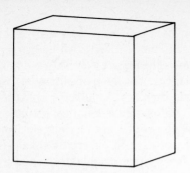

75a The cube, an example of a simple, closed form.

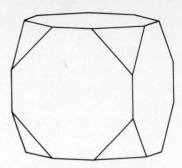

75b A combination of cube and octahedron, consisting of two closed forms.

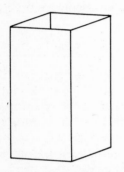

76 The tetragonal prism, an open form.

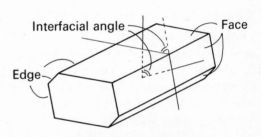

Interfacial angle — Face

Edge

77 Diagram illustrating crystal faces, edges and the interfacial angle.

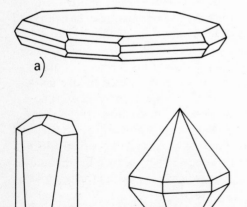

a)

b)

c)

78 Diagrams illustrating crystal habit: (a) tabular; (b) columnar; (c) pyramidal; (d) acicular; (e) prismatic.

d)

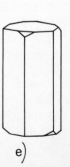

e)

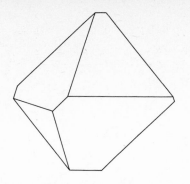

crystal along which the atomic density is high. For all crystals of the same substance, sharing the same lattice structure, corresponding interfacial angles are constant—even though, as mentioned above, the external shape of the crystal may be distorted (fig. 79). This law, the constancy of interfacial angles, is fundamental to the study of crystals.

The regularity of the atomic structure provides a crystal with symmetry which is highest in the simple cube. The accompanying diagram (fig. 80) illustrates that, in the lattice of rock salt, there are nine PLANES OF SYMMETRY; these are imaginary planes each of which, cutting the crystal, divides it into two halves which are mirror images of one another. Again, AXES OF SYMMETRY are lines about which a crystal can be rotated so that it takes up an identical position in space (i.e. presents a similar set of faces to the viewer) more than once in a complete revolution of 360 degrees. When this occurs twice, the axis is termed a DIAD, when three times it is a TRIAD, when four times in a revolution the axis is a TETRAD (fig. 81) and when six times a HEXAD. Finally, a crystal is said to possess a CENTRE OF SYMMETRY when it is bounded entirely by pairs of parallel, like faces.

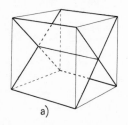

a)

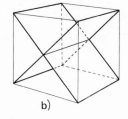

b)

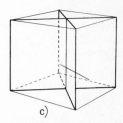

c)

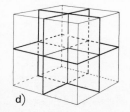

d)

80 Diagrams illustrating the planes of symmetry in a cube: there are two diagonal planes each in (a), (b) and (c), while in (d) there are three axial planes.

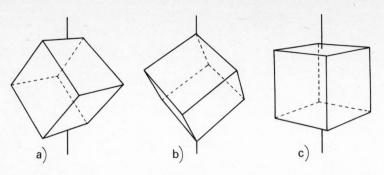

81 Diagrams illustrating axes of symmetry: (a) is a diad, (b) a triad, while (c) is a tetrad axis.

In order to describe three-dimensional crystal structure it is necessary to be able to relate the position of each face to a central scaffolding. This scaffolding is made up of three (or four) lines or CRYSTALLOGRAPHIC AXES whose common point of intersection is the ORIGIN. F. Coles Phillips has defined these axes as 'straight lines, not in the same plane, parallel to actual or possible edges of the crystal'. They are chosen to coincide with prominent axes of symmetry when the latter are present. Each crystal face, produced if necessary, cuts one or more of these axes. The length between the origin and the point where the face cuts the axis, is in each case described as an INTERCEPT (fig. 82).

The accompanying diagram represents a hypothetical crystal lattice (fig. 83). *ABC* would be a likely crystal face because its plane contains a concentration of atoms. *DBE* is a possible, though less likely crystal face, because the atoms are less dense within its plane. In establishing the geometry of a crystal, a commonly occurring face which (produced if necessary) cuts all three axes should be chosen as a basis. Such a face is known as the UNIT or PARAMETRAL PLANE. In the case being considered, the face *ABC* would be an obvious choice for the parametral plane.

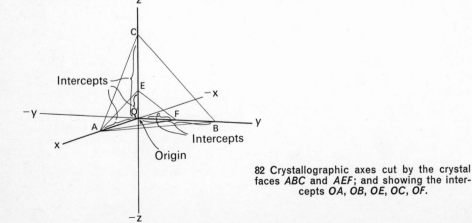

82 Crystallographic axes cut by the crystal faces *ABC* and *AEF*; and showing the intercepts *OA, OB, OE, OC, OF*.

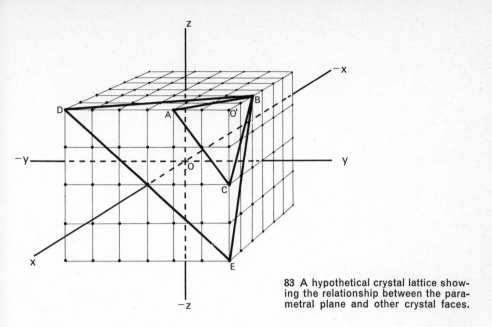

83 A hypothetical crystal lattice showing the relationship between the parametral plane and other crystal faces.

According to the definition given above, the three crystallographic axes will be set parallel to the three edges of the crystal, and therefore in this case at right angles to one another. As drawn, the origin lies within the lattice; the parametral plane ABC, if produced, will cut each of the three axes. However, for convenience in measuring the lengths of the intercepts, the origin could equally well be supposed to lie at O^1 and the intercepts of the parametral plane ABC could be expressed as O^1B, O^1A, O^1C. (By convention, intercepts are always considered in the order: front-to-back axis, side-to-side axis, vertical axis.) These special intercepts are known as the PARAMETERS. The intercepts of any other face are determined in a similar way; those for DBE will be O^1B, O^1D, O^1E and these can be expressed as O^1B, $3\ O^1A$, $2\ O^1C$. In other words, the intercepts for DBE are rational multiples of those of the parametral plane, reflecting the regularity of the crystal lattice. This simple relationship is always true for a crystal lattice and for faces to which it gives rise; it is defined as the LAW OF THE RATIONAL RATIO OF INTERCEPTS.

The relationship between the intercepts of any crystal face and the parameters of the parametral plane is established by dividing the former by the latter. The numbers which are obtained thereby are described as the INDICES. Thus, the indices of DBE are O^1B/O^1B, O^1D/O^1A, O^1E/O^1C which is the same as O^1B/O^1B, $3\ O^1A/O^1A$, $2\ O^1C/O^1C$ or $(1,3,2)$. This is the WEISS notation and the reciprocals 1, $\frac{1}{3}$, $\frac{1}{2}$ are known as the MILLER INDICES. Since the latter are ratios, it is possible and usual to clear the fractions and to express them thus: (623). Similarly the indices of the parametral plane will be O^1B/O^1B, O^1A/O^1A, O^1C/O^1C, which is (111). These figures, (111), always represent the indices for

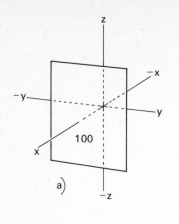

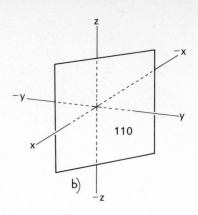

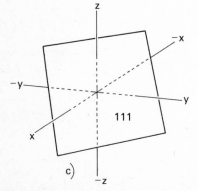

84 In (a) the face 100 cuts the *x* axis but it is parallel to *y* and *z*; in (b) the face 110 cuts the *x* and *y* axes but is parallel to *z*; in (c) the face 111 cuts all three axes.

the parametral plane, in any crystal, and they are expressed in words as 'one one one'. The indices of any other face are expressed in the same way, so that *DBE* would be 'six two three'. When the notation expresses the crystal form, rather than the crystal face, curly brackets, i.e. {111}, are used.

By convention, the sign of the forward extension of *x*, the front-to-back crystallographic axis, is positive, and of the backward extension, negative (−*x*). The right-hand-side of the *y* axis is positive while the left-hand-side is negative (−*y*). The upper extension of the vertical axis is positive (*z*) and the lower end is negative (−*z*), as shown in the diagram (figs. 82 and 83). The signs are shown when expressing the indices, so that if O¹ is the origin in figure 83, *ABC* would in fact be $(\bar{1}\bar{1}\bar{1})$* not (111), while *DBE* would be $(\bar{6}\bar{2}3)$. A face which makes equal intercepts on the *x* and *y* axes, but which is parallel to the *z* axis will have the indices (110); one which cuts the *x* axis but which is parallel to both *y* and *z* axes will be (100) as in figure 84.

If the actual lengths of the parameters O¹B, O¹A, O¹C (fig. 83) for a particular crystal were measured in figures, and were found to be in the ratio 1 : 1·442 : 1·641,

* In words, this would be expressed as 'bar one, bar one, bar one'.

70

then these figures would constitute the AXIAL RATIO. On the other hand, if *DBE* were chosen as the parametral plane, the axial ratio would be

$$1:1\cdot442\times3:1\cdot641\times2=1:4\cdot326:3\cdot282.$$

Expressed in the conventional form, with the *y* parameter as unity, this would be:

$$0\cdot2313:1:0\cdot7586.$$

Classification. All known crystals can be assigned to one of six different SYSTEMS within which there are thirty-two possible, but only eleven commonly occurring, SYMMETRY CLASSES. This classification is based upon symmetry and upon the ratio of the intercepts of the principal crystal faces. Each system is introduced below by reference to a form in which faces cut all three axes.

The Cubic System. A common form is the OCTAHEDRON, each of whose faces constitutes the parametral plane. The crystallographic axes pass through the opposite corners of the octahedron and intersect one another at right angles (fig. 85). The parametral intercepts *a*, *b*, *c*, are here equal to one another; that is to say, the axial ratio is $1:1:1$.

In the octahedron, each corner may be modified by the development of a face of the cube or HEXAHEDRON, which may be of such a size as to reduce considerably the faces of the octahedron, or to eliminate them altogether (fig. 86). In the hexahedron, each face is parallel to two of the crystallographic axes, with indices (100), etc.

There are five symmetry classes in the cubic system, of which three will be considered here. The class showing the highest symmetry, represented by galena has (like rock salt) nine planes. Of these, six are diagonal, while the other three each contain two crystallographic axes and are therefore described as axial planes (see fig. 80). There are also thirteen axes of symmetry; three of these

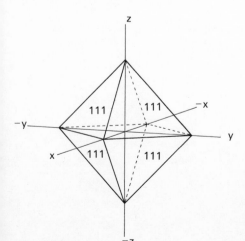

85 The octahedron, illustrating the cubic system; each face being named according to to the Millerian system of indices.

71

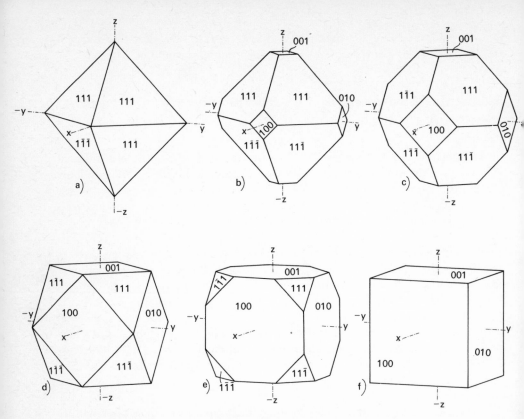

86 Diagrams of cubic crystals, showing the progressive development from the octahedron to the cube.

87 Diagrams illustrating symmetry in the pyritohedron. In (a) the three planes of symmetry are shown; in (b) the three diad axes, and in (c) the four triad axes of symmetry.

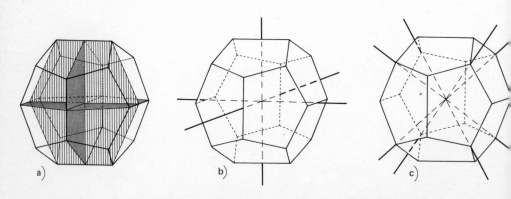

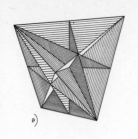 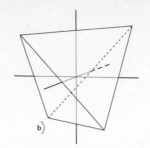 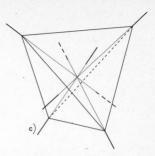

88 Diagrams illustrating symmetry in the tetrahedron. In (a) there are nine planes of symmetry, in (b) the three diad axes, and in (c) the four triad axes.

89 Diagrams illustrating some possible combinations of faces in the cubic system: (a) the tetrahexahedron, (b) the hexoctahedron, (c) the trisoctahedron, and (d) the rhombdodecahedron.

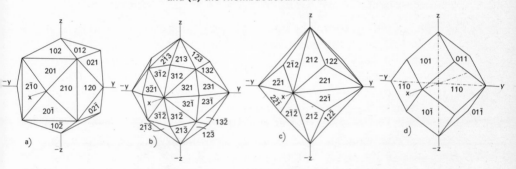

coincide with the crystallographic axes and are tetrads, four others are diagonal and are triads, while six are diads (see fig. 81). These facts can be simply expressed as 4^{III}, 3^{IV}, 6^{II}. The class has a centre of symmetry. Some crystals in this symmetry class, such as magnetite, develop as octahedra while others, including galena itself, may show a combination of both the octahedron and hexahedron (see figs. 86 and **128**).

Pyrite is an example of the second symmetry class in the cubic system, with three planes, seven axes (3^{II}, 4^{III}) and a centre of symmetry (fig. 87). The mineral tetrahedrite represents the third symmetry class with six planes and seven axes (3^{II}, 4^{III}) of symmetry. In this class there is no centre of symmetry (fig. 88).

There are many possible combinations of faces in the cubic system. For example, the TETRAHEXAHEDRON has four triangular faces in place of each face of the cube, while the HEXOCTAHEDRON and the TRISOCTAHEDRON show six and three faces respectively in place of each face of the original octahedron. In the accompanying diagrams, Miller indices are given for some of the faces. In the RHOMBDODECAHEDRON each face cuts two axes and is parallel to one (fig. 89).

73

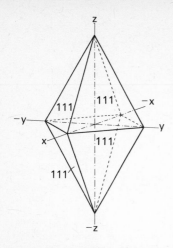

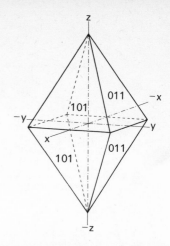

90a The tetragonal bipyramid (i.e. double pyramid) of the first order.

90b The tetragonal bipyramid of the second order.

The Tetragonal System. The three crystallographic axes are set at right angles to one another, but the intercept made by the face (1,1,1,) on the z axis, unlike the octahedron, may be greater or less than the two equal intercepts on the horizontal axis (fig. 90).

There are seven symmetry classes in the tetragonal system, though only one, that represented by zircon, will be considered here. All tetragonal crystals show a lower symmetry than substances crystallising in the cubic system; zircon has five planes, one tetrad and four diad axes of symmetry (1^{IV}, 4^{II}) and a centre.

The faces of the closed form shown in the diagram (fig. 90a) constitute the TETRAGONAL BIPYRAMID OF THE FIRST ORDER. In some tetragonal crystals the faces of the pyramid are parallel to one or other of the horizontal axes; they then constitute the TETRAGONAL BIPYRAMID OF THE SECOND ORDER

91 The ditetragonal bipyramid, with two faces developed on each face of the tetragonal bipyramid.

92 The ditetragonal prism, with two prism faces developed in place of each face of the tetragonal prism. Basal pinacoid also present.

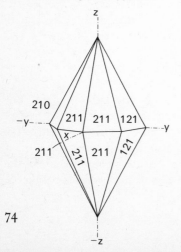

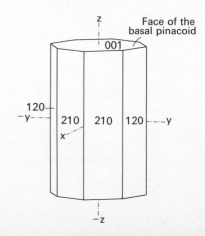

74

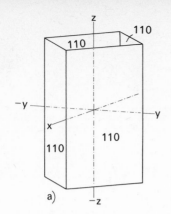

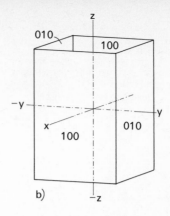

93 The tetragonal prism, an open form, with faces parallel to the vertical axis: (a) of the first order, with each face cutting two horizontal, and (b) of the second order, with each face parallel to one horizontal axis.

(fig. 90b). When two faces develop in the place of one, the result is the DITETRA-GONAL BIPYRAMID (fig. 91). Faces which are parallel to the vertical axis commonly occur, giving the open form known as the TETRAGONAL PRISM—of the first or second order according as they cut respectively two or only one of the horizontal axes (fig. 93). Then there is the DITETRAGONAL PRISM with which there may be developed the BASAL PINACOID. These are both open forms (fig. 92).

The Orthorhombic System. The three crystallographic axes lie at right angles to one another, but the intercepts made by the parametral plane (111) are all unequal.

There are three symmetry classes in the orthorhombic system of which two are considered here. Compared with the tetragonal system there is a further

94 The orthorhombic bipyramid (compare fig. 90a, b).

95 The orthorhombic bipyramid modified by the development of the orthorhombic prism and basal pinacoid.

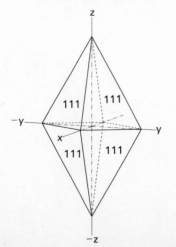

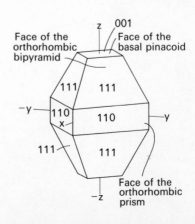

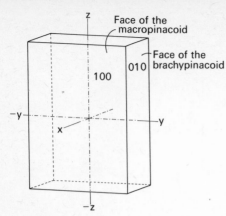

96 Diagram illustrating the combination of the brachypinacoid and the macropinacoid in the orthorhombic system.

reduction in symmetry in that there are three axial planes, three diad axes (3^{II}) and a centre of symmetry. Figure 94 illustrates a class represented by the ORTHORHOMBIC BIPYRAMID. However, faces parallel to the vertical but cutting the two horizontal axes, may be associated with the bipyramid; they are described as the ORTHORHOMBIC PRISM. The usual form has the symbol {110} but other prism faces may be (210), (120), etc. Barytes is a common example (fig. 95).

Another class in the orthorhombic system shows the development of an open form, namely, the PINACOID {100}. The faces which are parallel to the short axis form the BRACHYPINACOID, while those parallel to the long axis constitute the MACROPINACOID (fig. 96). In this class, instead of the pyramid, the dome is developed and has the symbol {101} or {011}. Following the nomenclature of the pinacoids of this class it is termed either a BRACHYDOME or a MACRODOME. The dome, however, may be replaced by the open form {001}, the basal pinacoid.

The Monoclinic System. Of the three crystallographic axes, the x axis is at right angles to the y but is set at an obtuse angle to z, while y and z lie at right

97 The negative hemi-pyramid (a), the positive hemi-pyramid (b), both open forms, and the two combined to form the monoclinic crystal (c).

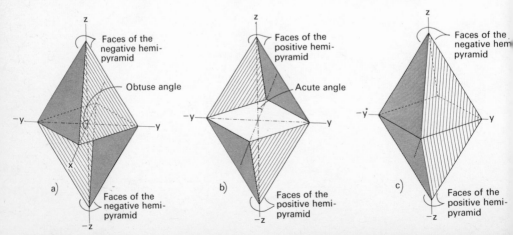

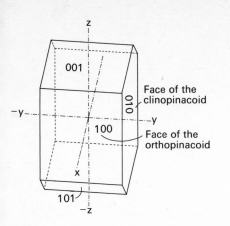

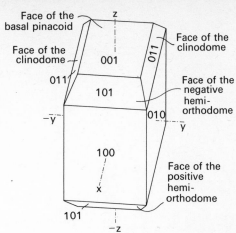

98 Diagram illustrating the development of the orthopinacoid and the clinopinacoid in a monoclinic crystal.

99 Diagram illustrating the development of the positive and negative hemi-orthodome, the clinodome and the basal pinacoid in a monoclinic crystal.

angles to one another. The intercepts made by the parametral plane (111) of the HEMI-PYRAMID, are of unequal length.

The monoclinic system has three classes of symmetry, of which the highest possesses a single plane, a diad axis of symmetry (1^{II}) and a centre of symmetry. The faces of the hemi-pyramid are of two kinds; the four which lie within the acute angle between x and z constitute the POSITIVE HEMI-PYRAMID, while the remaining four within the obtuse angle comprise the NEGATIVE HEMI-PYRAMID (fig. 97). Pinacoid faces which are parallel to the ortho (y) and the vertical (z) axes make the open form known as the ORTHOPINACOID, while those parallel to the clino (x, the inclined) axis and the vertical axis constitute the CLINOPINACOID (fig. 98). There are three distinctive forms of the dome: those lying within the acute angle between x and z constitute the POSITIVE HEMI-ORTHODOME, and within the obtuse angle, the NEGATIVE HEMI-ORTHODOME. The remaining four faces of the dome which are parallel to the clino-axis are all of the same shape and make up the CLINODOME. Faces which are parallel to the ortho- and clino-axes but which cut the vertical axis form the basal pinacoid (fig. 99). Common representatives of the monoclinic system include gypsum.

The Triclinic System. In this system, of which there are two classes, there is only a centre of symmetry, with no planes and no axes. The three crystallographic axes all intersect at angles other than 90 degrees, and the intercepts made by the parametral plane (111) are unequal in length.

The z axis is taken as the vertical, and of the two inclined axes x corresponds to the clino-axis of the monoclinic system while y, generally the longer, occupies the position of the ortho-axis; x and y are therefore described as the brachy- and macro-axes respectively.

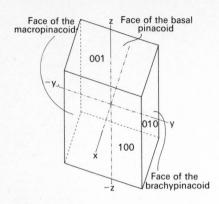

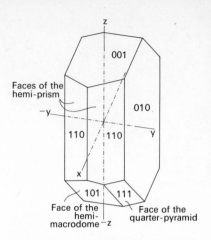

100 Diagram illustrating the macro-pinacoid, the brachypinacoid, and the basal pinacoid in a triclinic crystal.

101 Diagram illustrating the development of the hemi-prism, the hemi-macrodome and the quarter pyramids in a crystal of the triclinic system.

The faces of the triclinic crystal are named after those in the orthorhombic system, namely, the basal pinacoid, the macropinacoid and the brachypinacoid (fig. 100). However, the prism, the macrodome and the brachydome are each made up of two kinds of faces, differing in shape because of the absence of symmetry in this system; each of these two forms is described as the HEMI-PRISM, the HEMI-MACRODOME and the HEMI-BRACHYDOME respectively. The pyramid consists of four pairs of faces each pair having a different shape, and is therefore described as the QUARTER-PYRAMID (fig. 101). Albite is a representative of this system.

The Hexagonal System. The hexagonal system is sub-divided by some authorities into two—the hexagonal and the trigonal. It is unique among the

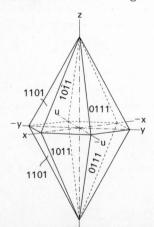

102 The hexagonal bipyramid of the first order.

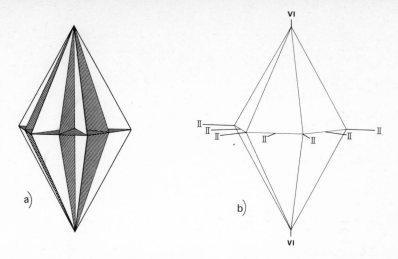

103 Diagrams showing: (a) the seven planes of symmetry, and (b) the seven axes of symmetry in the hexagonal bipyramid.

crystal systems in that there are three horizontal crystallographic axes. The parametral intercepts along these horizontal axes are equal in length and are set at 120 degrees to one another. The horizontal axes all lie at right angles to the vertical axis, which may be longer or shorter than the others. The three horizontal axes are, by convention, labelled x, y, u, with their positive and negative signs as indicated in the diagram (fig. 102).

There are 12 symmetry classes in the hexagonal system. In that with the highest symmetry there are four axial planes—one plane containing the three horizontal axes and three each containing the vertical and one horizontal axis. In addition there are three other vertical planes, diagonals, containing only the II axis (fig. 103). Of the axes of symmetry, there are six diads (of which three are diagonal and three axial) together with one vertical axis, a hexad (6^{II}, 1^{VI}). There is also a centre of symmetry (fig. 103).

The descriptive nomenclature is similar to that in the tetragonal system. In the HEXAGONAL BIPYRAMID OF THE SECOND ORDER (fig. 104), each pyramid face cuts all three horizontal axes, while that of the first order (fig. 102) cuts two horizontal axes but is parallel to the third. In place of each single face two faces may be developed, making a DIHEXAGONAL BIPYRAMID. Similarly, the faces of the HEXAGONAL PRISM may be first or second order and a further growth of faces leads to the DIHEXAGONAL PRISM. The basal pinacoid may be associated with these forms (fig. 105).

The crystal form representing the second symmetry class (assigned by some to the separate, trigonal, system) is commonly the RHOMBOHEDRON (i.e. see cleavage fragment of calcite, figs. 106 and **129**). The rhombohedron has three vertical planes, three horizontal diad axes and one vertical triad axis of symmetry (3^{II}, 1^{III}) together with a centre of symmetry. The faces of the rhombohedron

79

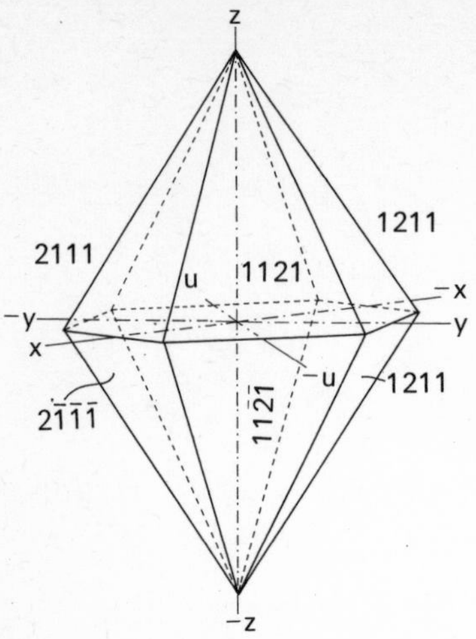

104 The hexagonal prism of the second order.

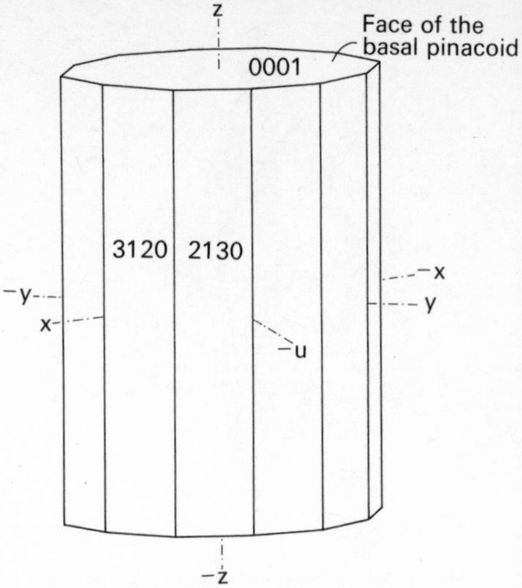

105 The dihexagonal prism with basal pinacoid.

constitute a closed form and are a development of the alternate faces of the hexagonal bi-pyramid of the first order (10$\bar{1}$1) as shown in the diagram (fig. 102). Calcite crystals sometimes show a combination of rhombohedron and prism forms (fig. 107). Yet another form is the SCALENOHEDRON (fig. 108).

Another symmetry class of the hexagonal system, that including quartz, develops forms which are a combination of the three already described. For example, the TRIGONAL TRAPEZOHEDRON (fig. 109) retains one in every four faces of the dihexagonal pyramid, while other forms resemble the rhombohedron and yet others the beryl type.

106 The rhombohedron.

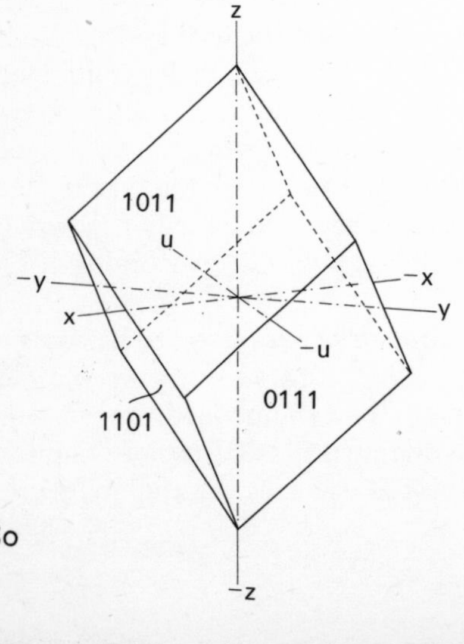

107 Diagram showing a combination of the rhombohedron and the prism in a hexagonal crystal.

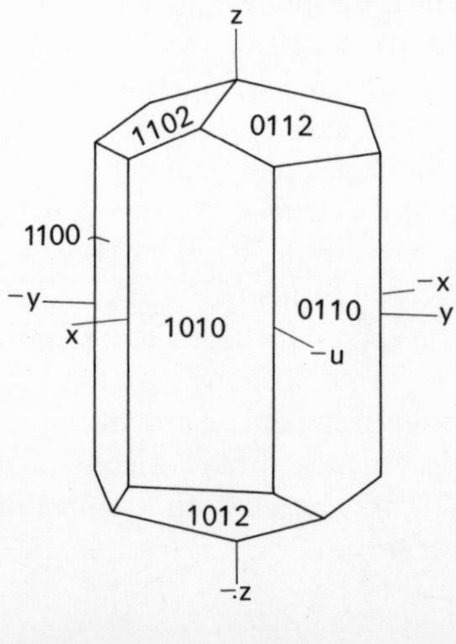

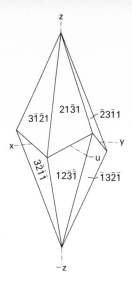

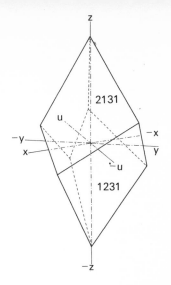

108 The scalenohedron.

109 The trigonal trapezohedron.

Twinning. Some crystals consist of two equal parts joined together along a plane in such a way that one half of the crystal is a reflection of the other; these are described as SIMPLE TWINS (fig. 110a). In another form, the two halves are grown into one another, and are INTERPENETRATION TWINS (fig. 110c). A third variety is present in the plagioclase feldspars, described as REPEATED TWINS, which is simply a repetition, numerous times, of simple twinning. There are examples of twinning among crystals from each of the crystal systems and there are many characteristic and distinctive forms which can be recognised both in the hand specimen and under the microscope.

110 The position of the twin plane in an octahedral crystal (a), and the development of the twin plane (b).

110c Interpenetration twins in a simple cube.

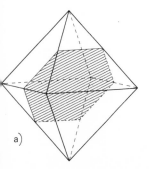

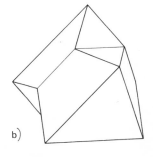

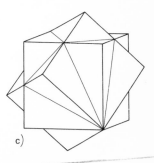

a)

b)

c)

111 Hematite. (Natural size)

112 Chalcopyrite. (Natural size)

113 Cinnabar. (Natural size)

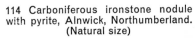

114 Carboniferous ironstone nodule
with pyrite, Alnwick, Northumberland.
(Natural size)

115 Nailhead spar. (Natural size)

116 Azurite. (Natural size)

117 Siderite on hematite. (Natural size)

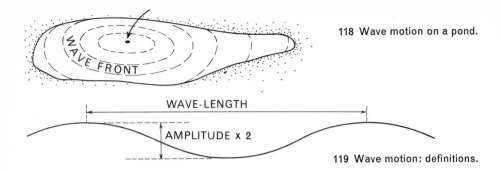

118 Wave motion on a pond.

WAVE-LENGTH

AMPLITUDE x 2

119 Wave motion: definitions.

THE OPTICAL PROPERTIES OF CRYSTALS

Wave Motion. Light consists of electromagnetic waves which vibrate in all directions within a plane at right angles to the direction of its transmission. Waves from a source of light, in air, for example, spread outwards at a uniform velocity in every direction. Every point on a circle, whose centre coincides with a source of light, is said to lie on the WAVE-FRONT of that source.

This can be more easily visualised by considering the wave-motion of water: if a stone is dropped into the still waters of a lake it causes the surface to vibrate outwards in the form of waves, in ever-widening circles from the point of impact. The body of the water does not itself move outwards from the centre, as can be shown by the fact that a cork floating on the surface is not carried forward, but simply oscillates up and down as successive waves pass it. As with light, the particles within the water vibrate at right angles to the direction of transmission of the wave motion and the wave-front is a circle around the centre of disturbance (fig. 118). The horizontal distance from crest to crest is the WAVE-LENGTH, while the vertical distance from crest to trough is the AMPLITUDE (fig. 119). The time taken for the disturbance to travel one wave-length is called the PERIOD. Whereas the wave-length of the disturbed surface of the lake is measured in feet, that of light is measured in ten-millionths of a millimetre (page 64); whereas the velocity of the waves across the lake is a few feet per second, that of light is 186,000 miles per second.

Single Refraction. The velocity of light varies according to the medium through which it passes. When a beam of light, consisting of innumerable parallel rays, enters a slab of glass from air it is bent or REFRACTED towards the normal to the surface (XY in fig. 120), and is then refracted away from the normal as it leaves the glass, to emerge parallel to its original course. In air, in a given time, light travels from B to D, but in glass the distance covered in the same time is less, namely, AC. The ratio of BD/AC, that is, the velocity of light in air (strictly speaking, *in vacuo*) divided by the velocity of light in glass, is described as the REFRACTIVE INDEX of glass. Thus, the slower the velocity, the higher the refractive index of a medium.

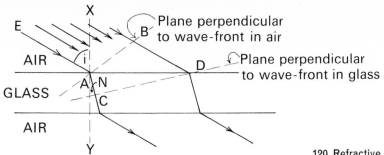

Plane perpendicular to wave-front in air

Plane perpendicular to wave-front in glass

120 Refractive index defined.

The ratio BD/AC can be expressed in another way: The angle made by the beam with the normal to the surface of the glass is termed the angle of incidence, i, and the angle which the beam makes after being refracted is the angle of refraction, r. From the diagram (fig. 120), angles $EAX + XAB =$ angles $XAB + BAD =$ 90 degrees. Therefore angle $EAX =$ angle BAD. Similarly, angles $YAC + CAD = CDA + CAD =$ 90 degrees. Therefore angle $YAC =$ angle CDA. But $BD/AD = \sin BAD = \sin i$, and $AC/AD = \sin CDA = \sin r$. Therefore the refractive index $BD/AC = AD \sin i/AD \sin r = \sin i/\sin r$.

Double Refraction. If the slab of glass is replaced by a crystal of calcite so that light passes through two of its parallel rhomb faces, then a more complicated pattern of refraction occurs. Each ray on entering the crystal is broken into two component rays having different velocities (fig. 121). These two rays emerging from the surface of the crystal of calcite each vibrate in one direction only, within a plane perpendicular to the direction of transmission, and their directions of vibration lie at right angles to one another. In calcite, the slower of the two rays is described as the ORDINARY RAY. while the faster one is named the EXTRAORDINARY RAY. This property of DOUBLE REFRACTION is possessed by all crystals except for those which crystallise in the cubic system. Crystals having double refraction are said to be ANISOTROPIC. Singly refracting substances (from which light emerges vibrating in every direction within a plane) include all gases, liquids and glasses. These substances are described as ISO-TROPIC. Anistropy in crystals depends upon internal atomic structure.

There is a synthetic material known as POLAROID, which behaves as an anisotropic substance. It also possesses the property of absorbing one of the

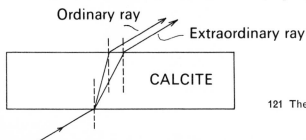

Ordinary ray

Extraordinary ray

CALCITE

121 The double refraction of calcite.

85

122 Rock crystal. (Natural size)

123 Amethyst. (Natural size)

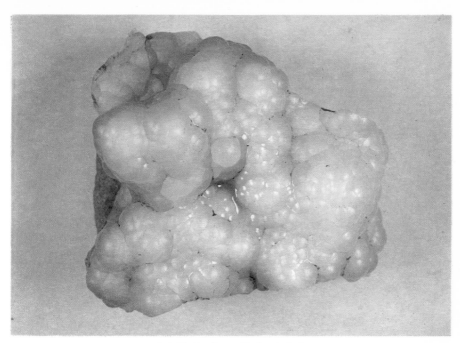

124 Chalcedony. (Natural size)

125 Amethyst and chalcedony in geode. (Natural size)

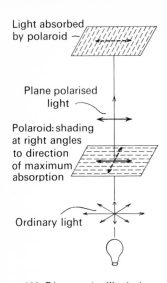

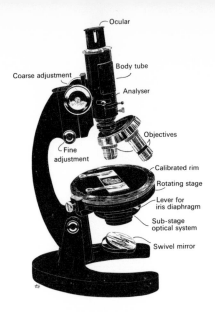

126 Diagram to illustrate the property of polaroid.

127 The polarising microscope.

two rays into which light is broken as it is transmitted through it. (This property of ABSORPTION is common to certain natural substances also, including biotite and tourmaline.) The other ray, vibrating at right angles to its absorbed mate, emerges from the polaroid. This is described as POLARISED LIGHT. If a second sheet of polaroid is interposed between the light source and the viewer, so that its direction of absorption lies parallel to the direction of vibration of the polarised light emerging from the first sheet (and therefore at right angles to the direction of absorption in that sheet), then there will be complete absorption and no light will reach the eye (fig. 126). This is a very important fact which is fundamental in the use of the polarising microscope.

The Polarising Microscope (fig. 127). The polarising microscope consists of a heavy base on which is hinged the body tube with the rotating stage and the substage optical system; the latter includes a disc of polaroid, described as the polariser. The objective lens is attached at the base of the body tube. Provision is made for objectives of different magnifications, which may be exchanged as required. The ocular or eye-piece is housed at the top of the tube and contains two cross-wires set at right angles to one another. A second disc of polaroid, known as the analyser, is set in the body tube between the ocular and the objective; it can easily be withdrawn from the optical system. The body tube can be raised or lowered for focusing either by means of the coarse or by the fine adjustment device. The rim of the stage is calibrated in degrees so that the angle of its rotation may be determined. At the base of the instrument there is a swivel

88

mirror which can be adjusted to reflect the maximum amount of light upwards to the eye through the lens system. Also, close beneath the stage, an iris diaphragm is set; it can be used to control the amount of light passing through the specimen on the stage, the so-called THIN SECTION.

The polaroid sheets, comprising the polariser and the analyser, are set so that their directions of maximum absorption are at right angles to one another and parallel to the cross-wires. Therefore with the analyser inserted in the body tube, no light will reach the eye of the viewer as explained in figure 126.

In the preparation of a thin section, a slice of rock about 2 cm square and 3 mm thick, polished on one side, is cemented on to a glass slide by means of a transparent substance of known refractive index, such as canada balsam or 'lakeside 70'. The slice is then ground down with increasingly fine grades of carborundum powder until it is of standard thickness (0·03 mm); only the iron oxides then appear opaque in transmitted light, while the other common rock-forming minerals are transparent.

Minerals in Thin Section. Part of the investigation of minerals in thin section is carried out in plane polarised light, that is, with the polariser under the stage but with the analyser removed. Some minerals like quartz, the feldspars, muscovite, olivine, etc., are colourless in thin section (figs. **54-57**); others may have distinctive colours. Some of the anisotropic coloured minerals exhibit, like polaroid, the property of absorption and, as mentioned above, biotite mica is one of the minerals which shares with polaroid this property. If, with the analyser removed, a thin section of biotite is placed on the microscope stage; if its direction of maximum absorption is parallel to the direction of vibration of the polarised light emerging from the polariser (and therefore at right angles to the direction of maximum absorption of the latter), then the effect will be exactly as though the analyser were in position, and the biotite will appear dark. If the stage is rotated, the biotite will gradually become lighter until it reaches the point (at right angles to its first position) of minimum absorption. This property, known as PLEOCHROISM, is shared by many coloured minerals, but not by any of those crystallising in the cubic system.

The determination of the refractive index of a non-opaque mineral in thin section is often an important guide to identification. If a mineral like muscovite, for example, is immersed in a medium of lower refractive index (canada balsam), then on raising the body tube so that the edge of the mineral is slightly out of focus, a white line of light appears to detach itself from the mineral boundary and to move into the mineral itself. The converse is the case for a mineral of lower refractive index. The simple rule is: raise the body tube and the line passes into the medium of higher refractive index (fig. 132). It is known as the BECKÉ TEST, and is an extremely sensitive test for determining differences in refractive index; this is especially the case under the high power objective with the iris diaphragm partially closed. The phenomenon is produced by the refraction of

128 (1) Native copper, (2) galena with dolomite, (3) graphite, (4) fluorspar (5) asbestos.

129 (1) Garnet, (2) rose quartz, (3) calcite rhomb, (4) selenite, (5) apatite, (6) native sulphur.

130 (1) Orthoclase feldspar, (2) muscovite, (3) witherite, (4) smoky quartz.

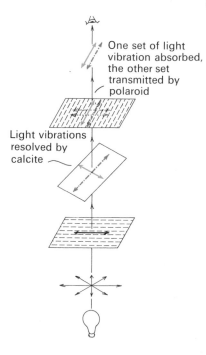

One set of light vibration absorbed, the other set transmitted by polaroid

Light vibrations resolved by calcite

131 Calcite, as on the microscope stage, resolving light vibrations from the polariser.

light across the boundary between the two media. The Becké test may be used not only along the edge of the rock section where minerals are in contact with canada balsam, but also within the section itself, where two different mineral species may lie in juxtaposition.

If a mineral in a thin rock section happens to lie with its cleavage planes (page 65) at right angles to the plane of the section, then the cleavage lines, (that is, the trace of the cleavage planes) will be clearly seen. If, however, the section is cut obliquely to the planes of cleavage then the lines will appear faint or invisible. However, since minerals are generally scattered in random positions through the section, there will always be some individuals which happen to be orientated in a direction which clearly shows their cleavage lines.

In the mineral hornblende there are two sets of cleavage planes, parallel to the faces of the monoclinic prism, which intersect at an angle of about 120 degrees. In sections cut parallel to the pinacoid, the cleavage can be clearly seen. Similar sections of augite, however, show two sets of cleavage planes which intersect at right angles to one another. Cleavage and absorption are related to one another; in biotite, for example, the cleavage is parallel to the direction of maximum absorption. Determination of cleavage may be an important aid in identification.

In thin section, the degree of ALTERATION undergone by a mineral can be studied in detail. Biotite, when chemically fresh, shows strong pleochroism, but if altered it presents a dull, non-pleochroic brown or green. Olivine, a chemically unstable mineral, usually undergoes extensive alteration to a black iron oxide or a green chlorite, especially along its lines of fracture (fig. **56**). Feldspars also vary in the degree of alteration to clay minerals, and the effect is clearly seen in thin section.

If an isotropic substance is placed on the stage with the analyser in position, then the polarised light from the polariser will pass uninterrupted through the substance, but will be absorbed by the analyser. If an anisotropic crystal, calcite for example, is placed on the stage in such a position that one or other of its permitted directions of light vibration is parallel to that of the polarised light from the polariser, then the light from the latter will pass through the calcite without being interrupted and will be absorbed by the analyser. Under these conditions, calcite is said to be in the position of EXTINCTION (fig. 133). If a mineral is in the position of extinction when the cleavage lines are parallel to either cross-wire, it is then said to exhibit STRAIGHT EXTINCTION. If otherwise, it is said to possess OBLIQUE EXTINCTION.

The case should now be considered when neither of the two permitted directions of vibration in the calcite section coincides with that of the light vibrations from the polariser: The light from the polariser (vibrating in one direction only) will be resolved into two rays as it passes through the calcite, vibrating at right angles to one another. On reaching the analyser, there will be a further resolution of each of these two components, parallel and at right angles respectively to the direction of maximum absorption of the polaroid. One pair

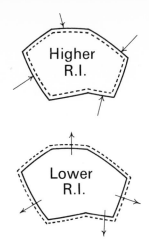

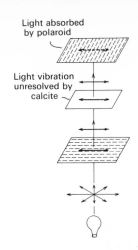

132 Illustrating the Becké test.

133 Calcite, as on the microscope stage, leaving light vibrations from the polariser unresolved.

of these components will therefore be absorbed by the analyser, while the other pair will reach the eye (fig. **131**).

The pair of component rays which reach the eye are rays which passed through the calcite section with different velocities. This being the case, the vibrations of the two rays will not coincide but will be OUT OF PHASE. In other words, one ray will have undergone RETARDATION with respect to the other. But this is white light which consists of a rainbow of colours, each with its own specific wave-length; because of the difference in phase of these vibrations, the wave-amplitudes of some of these colours will be increased, others reduced, yet others will be cancelled out. Certain shades will therefore be eliminated; there may be a predominance of yellows or blues or only greys (figs. **55–57**). These are described as POLARISATION COLOURS and their evaluation, which affords a further means of identification of anisotropic substances, is expressed numerically as BIRE-FRINGENCE. Many other techniques are employed to determine the optical properties of minerals under the polarising microscope, which are beyond the scope of the book.

THE PHYSICAL PROPERTIES OF MINERALS

Minerals which occur as the constituents of igneous and metamorphic rocks are generally much too small to be examined in the hand. However, in veins many minerals are found to be of hand specimen size and they can be identified by a number of simple physical tests.

Many minerals exhibit a characteristic COLOUR in reflected light. Sapphires are blue, garnets red, malachite is green, sulphur is yellow. Yet other minerals like quartz and feldspar vary in colour according to the proportions of minute traces of other elements in them. Though quartz, in the form of rock crystal, is

93

134 Garnetiferous hornfels, Scottish Highlands. (Natural size)

135 Garnetiferous mica schist, Scottish Highlands. (Natural size)

136 Staurolite schist, Scottish Highlands. (Natural size)

137 Slate, Skiddaw, Cumberland, showing minute thrust. (Natural size)

138 Slate, showing cleavage. (Natural size)

139 Gossan. (Natural size)

colourless and transparent, this mineral also occurs as rose quartz (a pink shade) amethyst (purple) and as smoky quartz (dark grey to black). Similarly, the characteristic shade of fluorspar is purple, but sometimes its crystals are light green or even colourless (figs. 111–117, 122–125, 128–130).

The powder or STREAK of a mineral, obtained either by scratching the surface with a hard steel point or by drawing the specimen across unglazed porcelain, is a rather more sensitive test than that of colour. For example, hematite and magnetite, which are oxides of iron, both appear black in the hand specimen, yet powdered hematite is red while that of magnetite is black.

The LUSTRE of a mineral is the term used to describe the intensity of light reflected from its surface. Minerals with very shiny, glassy surfaces like quartz, feldspar, iceland spar, etc., are said to possess VITREOUS lustre. Metallic minerals like galena and pyrites exhibit METALLIC lustre. Amber has a RESIN-OUS lustre while that of selenite is PEARLY. The fibrous appearance of satin-spar, asbestos and gypsum is described as a SILKY lustre. A surface without lustre is described as DULL.

An important test is that of HARDNESS, which increases with increasing density of the crystal lattice. Some minerals, like graphite and talc, can be scratched with the finger-nail; the surfaces of others, like calcite, can be indented with the point of a knife, while others—corundum and diamond—resist abrasion by even the hardest steel. Mohs, an Austrian mineralogist, early last century devised a scale of hardness within which he found he could assign a place for every known mineral. The scale is represented by ten minerals, most of which are commonly occurring, and runs as follows: 1. Talc; 2. Gypsum; 3. Calcite; 4. Fluorspar; 5. Apatite; 6. Feldspar; 7. Quartz; 8. Topaz; 9. Corundum; 10. Diamond. Each of these minerals has the hardness value represented by its number in the scale, and can be scratched by its neighbour which bears the higher number. All other mineral substances can be placed at some point in the scale. For example, hornblende scratches apatite, whilst it is itself scratched by feldspar. Thus it has a hardness of 5–6.

When a piece of glass is smashed, the broken surface or FRACTURE tends to be curved or CONCHOIDAL. Glass has no regular pattern of atomic structure, and therefore, though fracture occurs in crystalline substances also, it is inde-pendent of the crystal lattice and therefore quite distinct from cleavage (page 65). Quartz, which possesses no cleavage, shows marked conchoidal fracture while pyrite, for example, presents a flat but irregular fracture surface, described as UNEVEN. A break in cast iron, with its highly irregular and knobbly surface, is a good example of HACKLY fracture. When the fracture is BRITTLE, the mineral tends to fly into small pieces.

The SPECIFIC GRAVITY of a substance, a comparison of its weight with that of an equal volume of water, is commonly used in mineral identification. The mineral is first weighed in air and then in water. The buoyancy of the water causes an apparent loss in weight of the mineral, and this loss is equal to the

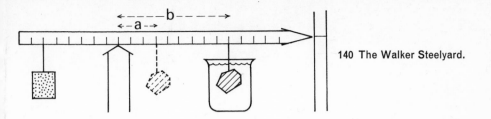

140 The Walker Steelyard.

weight of water displaced. Since the mineral is completely immersed, the volume of displaced water must equal that of the mineral itself. That is to say, apparent loss in weight = weight of an equal volume of water. Therefore, where Wa is the weight in air and Ww the weight in water, the specific gravity (S.G.) = $Wa/Wa-Ww$.

Walker's Steelyard (Fig. 140) is a simple apparatus for determining the specific gravity of minerals in the hand specimen. It consists of a graduated beam supported by a pivot near one end, dividing it into a short and a long arm. The mineral specimen is suspended by means of a thread from the long arm so that it exactly balances the weight attached to the short arm. The distance, a cm, of the mineral from the fulcrum, is noted.

The mineral is then suspended in a beaker of water and moved along the arm —the weight on the short arm being kept at the same point of attachment—until the system is in balance again. The length, b cm, which is greater than a, is noted. In fact the weight of the mineral is inversely proportional to the length of the arm. That is, $Wa \propto 1/a$ and $Ww \propto 1/b$. Therefore

$$\frac{Wa}{Wa-Ww} = \frac{\dfrac{1}{a}}{\dfrac{1}{a}-\dfrac{1}{b}} = \frac{\dfrac{1}{a}}{\dfrac{b-a}{ab}}, = \frac{b}{b-a}$$

and the specific gravity of any solid can thus be obtained from two readings with the aid of Walker's Steelyard.

The specific gravity of mineral grains can be obtained by immersing them in a 'heavy liquid' whose specific gravity can be altered by adding dense, or less dense, miscible solutions to it. This is carried out until the mineral neither sinks nor floats in the mixture, whereupon liquid and solid will have the same specific gravity. The specific gravity of the liquid can then be readily obtained by standard procedure, using a specific gravity bottle.

The accompanying table (fig. 141) illustrates the distribution of some of the common mineral substances according to their chemical associations. The properties of these minerals are then summarised in the table (fig. 142) on the succeeding pages and brief reference is included on their mode of occurrence and uses. Those minerals which are included among the colour photographs are marked with an asterisk.

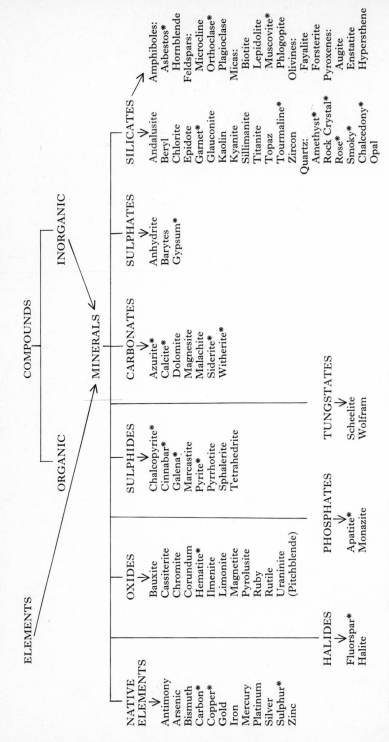

COMPOUNDS

ELEMENTS

ORGANIC INORGANIC

MINERALS

NATIVE ELEMENTS
Antimony
Arsenic
Bismuth
Carbon*
Copper*
Gold
Iron
Mercury
Platinum
Silver
Sulphur*
Zinc

HALIDES
Fluorspar*
Halite

OXIDES
Bauxite
Cassiterite
Chromite
Corundum
Hematite*
Ilmenite
Limonite
Magnetite
Pyrolusite
Ruby
Rutile
Uraninite
(Pitchblende)

PHOSPHATES
Apatite*
Monazite

SULPHIDES
Chalcopyrite*
Cinnabar*
Galena*
Marcastite
Pyrite*
Pyrrhotite
Sphalerite
Tetrahedrite

TUNGSTATES
Scheelite
Wolfram

CARBONATES
Azurite*
Calcite*
Dolomite
Magnesite
Malachite
Siderite*
Witherite*

SULPHATES
Anhydrite
Barytes
Gypsum*

SILICATES
Andalusite
Beryl
Chlorite
Epidote
Garnet*
Glauconite
Kaolin
Kyanite
Sillimanite
Titanite
Topaz
Tourmaline*
Zircon
Quartz:
Amethyst*
Rock Crystal*
Rose*
Smoky*
Chalcedony*
Opal

Amphiboles:
Asbestos*
Hornblende
Feldspars:
Microcline
Orthoclase*
Plagioclase
Micas:
Biotite
Lepidolite
Muscovite*
Phlogopite
Olivines:
Fayalite
Forsterite
Pyroxenes:
Augite
Enstatite
Hypersthene

*These minerals are illustrated in colour (figs. 111–117, 122–125, 128–130).

141 Minerals grouped according to chemical composition.

below: 142 Table listing the principal physical properties of minerals.

MINERAL	STREAK	LUSTRE	HARD-NESS	CLEAVAGE	FRACTURE	SP.G.	CRYSTAL SYSTEM	OCCUR-RENCE	USES
				NATIVE ELEMENTS					
Antimony (Sb)	white	metallic	3–3·5	perfect (basal)	uneven	6·6	hexagonal	veins (rare)	alloys, medicine
Arsenic (As)	white	metallic	3·5	—	uneven	5·7	hexagonal	sulphide ore veins	insecticides
Bismuth (Bi)	white	metallic	2·5	perfect (basal)	brittle	9·7	hexagonal	veins	alloys, medicine
Carbon (C): Diamond	white	vitreous	10	perfect (octahedral)	conchoidal	3·5	cubic	igneous rocks, placers	gems, abrasives
Graphite	black	metallic	1–2	perfect (basal)	—	2·3	hexagonal	veins	lubricant, electrodes, pencils
Copper (Cu)	red	metallic	2·5–3	—	hackly	8·8	cubic	volcanic rocks	alloys electrical app.
Gold (Au)	yellow	metallic	2·5	—	hackly	12–20	cubic	veins, placers	jewellery, coins
Iron (Fe)	grey	metallic	4·5	perfect (cubic)	hackly	7·5	cubic	igneous rocks placers	steel industry
Mercury (Hg)	—	metallic	—	—	—	13·6	hexagonal	volcanoes	medicine, electrical apparatus
Platinum (Pt)	grey	metallic	4·5	—	hackly	21·5	cubic	igneous rocks, veins, placers	chemicals, electrical, apparatus
Silver (Ag)	white	metallic	2·5	—	hackly	11·1	cubic	veins, placers	jewellery, coins
Sulphur (S)	yellow	resinous	2·5	imperfect (prismatic)	—	2·0	ortho-rhombic	volcanoes	chemicals
Zinc (Zn)	—	—	—	—	—	—	hexagonal	very rare (in basalt?)	galvanising processes
				OXIDES					
Bauxite ($Al_2O_3 \cdot 2H_2O$)	grey-brown	—	—	—	—	—	amorphous	igneous rocks also as Gibbsite ($Al_2O_3 \cdot 3H_2O$)	source of aluminium
Cassiterite (SnO_2)	grey-brown	vitreous	6–7	—	uneven	6·8	tetragonal	veins, greisen	source of tin
Chromite ($FeO \cdot Cr_2O_3$)	brown	metallic	5·5	—	brittle	4·5	cubic	igneous rocks placers	source of chromium

continued overleaf

MINERAL	STREAK	LUSTRE	HARD-NESS	CLEAVAGE	FRACTURE	SP.G.	CRYSTAL SYSTEM	OCCUR-RENCE	USES
OXIDES (*continued*)									
Corundum (Al_2O_3)	grey	vitreous	9	—	uneven	3·9	hexagonal	igneous, metamorphic rocks	abrasives
Hematite (Fe_2O_3)	red	metallic	5·5–6·5	poor	uneven	4·9–5·3	hexagonal	diagenetic	source of iron
specular iron ore—needle-like crystals									
kidney iron ore—radiating crystals									
Ilmenite ($FeO.TiO_2$)	black	dull	5–6	—	conchoidal	4·5–5	hexagonal	basic igneous rocks	source of titanium
Limonite ($2Fe_2O_3.3H_2O$)	yellow	dull	5–5·5	—	—	3·6–4	amorphous	alteration	source of iron
Magnetite (Fe_3O_4)	black	metallic	5·5–6·5	poor	uneven	5·2	cubic	igneous rocks	source of iron (magnetic ore)
Pyrolusite (MnO_2)	black	metallic	2–2·5	—	brittle	4·8	?amorphous	product sedimentary rocks	source of manganese
Ruby—red variety of corundum (Al_2O_3)									
Rutile (TiO_2)	brown	metallic	6–6·5	poor	uneven	4·2	tetragonal	igneous rocks	gems, source of titanium
Uraninite ($2UO_3.UO_2$)	black	resinous	5·5	—	—	6·4–9·7	cubic	igneous rocks	source of radioactive minerals
SULPHIDES									
Chalcopyrite (Copper pyrite, $Cu_2S.Fe_2S_2$)	green	metallic	3·5–4	—	uneven	4·2	tetragonal	veins, sedimentary rocks	source of copper
Cinnabar (HgS)	scarlet	vitreous	2–2·5	perfect (prismatic)	uneven	8·1	hexagonal	veins, volcanoes	source of mercury
Galena (PbS)	grey	metallic	2·5	perfect (cubic)	even	7·4	cubic	veins	source of lead
Pyrite (FeS_2)	green-brown	metallic	6–6·5	—	uneven	4·8	cubic	veins, sedimentary rocks	source of sulphur
Marcasite (FeS_2)	grey	metallic	6–6·5	—	uneven	4·9	orthorhombic	sedimentary rocks	source of sulphur

Mineral	Colour	Lustre	Hardness	Cleavage	Fracture	Density	Crystal system	Occurrence	Uses
Pyrrhotite ($FeS_2 + Ni$)	grey	metallic	3·5–4·5	imperfect	uneven	4·5	hexagonal	segregations (igneous rocks)	source of nickel
Sphalerite (blende, ZnS)	brown	resinous	3·5–4	perfect	conchoidal	3·9	cubic	veins	source of zinc
Tetrahedrite ($4Cu_2S.Sb_2S_3$)	grey	metallic	3–4·5	—	uneven	4·5–5·1	cubic	veins	source of copper
CARBONATES									
Azurite ($2CuCO_3.Cu(OH)_2$)	blue	vitreous	3·5–4	—	conchoidal	3·7	monoclinic	veins	source of copper
Calcite ($CaCO_3$) nail-head spar, dog-tooth spar, iceland spar } common varieties of calcite	white	vitreous	3	perfect (rhombohedral)	conchoidal	2·7	hexagonal	sedimentary rocks	cement, agriculture
Dolomite $CaCO_3.MgCO_3$	yellow	pearly	3·5–4	perfect	uneven	2·8	hexagonal	diagenetic	agriculture
Magnesite ($MgCO_3$)	grey	vitreous	3·5–4·5	perfect (rhombohedral)	conchoidal	2·8	hexagonal	diagenetic	source of magnesium
Malachite ($CuCO_3.Cu(OH)_2$)	green	silky	3·5–4	—	—	3·9	monoclinic	veins	source of copper
Witherite ($BaCO_3$)	grey	vitreous	3·5	poor	uneven	4·3	orthorhombic	veins	source of barium
Siderite ($FeCO_3$)	white	pearly	3·5–4·5	perfect (rhombohedral)	uneven	3·7	hexagonal	veins	source of iron
HALIDES									
Fluorspar (CaF_2)	white	vitreous	4	perfect (octahedral)	uneven	3–3·2	cubic	veins	glass, flux in steel manufacture
Halite (rock salt, $NaCl$)	white	vitreous	2–2·5	perfect (cubic)	conchoidal	2·2	cubic	evaporites	chemical industry
PHOSPHATES									
Apatite: Fluor-($3Ca_3P_2O_8.CaF_2$) Chlor-($3Ca_3P_2O_8.CaCl$)	white	vitreous	5	poor	uneven	3·2	hexagonal	igneous rocks residual deposits	fertiliser
Monazite (($CeLaYt)PO_4 + ThO_2.SiO_2$)	white	resinous	5·5	imperfect	uneven	5·2	monoclinic	igneous rocks	source of thorium

continued overleaf

MINERAL	STREAK	LUSTRE	HARD-NESS	CLEAVAGE	FRACTURE	SP.G.	CRYSTAL SYSTEM	OCCUR-RENCE	USES
SULPHATES									
Anhydrite ($CaSO_4$)	white	pearly	3–3.5	perfect (pinacoidal)	uneven	2.9	ortho-rhombic	evaporites	fertiliser, cement, plaster
Gypsum ($CaSO_4.2H_2O$)	white	pearly	1.5–2	perfect (pinacoidal)	—	2.3	monoclinic	evaporites	fertiliser, cement, plaster
selenite, alabaster—varieties of gypsum									
Barytes ($BaSO_4$)	white	vitreous	3–3.5	perfect (basal)	uneven	4.5	ortho-rhombic	veins	paint, paper
TUNGSTATES									
Scheelite ($CaWO_4$)	white	vitreous	4–5.5	perfect (pyramidal)	uneven	6.0	tetragonal	veins	source of tungsten tools
Wolfram (($Fe.Mn)WO_4$)	brown	vitreous	5–5.5	perfect (pinacoidal)	uneven	7.1–7.9	monoclinic	veins	source of tungsten tools
SILICATES									
Amphibole:* asbestos (fibrous) hornblende	green-black	vitreous	5–6	perfect (prismatic)	uneven	3.3	monoclinic	igneous rocks	
Andalusite ($Al_2O_3.SiO_2$)	grey	vitreous	7.5	poor	uneven	3.1	ortho-rhombic	metamorphic rocks	
Beryl ($3BeO.Al_2O_3.6SiO_2$)	white	vitreous	7.5	poor	uneven	2.7	hexagonal	igneous rocks	gems
Chlorite ($4H_2O.5(MgFe)O \ Al_2O_3.3SiO_2$)	green	pearly	1.5–2.5	perfect (basal)	—	2.6	monoclinic	alteration in igneous rocks	
Cordierite ($H_2O.4(Mg,Fe)O.4Al_2O_3.10SiO_2$)	white	vitreous	7.5	poor	brittle	2.7	ortho-rhombic	metamorphic rocks	
Diopside ($CaO.MgO.2SiO_2$)	green	vitreous	5–6	good	—	3.3	monoclinic	igneous rocks	
Epidote ($Ca_2(AlOH)(AlFe)_2(SiO_4)_3$)	green	vitreous	6–7	perfect (basal)	uneven	3.5	monoclinic	metamorphic rocks	
Feldspars:* Microcline	grey	vitreous	6–6.5	perfect (basal)	uneven	2.5	triclinic	igneous rocks	
Orthoclase	grey-red	vitreous	6	perfect (basal)	uneven	2.5	monoclinic	igneous rocks	
Plagioclase: Albite	grey	vitreous–resinous	6–6.5	perfect (basal)	uneven	2.6–	triclinic	igneous rocks	
Anorthite	grey		6–6.5	perfect (basal)	conchoidal	2.74	triclinic	igneous rocks	

Mineral (composition)	Colour	Lustre	Hardness	Cleavage	Fracture	Specific gravity	Crystal system	Occurrence	Uses
Glauconite (Fe+K+Si mainly)	green	dull	2	—	—	2·4	amorphous	sedimentary rocks	
Garnet (CaO) or (MgO) or (FeO) or (MnO) or (CaO, FeO) or (CaO, Cr₂O₃) aluminium silicate	pink, red or green	vitreous	7-7·5	—	conchoidal	3·5	cubic	igneous rocks, metamorphic rocks	abrasives, gems
Kaolin (Al₂O₃.2SiO₂2H₂O)	white	dull	2·5	perfect (basal)	—	2·6	monoclinic	alteration of feldspars	source or chinaware
Kyanite (Al₂O₃.SiO₂)	white	pearly	4-7	imperfect	—	3·6	triclinic	metamorphic rocks	
Micas:*									
Biotite	black	vitreous	2·5-3	perfect (basal)	—	3	monoclinic	igneous rocks, metamorphic rocks	electrical industry
Muscovite (variety: sericite)	white	vitreous	2-2·5	perfect (basal)	—	3	monoclinic		
Olivines:*									
Fayalite } Forsterite }	white	vitreous	6-7	poor	conchoidal	3·2-4·3	ortho-rhombic	igneous rocks	
Pyroxenes:*									
Augite	black	vitreous	5-6	good	—	3·2	monoclinic	igneous rocks	
Enstatite } Hypersthene }	green	vitreous	5·5-6	good	uneven	3·1-3·5	ortho-rhombic	igneous rocks	
Quartz (SiO₂) Chalcedony-cryptocrystalline and amorphous; Opal-amorphous	white	vitreous	7	rare	conchoidal	2·6	hexagonal	igneous rocks	furnace moulding, glass
Sillimanite (Al₂O₃.SiO₂)	white	vitreous	6-7	perfect (pinacoidal)	uneven	3·2	ortho-rhombic	metamorphic rocks	
Staurolite (H₂O.2FeO.5Al₂O₃.4SiO₂)	grey	vitreous	7·5	imperfect	conchoidal	3·7	ortho-rhombic	metamorphic rocks	
Titanite or Sphene (CaO.TiO₂.SiO₂)	white	resinous	5-5·5	good (prismatic)	uneven	3·5	monoclinic	igneous rocks	
Topaz (Al₂F₂SiO₄) (ZrSiO₄)	white	vitreous	8	perfect (basal)	uneven	3·5	ortho-rhombic	igneous rocks	gems
Tourmaline complex silicate	white, green, blue	vitreous	7-7·5	poor	uneven	2·98	hexagonal	igneous rocks	gems
Wollastonite (CaO.SiO₂)	white	vitreous	4·5	perfect	—	2·9	triclinic	metamorphic rocks	gems
Zircon (ZrSiO₄)	white	vitreous	7·5	poor	conchoidal	4·7	tetragonal	igneous rocks	gems

* The rock-forming minerals. For chemical composition see page 50.

V. Degradation and its Consequences

The surface of the earth, like the circumstances of man's life, is for ever exposed to the forces of change. These forces, when manifested in a volcanic eruption, in an earthquake with its accompanying tidal wave, in a tornado or in floods, may be swift and catastrophic. When they occur through the action of the wind upon the desert surface, the sea against a rocky shore, a highland torrent or a mountain glacier, they are slow and their effects are barely perceptible during the course of a lifetime. Nevertheless, it is these slow, steady forces of change which, in the course of geological time, have again and again transformed the face of the earth.

This transformation is initiated by the loosening of the hard rock of the land surface and by its transport and deposition elsewhere, both on land or in the sea. This breaking-up of the land surface is described as WEATHERING, while the process of removal, transport and the further disintegration during transport, is known as EROSION. Erosion is a destructive process; deposition is constructive, leading to the formation of new rocks. Where the forces of wind or ice are involved, the action is dominantly mechanical. In erosion and deposition by water, both mechanical and chemical changes occur.

Some authorities regard the term DENUDATION as synonymous with erosion. Others, including Holmes, consider that denudation should embrace both weathering and erosion, with the same meaning as DEGRADATION. The latter view of the use of the term—the position is well summarised by Challinor—is used in the present text.

SOILS

Considerable advances have been made in recent years in the investigation of the properties of soils. In civil engineering, where the strength of building foundations is all-important, it is the physicist and the engineer who collaborate within the discipline of soil mechanics. On the other hand, soils in agriculture require the co-operation of the geologist, the chemist, the biologist and the physicist.

Immature soils develop through the process of weathering, and these soils reflect the chemical content of the rocks from which they have been derived. But the character of older, more mature soils increasingly depends upon factors other than the composition of the rock. These factors include climate, topography, vegetation and time. In the end, thoroughly mature soils which have developed under similar environmental conditions, are likely to have similar chemical characteristics, irrespective of the nature of the underlying rock whose disintegration provided the substance of the soil in the first place.

The vertical section from the surface down to the solid rock (BEDROCK) is known as the SOIL PROFILE. It is made up of a number of horizons. These soil horizons vary in character and in thickness according to the interplay of the factors of environment mentioned above. The WASTE MANTLE is the broken material which immediately overlies and is derived from the bedrock. This layer often shows the beginnings of chemical change as well as mechanical disintegration, but is as yet unaffected by vegetation and animals. Above the waste mantle lie the lower horizons of the soil. These are of variable thickness whose character depends very much upon the extent to which organic solutions from the surface have reacted upon what was formerly the waste mantle. The surface soil, lying at the top of the profile, is rich in humus with only the most chemically resistant minerals of the bedrock still present.

Three important soils of the world are the PODZOLS (the grey soils of the humid temperate regions), the CHERNOZEMS (the black soils of the regions of lower rainfall, including the Russian steppes) and the RED EARTHS (soils of the tropical regions where rainfall is seasonal). In the development of each of these types, climate is the decisive factor, and this governs not only the nature of the vegetation but also the extent of the chemical action provided by the surface solutions within the soil profile.

The podzols develop as a result of the removal by percolation of bases, humus, iron and aluminium compounds. This leaves an impoverished bleached zone in the upper part of the subsoil. The base of this zone (one or two feet below the surface) is often marked by a hard black layer where the leached materials have accumulated, forming HARDPAN.

In regions of chernozem development, the dominant factor is the influence of the long dry and hot summers which retards both leaching and the breakdown of organic matter. As a consequence the soils are neutral, whilst the high content of humus imparts to them its characteristic black colour.

Red earths develop in regions of heavy tropical rainfall which causes intense downward leaching. This process is so complete that only the most resistant minerals survive in the soil. The result is that the insoluble hydroxides and oxides of aluminium and iron become relatively concentrated to form a red-brown earth. Occasionally, the iron hydroxide is absent, leaving BAUXITE, a valuable source of aluminium.

These are three of the important examples of the world's mature soils. There are many others. Much research is still being carried on into the complex chemical reactions with which they are associated. In addition, there are great areas of the earth's surface where the soils are still immature; this may be due to topographical conditions resulting in bad drainage or to parent rocks unproductive in breakdown products, such as limestones or quartzose sandstones. On the other hand, conditions may be as in Britain, where much of the high ground was rubbed bare of its waste mantle during the Ice Age; in these regions it is the bedrock which, under the process of weathering, is still the dominant influence in the provision of soil.

WEATHERING

Weathering depends upon both the climate and the composition of the rock outcropping on the surface. It may come about through the mechanical disintegration of the rock or from chemical changes in its constituent minerals.

Mechanical changes. Under desert conditions, the sun's heat can raise the temperature of a bare rock surface to such a degree that it becomes uncomfortable to the touch. Yet only a few inches below the surface, the rock remains many degrees cooler. At night the surface temperature falls, and this repeated daily variation causes expansion and contraction in the rock which, in turn, sets up internal stresses. Eventually, fracturing develops and the rock surface flakes off in plate-like masses (fig. 143). This phenomenon, known as EXFOLIATION, occurs only in igneous (especially granite) and in metamorphic rocks, whose crystals are tightly packed, without adequate room for expansion. It may be that chemical alteration also plays a subsidiary part. There are many examples of exfoliation from Africa. A similar mechanism is at work on the pebbles and boulders on a desert surface which also break apart through changes in temperature.

Under freezing conditions in humid regions, the destructive power of mechanical weathering is much greater. Water percolates into joints and crevices

143 The exfoliation of a granite surface under hot, dry conditions. (After photograph in Holmes' *Principles of Physical Geology*)

144 Tree, rooted in the joint of a large glacial erratic, gradually forcing the two halves asunder.

in the rock and also between the grains of sedimentary formations. On freezing, the water expands and breaks open the rock, as it does when, turned to ice, it bursts a domestic water-pipe. This FROST SHATTERING produces a very characteristic topography on the bare hill-tops in many parts of the world (figs. **170**, 188, **224, 230**).

The roots of trees and shrubs, during growth, also help in this process of wedging rock apart. Roots often find their way down into joints and as they thicken, the walls of the joint are forced apart (fig. 144).

Chemical changes. Rain-water is the chief agent of chemical change in rocks. Pure rain-water is a poor solvent, but if it should contain carbon dioxide in solution, then it is able to dissolve limestone. Solution readily takes place down joint-planes, producing the topography which takes its name from the Karst region of Jugoslavia (fig. 145). As the solution along the joints increases, streams and rivers find their way underground, and enormous caverns are produced. Unless there are impurities in limestone, the soil derived from their solution is poor, and wide surfaces of bare rock are characteristic of limestone country (fig. 145).

Rain-water, bearing carbon dioxide in solution, causes chemical changes among the less stable minerals of igneous rocks. Potash and soda feldspars are broken down, and a clay residue is left. The ferromagnesian minerals, especially olivine, are susceptible to this kind of chemical change, and basic igneous rocks can be reduced to a crumbling mass. In dolerites, for example, solutions migrating

107

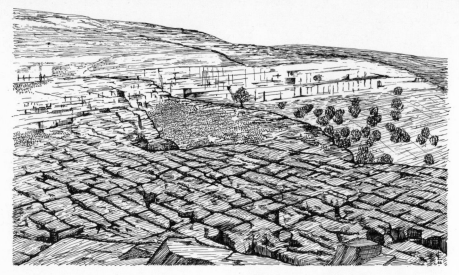

145 Karst topography in the limestone of Malham, Yorkshire. (After photograph in Holmes' *Principles of Physical Geology*)

down joint-planes attack the surface of each joint, causing the rock to flake off
in a series of shells and producing SPHEROIDAL or ONION WEATHERING
(figs. **43** and 146).

When ferromagnesian minerals are broken down in this way, in the presence
of oxygen, the mineral limonite is formed. This is yellow-brown, and is very
widely distributed. Frequently it is precipitated between the grains of a sandstone, giving the colour which is characteristic of many of these rocks. If this
mineral is dehydrated through heating, it is transformed into the red oxide,
hematite. Desert soils, which have been subjected to prolonged dehydration, are

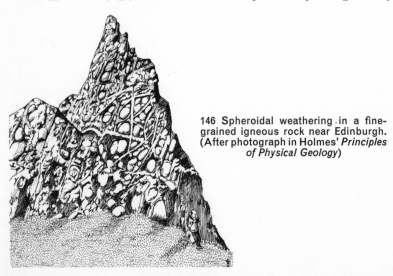

146 Spheroidal weathering in a fine-
grained igneous rock near Edinburgh.
(After photograph in Holmes' *Principles
of Physical Geology*)

generally red. Both limonite ($Fe_2O_3.H_2O$) and hematite (Fe_2O_3) are ferric oxides. If they are subjected to reducing action, for example, by chemicals produced from growing plants, they are changed to the black ferrous (Fe_3O_4) form, known as magnetite.

THE ACTION OF THE WIND

Wind is directly responsible for sculpturing the surface in the arid deserts of the world. It is also indirectly responsible for the processes of denudation by water and ice, in that it transports water-vapour in the atmosphere to regions where it is eventually precipitated as rain or snow. Furthermore, wind creates the ocean waves which erode the fringes of the land-masses and form the shorelines of the world.

In a desert region, the destructive work of the wind involves DEFLATION, the removal of particles from the dry surface; also ABRASION or CORRASION, the wearing away of rock surfaces through the bombardment of sand-laden wind; and ATTRITION, the breaking and wearing of the particles during transport, as they collide with one another and with rock surfaces.

Deflation. Deflation can occur only across a dry surface. In areas where the rainfall is distributed throughout the year, it is negligible. Where rainfall is confined to certain periods of the year, it follows that deflation, too, is seasonal, while in areas where there is little or no precipitation, deflation is a continuous and active process so long as there is wind.

The power of the wind to transport particles varies according to its velocity. A strong wind will carry forward small pebbles (1 cm or more in diameter) in a bouncing movement. Coarse sand may be swept along several feet above the dry surface. Upward currents raise fine dust and sand particles so that they may remain indefinitely in suspension. It is in this way that dust-storms are formed, and material can be carried across a continent. Sand from the Middle West of North America is deposited in the eastern part of that continent. Sand from the Sahara is borne across the Mediterranean and is shed over the countries of southern Europe. African dust is known to have fallen even in England. The fine ash from volcanic eruptions, such as that of Krakatoa in 1883 (page 29), may encircle the globe and remain in suspension in the atmosphere for several years.

The capacity of the wind to transport great volumes of dust from one area to another is enormous. It has been calculated that a cubic mile of air will support as much as 4,000 tons, and a large storm will involve tens of millions of tons of dust.

The chief factor in ridding the air of the light suspended particles of dust is rainfall. Just as rain washes out soot from the air over a large city, and deposits it upon its buildings (and the housewife's washing), so over the humid regions of the world, the dust derived from the neighbouring deserts is deposited; it has

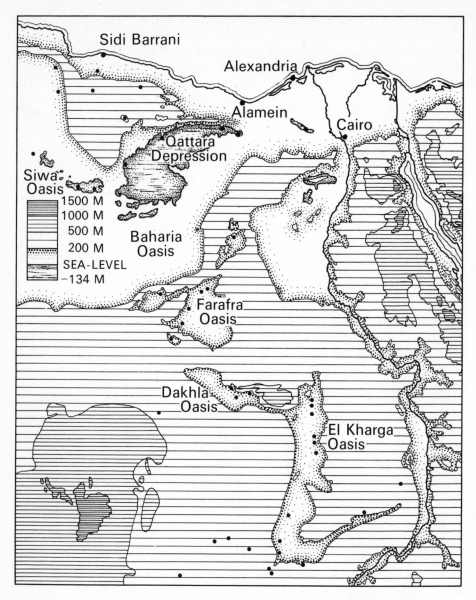

Siwa
Oasis

1500 M
1000 M
500 M
200 M
SEA-LEVEL
−134 M

Sidi Barrani

Alexandria

Alamein

Cairo

Qattara
Depression

Baharia
Oasis

Farafra
Oasis

Dakhla
Oasis

El Kharga
Oasis

147 The great **Qattara Depression** in the Western **Desert** of **Egypt**, and the
chief oases, cut out by the deflationary action of the wind.

been calculated that in these regions a layer, on average 1 cm thick, accumulates in the course of two centuries.

Where the wind crosses an area of desert over which soft shaly rocks outcrop, great hollows may be scooped out, and this process will continue downwards, until the water-table is reached. In Egypt, the Qattara Depression and the many oases in the Western Desert (fig. 147), are examples of this process, as also is the Kalahari of South Africa.

Abrasion. Sand-blasting provides the main abrasive power of the wind. This is most effective within a few feet of the ground, where sand-laden winds pound rock surfaces, boulders, telegraph poles and fence posts. Timber is cut through, and has to be protected by metal sheeting. Vehicles can have their paint removed and their wind-screens frosted in a severe sand-storm. Unevenness in the distribution of cementing materials in sandstones is picked out by abrasion and produces a honeycomb pattern. Limestones become fluted, nodules and fossils stand out on the rock face. Fantastically shaped ROCK PINNACLES are formed (figs. 148 and 152), while on a larger scale INSELBERGE, or island mountains, left by a retreating desert plateau, owe their origin in part to stream as well as to wind erosion (fig. 153).

On the desert surface, the sand is removed from layers of mixed sand and gravel, leaving the latter to form what is termed a DESERT PAVEMENT. Each pebble, should its position be shifted by a stronger gust, becomes fluted first on one side and then another. In its final shape the pebble possesses three or more flat surfaces, separated by sharp, sinuous ridges. Such pebbles are commonly known as VENTIFACTS or DREIKANTER (fig. 149).

148 El Zobr, a rock pinnacle fashioned by the blast of the sand-laden wind, Sinai, Egypt.

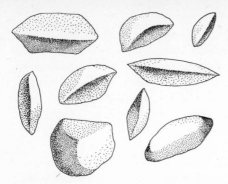

149 Dreikanter, abraded pebbles, on a desert surface.

In the process of attrition, grains of sand, originally angular when broken from the parent rock, become slowly rounded and their surfaces frosted. This is particularly the case with quartz, which is high in the scale of hardness. Other minerals, especially those with well-developed cleavage like mica, are ground down, reduced to a very fine powder and are winnowed away from the heavier quartz grains. Absence of mica, together with frosted grains of quartz, are characteristics common to all desert sands, both ancient and modern.

Deposition. Sand and dust is deposited by the action of the wind. The sand accumulates to form DUNES, and is material of local origin. The dust may be carried many hundreds of miles before being laid down as LOESS.

Any accumulation of sand with a crest is described as a dune. Whenever sand-bearing wind meets an obstruction—it may be an established dune or vegetation, pebbles or boulders—an eddy is formed and sand is deposited around it. DESERT DUNES are formed only in regions of very low rainfall; RIVER DUNES are built up along the banks of water-courses where rainfall is seasonal, while SHORE DUNES occur along the coasts of the world, irrespective of rainfall.

Shore Dunes. Sand raised from the sea-bed by bottom currents may be carried towards the shore and deposited above low water, forming a sandy beach. In areas where persistent on-shore winds occur, this beach sand is carried forward in the air and deposited on the low ground adjoining the beach, where it accumulates as a dune. High cliffs reduce the velocity of an on-shore wind, and generally prevent the formation of dunes on the landward side.

Shore dunes are usually halted, and become fixed, by the growth of coarse grasses and reeds, whose roots form a ramifying network through the sand. Around the coasts of the British Isles, they commonly occur in belts a few hundred yards wide, parallel to the shore. Occasionally, as along the north-facing shore of the Moray Firth, strong winds have promoted the landward migration of dunes, submerging woodlands and farm buildings. Strategic planting of thick belts of conifers can do much to halt this process. The best and most often-quoted examples of shore dunes occur along the coasts of the Bay of Biscay, where they extend inland for five miles, and reach a height of several hundred feet.

River Dunes. In countries with a long rainless season, rivers dry up and their sandy beds therefore become exposed. In wide, open valleys, the sand is raised by the wind and is deposited on the adjacent flat ground, forming groups of dunes. In the south of France, in Spain, in the Great Plains of the United States, in the south of Russia and elsewhere, there are abundant examples of this type of dune formation. Unless, like the shore dunes, it is controlled by tree planting, it can be ruinous to agricultural land.

Desert Dunes. In the truly desert areas of the world, there is little or no rainfall and therefore there is a lack of vegetation to impede the accumulation and movement of sand. The popular conception of the desert as a sea of sand is misleading. Sand seas occupy only about one-fifth of the total desert surface. The rest is rocky or stony ground, the so-called 'HAMMADA' desert (fig. **156**), with occasional belts or colonies of dunes. Sand seas, such as that across the northern part of the Sinai isthmus, or (on a much larger scale) the Empty Quarter of Arabia, are formed by inconstant winds which concentrate the sand within a particular area and fashion its surface into great hollows and crests (fig. **151**).

Where the wind is constant, but the amount of sand limited, the isolated dune, known as the BARCHAN, is formed (fig. 150). The barchan has a long, gentle windward slope with a steep lee slope. The sharp ridge between the two slopes is highest in the centre and on either side it curves forward into a CUSP. The mechanism of formation is simple: the prevailing wind lifts the sand from the windward face, forms an eddy as it reaches the ridge, so that the sand falls out, and accumulates on the leeward side at its natural angle of rest, about 35 degrees. Along either edge of the barchan the wind meets less resistance and therefore it carries the sand further forward. Barchans are often perfectly symmetrical, and during the course of a storm the smaller ones may migrate 20 feet down wind. They vary in size from two or three feet in height and 40 feet across, to a height of 100 feet and with a width in proportion.

150 A small barchan, five feet high, lying athwart a desert road.

Sand grains carried forward   Deposited in eddy

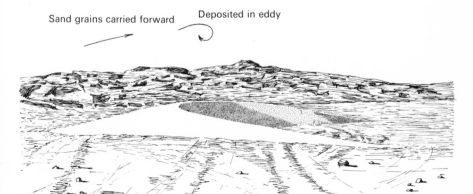

151 A sand sea in south-east Arabia.

152 Horizontally stratified sandstone fashioned by wind-abrasion in the Badlands of Drumheller, Alberta. The topmost layer, being more firmly cemented, forms a prominent feature.

153 Hammada topography in the Libyan Sahara. The small inselberg in the middle distance consists of horizontally stratified shale capped by more resistant sandstone.

154 Two parallel seif dunes, with the stony deflated area between them.

The SEIF (in Arabic 'sword-like') dunes with their long, parallel ridges are well developed in the Western Desert of Egypt. In that region, the prevailing northerly wind from the Mediterranean bears the sand from the coastal belt, leaving a gently rising hammada surface. (It was across this gravel surface that the opposing armies moved back and forth in the battles which culminated, in 1942, at Alamein.) Southwards, deflation has bitten deep into the outcropping shales, creating the great Qattara Depression. Further south, as its velocity decreases, the wind drops much of its load and forms the great parallel seif ridges—a series of dune barriers which are altogether 200 miles long and over 50 miles wide (fig. 147).

When the prevailing wind strikes the seif, its velocity is reduced, whereas across the flat ground between the seif and its neighbour, it meets less resistance. Therefore, lateral eddies are set up and sand is transferred from the flat to the seif surface on either hand (fig. 154). Seif dunes commonly reach a height of 200 or 300 feet. In the Western Desert, they sometimes rise as much as 700 feet above the desert plain. Small and solitary seif-like dunes may also be built up in the wind-shadow area of a cliff (fig. 155).

Loess. The dust which finally settles out of the air, often hundreds of miles from its source, forms an extremely fine-grained deposit, sometimes accumulating to a thickness of several hundred feet. It is almost as fine-grained as a clay, though, unlike the latter, its composition and structure proves it to be of aeolian rather than of aqueous origin.

The composition of loess varies according to its area of origin. The loess of North America is derived from the arid Middle West, of North Argentina from the desert regions in the west of South America, of eastern Europe from the vast glacial deposits which covered western Europe at the end of the Ice Age, and of China from the Gobi Desert.

Loess areas are often of great agricultural importance. Because loess is so soft and unconsolidated, it can easily be eroded by water. Indeed, it is often the flats of redeposited loess in river valleys—as in the Yellow River valley of China, for example—which prove of greatest value to the farmer. Not only does he wrest his living from soil derived from loess, but he sometimes fashions his home out of its cliffs.

THE ACTION OF THE SEA

Of all the agents of erosion, that of the sea, because of its rapidity of action, can be the most dramatic. The great North Sea 'surge' of 1953, for example, wrought havoc along the east coast of England. On that occasion exceptionally high tides, combined with very heavy seas whipped up by a gale, eroded back the cliffs at one point along the Suffolk coast by as much as 90 feet almost overnight.

Shoreline Patterns. The effect of erosion by the sea depends not only upon the character of the rocks which form the coastline, but also upon the prevalence of earth-movements. A shoreline which has developed after the subsidence of the land, a SHORELINE OF SUBMERGENCE, is much more subject to erosion than one which has been created by uplift, a SHORELINE OF EMERGENCE, as is explained below.

The effect around the coasts of Britain, because of the geologically recent events associated with the Ice Age, are striking. The great weight of snow forming the ice-caps and ice-fields in the regions of high latitude depressed countries like Scandinavia and, to a lesser degree, Britain. Therefore in these regions there was a general encroachment of the sea on to the land. But this encroachment was itself lessened because the levels of the oceans had become lowered in providing snow for the ice-fields. Then again, when the ice began to

155 A solitary seif-like dune growing beneath the wind shadow formed by a cliff.

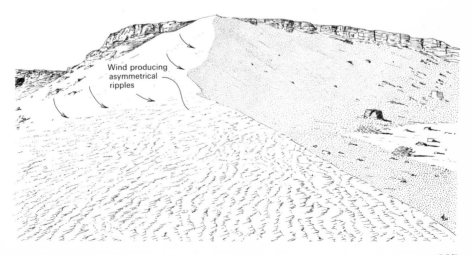

Wind producing asymmetrical ripples

156 Typical 'hammada' country—stony desert.

157 Miniature sand dunes developing on the leeward side of pebbles and shells as they lie on a beach swept by a sand-laden wind.

158 The estuary of the Gannel, Newquay; part of a submerged shore-line.

melt, a redistribution of weight took place and the land began to rise in isostatic compensation (page 181). The extent of subsidence or elevation varied in different parts of the same region, so that this process was frequently expressed in a tilting of the land. The result is that in Britain, shorelines are in some parts indicators of recent submergence, while in others of recent emergence. These movements will continue until compensation is fully achieved.

Below high-water mark, wave erosion produces a sea-bed which slopes gently down towards the deeper waters. Uplift raises the cliffs beyond the reach of the waves and exposes part of this sloping sea-bed. Because of the regularity of this slope, the new coastline remains straight and devoid of inlets. Furthermore, as the waves roll in towards the shore, much of their strength is dissipated against the shallowing slope, and little power is left in them to attack the new coastline

159 A stage in the development of a sea stack in the Jurassic sandstone along the north shore of the Isle of Eigg, Inner Hebrides. These sandstones are overlain by the Tertiary plateau basalts which, in the photograph, can be seen forming the distant skyline.

160 A raised beach, bounded on the landward side by old, abandoned sea-cliffs, and on the seaward side by the newly eroded cliffs.

itself. Eventually, however, a new cliff-line is developed, behind and above which is the old RAISED BEACH with its abandoned cliffs (figs. 160 and **165**).

On the other hand, subsidence of the land will cause the sea to invade the coastal areas, which may consist of hills and deep valleys. In such a case the new coastline will be much indented, with tongues of water running inland into the 'drowned' valleys. The south coast of Devon and Cornwall affords a good example of coastal submergence (figs. **158** and 161).

161 A 'drowned' coastline at Falmouth, S.W. England; the sea having invaded the river valleys.

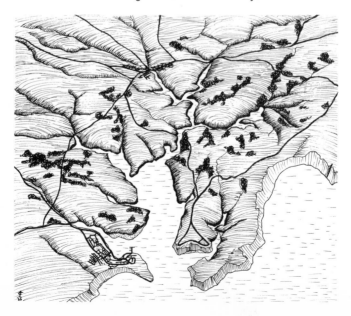

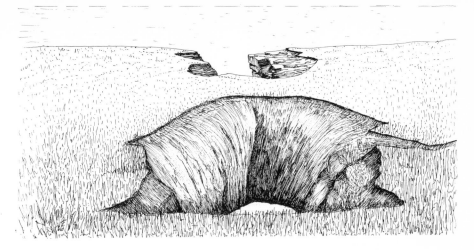

162 A view of a blowhole from the landward side.

Cliff Erosion. When a strongly consolidated rock of uniform composition—such as a limestone or a sandstone—forms a cliff along a shoreline of submergence, a very characteristic pattern of erosion develops. Waves, armed with pebbles, which break against a cliff of horizontal or gently tilted strata, force their way into the minute, parallel cracks, or JOINTS, which traverse all sedimentary rocks. These joints, of which there are generally two sets, extend vertically and more or less at right angles to one another. The gap between each joint (or

163 A sea-stack, soon to be reduced to two separate stacks by erosion along vertical joint planes.

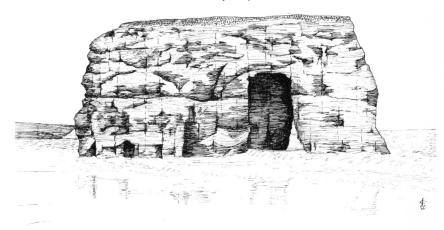

164 Two sea-stacks of Cretaceous Chalk, Isle of Purbeck, Dorset. A small cave is being eroded in the larger stack, which will eventually divide it in two.

165 The Scottish coast is a shoreline of emergence. Here, at Ardmair, Wester Ross, the raised beach can be seen beyond the bay, with farm cottages built upon it.

166 The Niagara Falls from the air. The long gorge cuts into horizontally bedded shales, which are capped by more resistant limestone. The bridge across the gorge linking Canada and the U.S.A. can be seen in the foreground. The American Falls spill over along the length of the gorge, while the Horse Shoe Falls lie at its head.

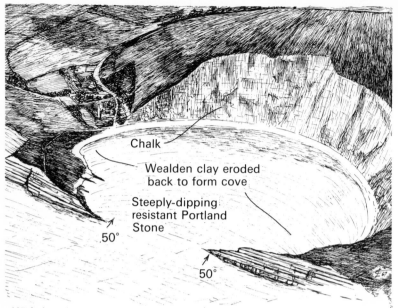

Chalk

Wealden clay eroded
back to form cove

Steeply-dipping
resistant Portland
Stone

50°

50°

167 Lulworth cove, a Pacific-type shoreline. (After a photograph by Aerofilms Ltd.)

between those better developed) is gradually widened, the rock falls away between them and a SEA-CAVE is formed. In sea cliffs where the strata approaches the vertical, this process takes place along adjacent, parallel bedding planes. The action is accentuated by the air which becomes trapped and compressed as the oncoming rush of water enters the cave. At length, the roof at the back of the cave may fall in, forming a BLOWHOLE (fig. 162). Further action leads to the collapse of the roof of the cave along its whole length. Meanwhile, if the cliff is part of a bluff, the sea may attack along the other set of major joints, forming a second cave running at right angles to the first. Eventually, the two caves will unite and a small portion of cliff will become entirely isolated. This island column is known as a SEA STACK (figs. 163 and **164**). Sea stacks are sometimes found preserved beside the abandoned cliffs bordering a raised beach.

As the cliffs retreat before the onset of the sea, a rocky floor is left, slightly below high-water level. This is known as the WAVE-CUT PLATFORM. In itself, this rocky platform reduces the force of the waves, and serves to protect the cliffs. Wave-cut platforms are common around the rocky coasts of Britain, extending seawards for perhaps half a mile. In Norway, the famous STRAND-FLAT, a platform 30 miles in width, is an extreme example of this process.

A cliff composed of alternating layers of hard and soft rock, much more than one of homogeneous strata, is a prey to erosion by the sea. The soft layers at or near high water are cut back and the hard rock is undermined. The latter, falling away in slabs, accumulates at the foot of the cliff and protects it from further immediate erosion—the sea has to break down the protecting slabs before it can again attack the cliff itself. Sea walls are often artificially protected in this way, by the dumping of large blocks of broken rock in front of them.

A cliff composed of uniformly soft rock provides only a feeble barrier against the processes of erosion. There is no protection against the force of the waves, and especially in times of storm (as in the North Sea 'surge' of 1953) great inroads can be made in a very short time. It is these soft strata which form the bays of a coastline, while the indurated rock creates the headlands.

In some coastal regions, the grain of the rock may run at right angles to the shore. In South-west Ireland the Carboniferous rocks are arched into a series of folds running almost west–east. The anticlines form topographical ridges, the synclines more readily form valleys (page 147). Subsidence of the land has caused the sea to invade the valleys, while the ridges remain above water-level. Therefore a series of bays, known as RIAS, form a deeply indented coastline, which has been given the name ATLANTIC TYPE (fig. **214**).

In other areas, as along the south coast of England, the coast of Jugoslavia and along parts of the west coast of America, the alignment of the strata runs parallel to the shore. Anticlines of hard rock form a barrier against the sea, and protect the soft rock on the landward side. In time, however, the sea breaks through this hard barrier—along joints and bedding planes, as already described —and once this occurs the landward soft rock is rapidly attacked. Along the south coast of England, Lulworth Cove is an example of this process in an early stage (fig. 167), while the numerous long islands lying in the Adriatic parallel with the shore of Jugoslavia, illustrate the process in its later stages. These are coastlines of the PACIFIC TYPE.

Deposition Across the Shore. Shorelines of emergence, as mentioned above, are characterised in their earliest stages by a straight coastline and by a gradually sloping sea-floor. The waves break offshore and therefore attack the sea-floor rather than the cliffs. The sand and silt which is derived from this process is built up into a bar running parallel with the shore, and eventually forms a lagoon. In the mature stage, the bar is cut away by the waves and a steepened sea-floor is formed, allowing the waves to attack the cliffs themselves.

Strong winds blowing off the land create a slight head of water out at sea, and this sets up a compensating undertow towards the land. Sand is shifted from the sea-bed by this current and is deposited on the shore. Likewise, a strong off-sea wind produces an undertow in a seaward direction, and the shore is swept clean of sand.

Waves breaking on the shore hurl pebbles and sand towards high-water mark. In the backwash, which lacks the mechanical power of the wave which preceded it, the sand is carried away while the pebbles are rolled back slightly, or remain stationary, forming a STORM BEACH. Pebbles whose shape is elongate often come to rest with their long axes parallel to the shoreline, forming a pattern

168 The deep fjord of Milford Sound, New Zealand.

169 The Goose River Falls, Labrador. The water can be seen cutting down through vertical joint planes in the rock. Note the glaciated land-surface.

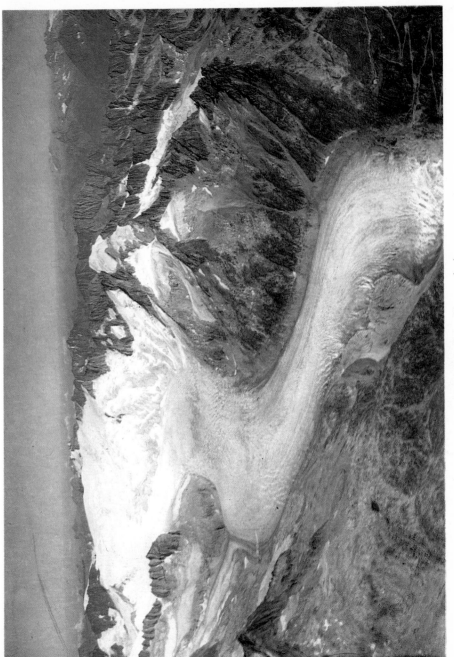

170 The head of the Rhone glacier.

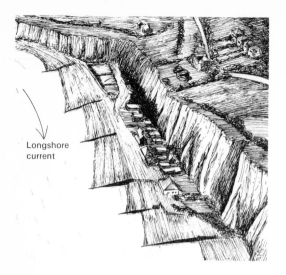

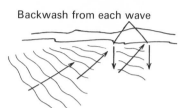

171 Groynes erected across the shore. The longshore drift is towards the viewer. (After a photograph by Aerofilms Ltd.)

Longshore current

Backwash from each wave

Waves approaching shore

172 Diagram illustrating the mechanics of transport of sediment along the shore.

known as IMBRICATION. In heavy seas, pebbles may be thrown well above high-water level, in the spray of the waves, forming an elongated barrier which cannot be removed by subsequent wave action. Chesil Beach, Portland, some miles west of Lulworth, affords a good example.

Deposition Along the Shore. When waves approach the shore obliquely, as for example in the English Channel where the prevailing wind is south-west, they curve round in a great arc as each point along their front slows down on meeting the resistance of the shallower sea-floor. The sand load of each wave therefore approaches the shore obliquely, but in the backwash it recedes at right angles to

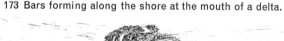

173 Bars forming along the shore at the mouth of a delta.

it (fig. 172). The overall movement of sediment is thus along the shore, described as LONGSHORE DRIFT. To reduce the effect of this drift, groynes are often set up at right angles to the shore. Sand piles up against them on the exposed side, but is swept clear on the leeward side, and the longshore movement is slowed down (fig. 171).

A change in the direction of the coastline causes the longshore drift to accumulate in the form of a SPIT, or promontory. Sometimes the presence of currents causes a spit to curve round landwards, producing a HOOK. At times, if the shore recedes to form only a narrow inlet, sand may be built right across its opening, forming a BAR (fig. 173).

THE ACTION OF RIVERS

In a river system, each stream has its source either in the swampy uplands which form the CATCHMENT AREA, or in a spring or series of springs bringing ground water to the surface in the manner described below (page 251). Streams unite as tributaries which, in turn, link up to form the main rivers of a region.

Erosion. Streams and rivers act as powerful agents of erosion in the following ways: the process of carrying debris downstream is known as HYDRAULIC ACTION, and this varies enormously according to the velocity of the water. A slow-running stream can transport only the finest mud; the same stream, swollen to a raging torrent after an exceptionally heavy storm, may move

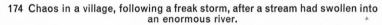

174 Chaos in a village, following a freak storm, after a stream had swollen into an enormous river.

boulders up to 10 feet in diameter (fig. 174). Rock material, including limestones and some evaporites, is carried in solution. This is described as CORROSION. The wearing of the sides and the floors of rivers by the scouring action of the material carried in the water is corrasion. The breaking-up of individual pebbles and boulders as they clash against one another and against the rocky banks and the floor is termed attrition. Hydraulic action, corrosion, corrasion and attrition are terms which are also used in describing the action of the sea.

Fine mud is carried downstream in SUSPENSION; sand grains are transported partly in suspension and partly by bouncing off the river-bed—a process described as SALTATION. Pebbles and boulders, being too heavy to be lifted by the water, are swept along the river-bed in a ROLLING movement. It is only during times of flood that the destructive force of hydraulic action, involving corrasion and attrition, really becomes significant.

It has been calculated that the rivers of the world transport 9,000 million tons annually, of which 30% is in solution. As described below, much of the insoluble load may be deposited within the lower part of a water-course and may fail to reach the sea. Some of the material in solution is precipitated at the river's mouth, where it flocculates as the fresh water comes into contact with the salt.

The classical description of river profiles was developed by W. M. Davis at the beginning of the century, and much of his work is still accepted by modern GEOMORPHOLOGISTS (those who study land-forms). Davis divided a river's course into three sections. These he called the MOUNTAIN TRACT, having steep gradients and walls and with interlocking spurs (fig. 175); the VALLEY TRACT, with a less steep gradient and a wider V-profile; the PLAIN TRACT, where the river's gradient is low and therefore its velocity much reduced (fig. 181). A river collects its load of material chiefly from the mountain tract, carries it, especially in times of flood, along the valley tract and deposits all but the finest fractions in the plain tract.

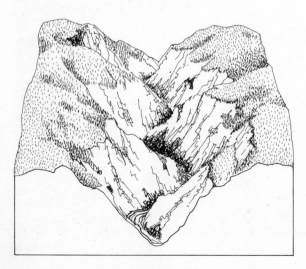

175 The mountain tract of a stream, with overlapping spurs and steep gradient.

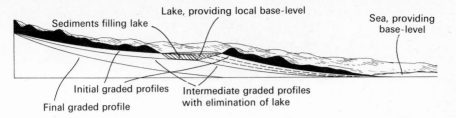

Sediments filling lake · Lake, providing local base-level · Sea, providing base-level

Initial graded profiles · Intermediate graded profiles with elimination of lake

Final graded profile

176 The establishment of a graded profile.

In a region where the crust is stable and not subject to elevation or subsidence, a river can develop a GRADED PROFILE. Here the three tracts merge one into another in a gradually slackening slope from source to mouth, where sea-level marks the downward limit of erosion. Sea-level is therefore described as the BASE LEVEL, while a lake along the course of a river provides a LOCAL BASE LEVEL (fig. 176). Such a lake is steadily filled-in by river deposits (fig. 177) and these deposits are themselves eliminated as the water-course is regraded from sea-level.

As a river erodes its course towards a graded profile, rocks of varying resistance may be encountered. WATERFALLS may develop across a succession of shales alternating with more indurated rock. As the water pours over a ledge of the more resistant rock, the underlying shale is cut back in the turbulent conditions at the

177 The site of a former lake, now filled in with, and displaced by, sediment which has been brought down by streams from the surrounding higher ground. (After photograph in Holmes' *Principles of Physical Geology*)

178 A waterfall, having eroded into shale and thus undercut the overlying limestone, leaves a long gorge in its wake.

foot of the waterfall. In time, the more resistant ledge is undermined and is cut away, so that a long gorge is formed, with the waterfall at its head (figs. **166, 169** and 178). Other types of strongly indurated rock, like an igneous dyke or a highly inclined sandstone or limestone bed, are more likely to form a series of rapids rather than a persistent waterfall.

One of the features commonly encountered in a developing river system is that of RIVER CAPTURE. Tributaries erode into the upland catchment areas by BACKWARD EROSION, the rate depending much upon the character of the rock. It may happen that the head of a tributary of a river cuts through the dividing ridge separating it from its neighbour and captures all but the lowest reaches of the latter. The point of capture, marked by a sharp bend, is termed the ELBOW OF CAPTURE, while the now abandoned valley is described as the WIND GAP. The small remnant stream in the wind gap is the MISFIT (fig. 179).

There are numerous examples of river capture; in Britain, the river system which is usually quoted in this connection is that of the Ouse. As the diagram shows (fig. 180), the River Aire flows eastwards to the sea and at one time a

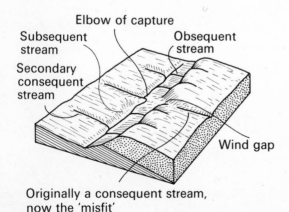

Elbow of capture

Subsequent stream

Obsequent stream

Secondary consequent stream

Wind gap

179 River capture: diagrammatic illustration.

Originally a consequent stream, now the 'misfit'

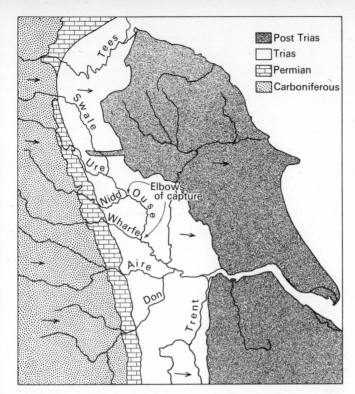

number of rivers on the north pursued parallel courses to the sea. However, these were in turn captured by a tributary of the Aire flowing south across the low ground occupied by the outcrop of the soft Trias. This tributary, now called the River Ouse, is augmented by the captured waters of Wharfe, Nidd, Ure and Swale. Only the Tees still maintains its eastward course to the sea.

181 A meander belt with oxbow lakes, flanked by river terraces—characteristic feature of a plain tract.

The Aire, with the lowest reaches of the Ouse, follows the dip of the rock and is a CONSEQUENT river; the main length of the Ouse, flowing across the dip, is termed SUBSEQUENT. The Wharfe, Nidd, Ure and Swale are each said to be SECONDARY CONSEQUENT. Streams which unite at an acute angle are termed INSEQUENT, while those which drain the ESCARPMENT formed by the subsequent, are described as OBSEQUENT.

Deposition. In the plain tract, the deposits of fine mud, sand and gravel become an obstacle to the progress of a river, causing it frequently to change its course in a series of wide sweeps. These form the MEANDER BELT, each individual loop being described as a MEANDER.

Meanders develop only in the soft, unconsolidated deposits of the plain tract, where a river can readily adjust its course to the path of least resistance. As undercutting progresses, the curve of each meander becomes sharper until the river breaks through to the neighbouring meander, leaving an isolated section known as an OXBOW LAKE (fig. 181). At each bend, too, there is a build-up of water, where the undercutting develops, creating a bottom current in the direction shown on the diagram (fig. 182). This not only restores the water-level but also transfers some of the undercut material to the opposing bank.

A river in time of flood is so loaded with debris that, towards its mouth, the channel becomes entirely filled with sediment. At this stage the river has to find its way through its own deposits by cutting out a series of channels. It is then said to be BRAIDED.

Also, in times of flood, a river overflows its banks, especially along the plain tract. As it swirls over the flooded shallows, its speed is reduced and therefore sediment in suspension is deposited. These deposits form ridges or LÉVÉES, running parallel with either bank. They help to confine succeeding flood waters but at the same time their effect is to restrict the accumulation of deposits to within the main channel. The river-bed is therefore raised above the level of the adjacent flood plain, and in times of severe flooding, the lévées may be breached, leading to very serious conditions indeed (fig. 183).

182 Undercutting in the soft deposits of a plain tract.

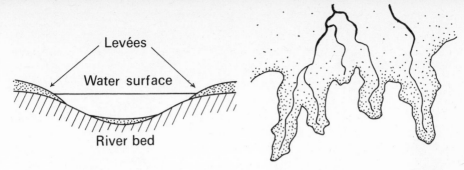

183 Cross-section of the plain tract of a river, with levées.

184 The pattern of a bird's foot delta.

River deposits reaching the open sea are carried away by currents. However, the deposits of a river which enters a partially land-locked and sheltered sea, like the Gulf of Mexico or the Mediterranean, suffer no such dispersal. Instead, sand and mud is dumped at the river mouth and is gradually built up, seawards, as a DELTA.

The name, delta, was first given by the Greeks to the great accumulation of deposits at the mouth of the Nile, because the ARCUATE spread bore the shape of the fourth letter of the Greek alphabet (fig. 173). Deltas vary in shape and extent according to local conditions. The region of the mouth of the Nile is subject to subsidence, and therefore the accumulating deposits do little more than keep the great delta surface up to sea-level; its seaward advance is only some 10 feet each year. In contrast, records show that the delta of the Po, which enters the Adriatic near Venice, an area of greater stability, has been advancing at the rate of 100 feet each year since A.D. 1200.

Like most of the world's deltas, the deposits of the Nile and the Po are sandy and porous. Such rivers, having blocked their own courses, reach the sea partly by percolation, partly by eroding new channels, or DISTRIBUTARIES, through the debris. Other deltas, with sandy deposits similar to those of the Nile and the Po, include those of the Rhine, the Danube, the Rhone and the Elbe in Europe, the Niger in Africa, the Volga, the Indus, the Ganges, the Irrawaddy, the Mekong, the Yellow River in Asia, and the Colorado in North America.

The Mississippi delta is markedly different. It does not conform to the arcuate Nile pattern. The fine clay of the Mississippi inhibits the development of the numerous distributaries characteristic of the sandy deltas. In fact, the seaward passages number only two or three, and these advance their deposits into the Gulf of Mexico at the rate of 200 feet each year. This pattern of distributaries forms the type known as the BIRD'S FOOT delta (fig. 184).

The Consequences of Earth-movement. In addition to the classification of river profiles, W. M. Davis was also the author of the concept of the maturity of a landscape. He described a newly uplifted region, just beginning to be

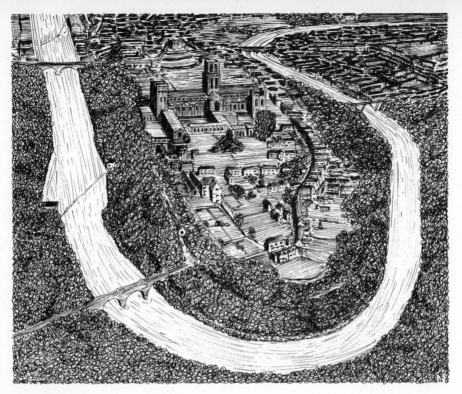

185 The incised meander of the River Weir at Durham City, with castle and cathedral built within the loop.

eroded by streams and rivers, as in the stage of YOUTH. MATURITY follows when the plateau has become deeply dissected so that rounded ridges now separate adjacent valleys, while erosion has removed the highest ground. OLD AGE closes the cycle when the land has been worn down almost to sea-level, forming a PENEPLAIN, drained by sluggish, meandering streams and rivers. Any isolated hills still remaining above the level of the peneplain were described by Davis as MONADNOCKS, from Mount Monadnock in New Hampshire, U.S.A.

It is now generally accepted that the concepts both of the graded profile and of the cycle of erosion may be true under certain climatic conditions and in regions of earth stability. However, there are many instances where this process is interrupted; for example, in a country like Britain, where the crust is subject to isostatic readjustment, rivers begin to undergo regrading before a graded profile is achieved—either through submergence or emergence of the coastline —and mature landscapes fail to reach peneplained old age.

The regrading of a river can often be clearly demonstrated along its plain tract when, through uplift of the land surface, it erodes into its own flood plain, leaving only remnants against either bank. These remnants are termed RIVER

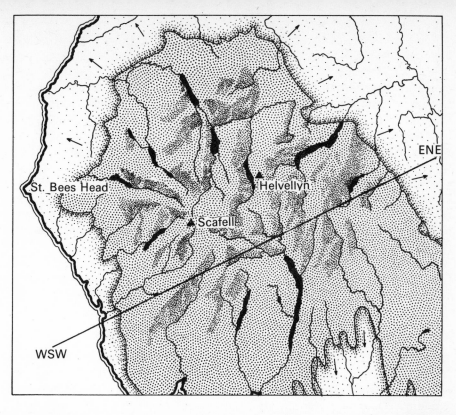

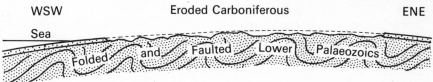

186 The superimposed drainage of the English Lake District.

TERRACES, and, like raised beaches, they may occur at several different levels (fig. 181).

When the land surface is uplifted by an amount exceeding the thickness of the deposits of the plain tract, the river cuts down and imposes the meander pattern on the solid rock beneath. This is then known as an INCISED MEANDER. The depth of the incised meander depends upon the amount of uplift; in the Colorado River of North America it exceeds 6,000 feet, while Britain's best example, on a much smaller scale, is the River Wear at Durham city (fig. 185). There is one famous instance where a tributary of the Colorado has tunnelled through the solid rock on the bend of an incised meander, and has joined its course on the far side. The great arch so formed is known as Rainbow Bridge.

Some river systems are of great age, so old in fact that they pre-date uplifted mountain chains. Raising of the land often changes the course of a river, but this is determined by the rate of uplift. In the Himalayan region, the rising mountain chain began to cut across the paths of the Brahmaputra and the Ganges rivers. But this process has been so slow that the rate of river erosion has kept pace with rate of uplift. The result has been that great gorges, up to 17,000 feet deep, have been cut by these rivers, and some of their tributaries, on their way south from Tibet to the plain of India. This pattern is called ANTECEDENT DRAINAGE.

In the English Lake District the Carboniferous, Permian and Trias deposits at one time covered the whole area, which was elevated as a great dome. Drainage from the dome developed a natural radial pattern, and as river erosion stripped off the Carboniferous rocks, the underlying Silurian and Ordovician strata were laid bare. The grain of these rocks, which is south-west to north-east, shows no relation to the drainage pattern, which is described as SUPERIMPOSED. The remnants of the dome structure can still be seen in the rocks of post-Silurian age where they outcrop on the fringes of the Lake District (fig. 186).

THE ACTION OF ICE

Accumulation. Year by year, the snow which falls over the highland areas of Britain melts away by late spring. Only occasional patches persist into the summer season. However, on higher mountains in similar or lower latitudes, as in Scandinavia and the European Alps, snow persists throughout the year, while in the polar regions vast deposits accumulate even at sea-level.

As snow accumulates season by season, its underlying layers become compacted and transformed into a solid frozen snow called NÉVÉ. The weight of further snowfall changes the névé into a WHITE ICE. This ice behaves in a manner similar to ice frozen under atmospheric pressure, though it differs in its physical character.

Adequate snowfall and sufficiently low temperature are conditions essential to the formation of white ice, on whatever scale. In fact, snow can accumulate throughout the year only if there is a fall in winter in excess of the amount melted during the summer months. The altitude below which it melts at any given time of the year is known as the SNOWLINE. On the equator, the snowline lies at approximately 18,000 feet, in the European Alps at 9,000 feet, in Scandinavia at 5,000 feet and in Greenland at about 2,000 feet. Over the poles the snowline descends to sea-level. Had Ben Nevis been 1,000 feet higher, its slopes would today be nourishing a permanent snowfield.

The term CONTINENTAL GLACIATION is used to describe accumulations of snow on the scale of that over Antarctica and Greenland. Snowfall in each of these areas produces an ICE SHEET, or on a smaller scale, as in Iceland, an ICE CAP. MOUNTAIN or VALLEY GLACIATION develops in all those moun-

187 Frost-shattered mountain peaks or nunataks, protruding through an ice-sheet.

tainous areas of the world in whose high valleys snow persists throughout the year.

Once the compacted snow has been transformed into ice, it begins to slide, under the influence of gravity, towards lower altitudes, in the form of great tongues of ice, known as GLACIERS (fig. 170). In the case of the Antarctic ice sheet, the whole ice front moves forward beyond the continental shore and floats on the ocean. Part of its margin, known as the Great Ross Barrier, forms a high, menacing, outward-facing cliff of ice rising over 100 feet above the sea. Enormous masses of ice break off this ice cliff and float away as ICEBERGS.

The ice sheets of both Antarctica and Greenland, as has been demonstrated by the seismic technique for depth estimation, bury the land surface to a depth of 10,000 feet, yet a frost-shattered mountain peak known as a NUNATAK may rise above the ice in an island-like protrusion (fig. 187).

Erosion. Frost shattering is very marked in all areas of mountain glaciation, but the rock surface which lies under the cover of the ice becomes smoothed and worn by the passage of the glacier over it. It is not, of course, the ice itself but rather the boulders of rock lying within it which, scraping along the surface, abrade it and produce STRIAE or STRIATIONS in the direction of ice movement. As the ice passes over outcrops of resistant rocks, it abrades and smooths their approaching slope while it freezes into the joints of the lee surface, pulling away or PLUCKING the rock face. Such rock-forms were first given the name ROCHES MOUTONNÉES one and a half centuries ago, because they resembled the wigs (moutonnées) which were then worn.

In regions of mountain glaciation, in contrast to continental glaciation, the influence of the glacier is confined to the narrow path of each valley. During the melting season, ice at the heads of the valleys slides forward, and deep

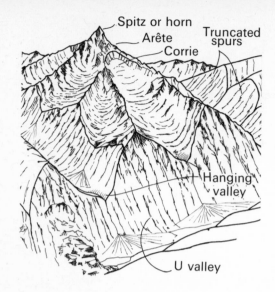

Spitz or horn
Arête
Corrie
Truncated spurs
Hanging valley
U valley

188 Diagram showing the effects of mountain glaciation.

crevasses, known as BERGSCHRUNDE, develop in an arc parallel to the enclosing rock walls (fig. 189). The walls become steepened as material is plucked away and the floor becomes deepened to form a great amphitheatre, known as a CORRIE or CIRQUE. The exit from a corrie is often marked by a prominent lip of rock, over which the ice slides at the beginning of its course down the valley.

The rate of movement of a valley glacier depends upon the gradient, upon the weight of ice pressing on from behind, upon the temperature and the load of rock waste trapped within the glacier. Whereas a river channel occupies only the valley floor, a glacier fills the whole valley and abrades both floor and sides. The

189 Bergschrunde developing parallel to a corrie wall.

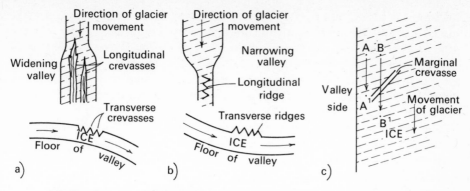

Widening valley — Direction of glacier movement — Longitudinal crevasses — Transverse crevasses — ICE — Floor of valley

a)

Direction of glacier movement — Narrowing valley — Longitudinal ridge — Transverse ridges — ICE — Floor of valley

b)

Valley side — A B — Marginal crevasse — A¹ — Movement of glacier — B¹ — ICE

c)

190 Development of (a) longitudinal and transverse crevasses, and (b) longitudinal and transverse ridges.

spurs characteristic of a river valley become TRUNCATED and its whole course is straightened. From a V-shape in cross-section, the valley becomes moulded into the form of the letter U (fig. 188).

Since a glacier tends to cut into soft rock on the valley floor while it rides up over the more resistant beds, an irregular valley profile is produced, known as a GLACIAL STAIRWAY. After the ice has melted or retreated, and the valley is

191 Mountaineers crossing a deep crevasse.

once more occupied by a river, long RIBBON LAKES fill the deepened parts of the glacial stairway. Glaciers occupying adjacent valleys gradually cut back into the ground separating them and form a sharp ridge or ARÊTE. Arêtes running up to the tops of valleys culminate in a SPITZ or HORN (fig. 224). When mountain glaciers develop in areas bordering the sea, the valley floor may be eroded to a depth below sea-level. If the ice eventually melts, the sea enters the deepened valley, forming a FJORD (fig. 168).

The surface of a glacier is generally broken by CREVASSES or deep fissures in the ice which may extend down to the base of the glacier (fig. 191). When the valley widens, LONGITUDINAL CREVASSES are formed; when it steepens, TRANSVERSE CREVASSES develop (fig. 190a). Similarly, a narrowing valley produces LONGITUDINAL RIDGES, and a decreasing floor gradient creates TRANSVERSE RIDGES (fig. 190b).

The varying rate of movement of different parts of a glacier down a valley can be demonstrated by driving in a line of stakes from bank to bank. The stakes adjacent to the bank move slowly because of the resistance to the ice produced by the solid bank, and in a given time the stakes in the centre of the glacier travel furthest. Similarly the resistance of the floor impedes the rate of movement, and the slowing-down of the glacier next to the banks causes the development of MARGINAL CREVASSES (fig. 190c).

192 A glacier with its train of moraines. The lateral moraines of each tributary become the median moraines of the main glacier.

193 A narrow, sinuous esker whose course is emphasised by the lake which now occupies the valley floor.

Deposition. A glacier terminates at the point well below the snowline, where rate of melting keeps pace with its advance. This is described as the SNOUT of the glacier (fig. 195), and it is at this point that the glacier deposits all the rock debris which it has carried within it. This consists of finely powdered rock, together with irregularly shaped, broken boulders. The deposit which accumulates as a barrier across the valley is called a TERMINAL MORAINE. If, through mellowing of the climate, the snout should retreat to successive points higher up a valley, a series of RECESSIONAL MORAINES are developed.

Rock debris falling as a scree from the hillsides on to the edges of a glacier, forms what are known as LATERAL MORAINES. When two tributary glaciers unite, their inner lateral moraines coalesce to form a MEDIAN MORAINE (fig. 192). Much of the material falling on the glacier surface becomes trapped in the depth of the crevasses, forming INTERNAL MORAINES, while the rock debris scooped up from the floor as the glacier advances is termed GROUND MORAINE.

The great continental glaciers, being very much thicker than valley glaciers, abrade on a much wider scale and produce a far greater thickness of rock debris, known as TILL or BOULDER CLAY. Moraines are simply localised accumulations of boulder clay. Boulder clay may cover many square miles of country to a depth of 100 feet or more, filling in pre-glacial valleys and levelling off what may often have been irregular topography. Sometimes it is moulded by the ice, in a manner

194 An overflow channel in process of formation as the waters from a lake erode a downward path between the hillside and the valley glacier. (After photograph in Holmes' *Principles of Physical Geology*)

not well understood, into a mass of rounded hummocks or DRUMLINS, one quarter of a mile or more in length and with intervening depressions whose floors may lie 50 feet below the level of the adjacent crests. This is described as BASKET-OF-EGG TOPOGRAPHY.

The melt-waters emerge from the snout of a glacier and deposit the rock debris as an OUTWASH FAN. Streams running along the floor within a glacier generally follow a sinuous course, leaving a deposit of water-worn material which, when the ice melts, forms a winding ridge known as an ESKER (fig. 193). A stream emerging from a point above the floor of a glacier may build up a pile of debris known as KAME. All these deposits, which are due to the action of water within or emerging from the ice, are termed GLACIOFLUVIATILE.

Long after the ice has melted from off the high slopes of a mountainous region, the great glaciers may still remain as STAGNANT ICE in the valleys. Tributary streams then entering the main valley become dammed back by the stagnant ice, and MARGINAL LAKES are formed. Eventually the lakes overflow and the water erodes a path for itself towards the sea, between the stagnant ice and the side of the valley (fig. 194). When the ice finally melts, the temporary path of the escaping water leaves a permanent record as a notch in the hillside known as an OVERFLOW CHANNEL or a DRY VALLEY. As the level of the stagnant ice falls, a number of successive overflow channels may be developed at different heights.

195 The melting snout of the Flatisen glacier, Norway, showing the fissured
surface of the ice; the melt waters are green with sediment
held in suspension.

Temporary lakes may be formed during the various stages of retreat of the ice,
through the damming of valleys by moraines as well as by the ice itself. Evidence
of the former existence of these lakes is seen in the rounded, pebbly deposits
which fringed their shores, in the fine mud which settled upon their floors, and
in the small deltas which were built up wherever a stream entered them. In Glen
Roy, in Scotland, several 'benches' of pebbly beds on the hillside—the famous
'parallel roads'—mark the successive levels of a lake which occupied the valley in
glacial times. By careful plotting of the levels of these former lakes, and of the
overflow channels, it is possible to build up a picture of the order of events
which accompanied the final retreat of the ice. This can be clearly demonstrated
in an area like the Pennines of northern England, which was glaciated during the
Ice Age.

VI. The Deformation of the Earth's Crust

GENERAL PRINCIPLES

Sedimentary rocks are laid down horizontally, or nearly so, as indicated earlier (page 13), but subsequent earth-movements almost invariably cause them to be either tilted, folded or fractured and torn apart. The accompanying diagrams (figs. **196a, b, c**) represent a block of country raised above water-level and illustrate the most fundamental terms which are used to describe the attitude of a layer of rocks. In figure **196a**, the tilted rocks appear horizontal only across the vertical face below AB, and the direction AB is known as the STRIKE. The rocks tilt away from the face in a direction parallel to BC; this direction of tilt, which is shown in perspective, lies at right angles to the strike and is termed the TRUE DIP. The angle of true dip, that is to say the inclination of the beds from the horizontal, is measured along the face BC and its value, in degrees, is indicated on the surface by an annotated arrow.

If the shales above the more indurated sandstone should be worn away by denudation, then the upper surface of that layer will form a DIP SLOPE; in figure **196b** the block has been slightly rotated in an anti-clockwise direction to reveal the dip slope to the viewer.

The dip along any other vertical face, such as $B'C$ (fig. **196c**), is the APPARENT DIP, and its value will always be less than the true dip. This fact can be demonstrated as follows: In figure **196a**, the top of the limestone outcrops along the surface of the block at AB, while along the hidden, vertical strike face below DC, the top of the same limestone is x feet lower, nearly at water-level. Now the shortest distance between the two parallel lines AB and DC is represented by the line BC which runs at right angles to them. Therefore, across the vertical section below BC, the top of the limestone falls x feet within the shortest possible distance; across any other vertical section, such as $B'C$ (fig. **196c**), the distance will be greater and hence the dip (apparent) will be less. In fact, a series of vertical sections could be cut along the lines $A'C$, $A''C$, etc., and each would in turn reveal a lower apparent dip—the final one coinciding with DC, when the beds would appear horizontal.

A region of country may have had strongly dipping beds outcropping on its peneplained surface; earth-movements may have lowered this surface so that it became covered by the sea. A series of new deposits may have been laid down across the tilted edges of the older rock; these deposits would then eventually have become indurated to form a stratified succession of rock. The relationship between two such sets of strata is described as an ANGULAR UNCONFORMITY (figs. **197** and **220**). If there should be no angular discrepancy between the two successions (i.e. if the earlier beds were lying horizontally at the time of subsidence), then they would be said to be separated by a DISCONFORMITY.

A NORMAL FAULT is a fracture in the earth's crust along which vertical displacement has occurred, due to forces of tension acting at right angles to the line of the fault, and the blocks of country on either side of the fault are described as the DOWNTHROW and the UPTHROW (fig. **198a**). The plane of a normal fault generally dips at a high angle (70 to 85 degrees), towards the downthrown side, but it may be as low as 45 degrees. When movement has taken place along a normal fault, the fault plane on the exposed, upthrown side forms a FAULT SCARP. However, the rate of erosion of the upthrown block is generally more rapid than that of the downthrown area and in time the scarp will be completely removed. In plan, it will then be seen that the younger rocks appear on the downthrown side (fig. **204**).

Horizontal stress may cause a sliding movement of one block of country past another, along a vertical or near-vertical plane. This shift is described as a TRANSCURRENT, WRENCH or TEAR FAULT, and the direction of movement is indicated by arrows (fig. **198b**). A combination of horizontal and vertical stress will produce an oblique movement along the fault plane (fig. **198c**). On the other hand, strong horizontal stress may cause the strata to fold into gentle SYMMETRICAL or ASYMMETRICAL ANTICLINES and SYNCLINES (figs. **201a** and **b**), according to the degree of compression. The highest part of the anticline is the CREST, while the rocks dipping away from the crest form the FLANKS. The lowest part of the adjacent inverted arch is the TROUGH. The imaginary plane which passes through the horizontal points of successive beds, both in an anticline and in a syncline, is described as the AXIAL PLANE, and the line of its outcrop on the surface is the anticlinal or synclinal AXIS. In a symmetrical fold the axial plane is vertical; in an asymmetrical fold, it is inclined. Repeated folds, in which the flanks are almost vertical, are described as ISOCLINAL.

In nature, anticlines and synclines are frequently PITCHING structures; that is, the strata are not only arched but the arches and inverted arches are tilted. The pattern produced by these pitching structures, as seen on a flat surface, is shown on the accompanying diagram (fig. **203b** and **c**). In these structures the direction of strike changes as the beds are followed towards the axis. It may help to visualise the pattern of outcrop of a pitching structure by imagining a tilted arch which is cut by a horizontal surface (fig. **203a**). When such a structure outcrops across undulating country, the pattern may become more complicated (fig. **212**).

Horizontal stress may become sufficiently strong to break the limb of an asymmetrical anticline, producing a REVERSED FAULT (fig. **202a**); or the stress may persist, causing the strata to override the underlying rocks along a THRUST PLANE (fig. **202b**). The structure is then described as an OVERTHRUST.

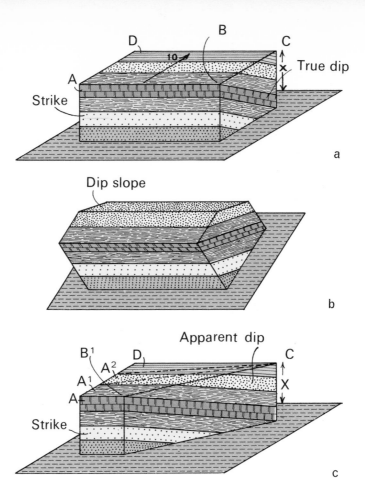

196a, b, c Block diagrams illustrating strike,
true and apparent dip.

197 Block diagram illustrating an angular
unconformity.

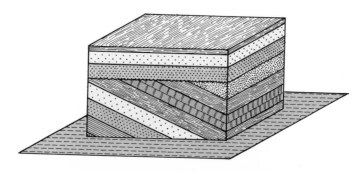

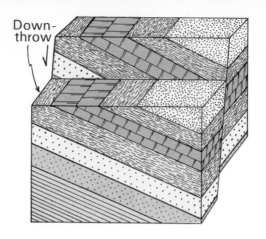

198a Block diagram illustrating a normal fault.

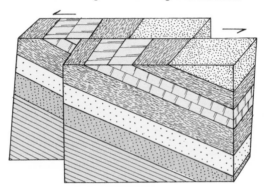

198b Block diagram illustrating a tear, transcurrent or wrench fault.

198c Block diagram illustrating an oblique
fault.

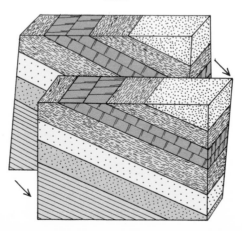

199 Geological map and section illustrating horizontal strata outcropping over an undulating countryside.

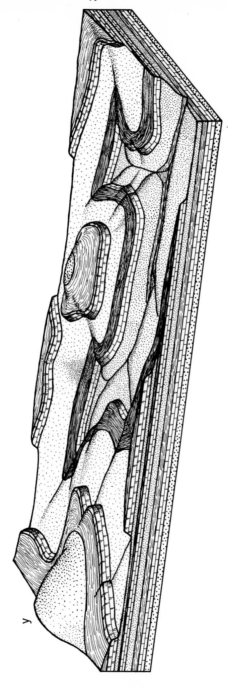

200 A perspective drawing, illustrating map shown as fig. 199.

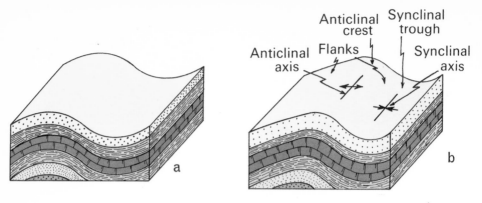

201 Block diagrams illustrating: (a) symmetrical anticlinal and synclinal folds, and (b) asymmetrical anticlinal and synclinal folds.

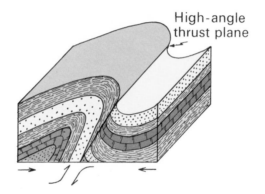

202a Block diagram illustrating a reverse fault.

202b Block diagram illustrating an overthrust fault.

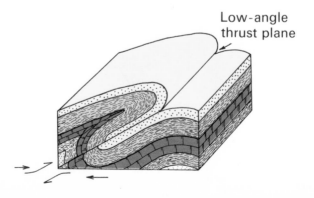

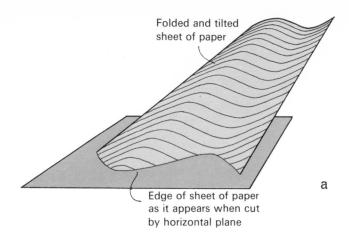

Folded and tilted
sheet of paper

Edge of sheet of paper
as it appears when cut
by horizontal plane

a

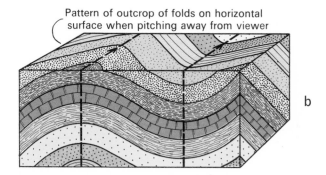

Pattern of outcrop of folds on horizontal
surface when pitching away from viewer

b

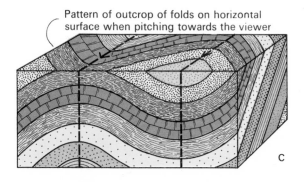

Pattern of outcrop of folds on horizontal
surface when pitching towards the viewer

c

203 Pitching folds: (a) explanatory diagram;
(b) and (c) block diagrams.

THE INTERPRETATION OF GEOLOGICAL MAPS

Figure 199 represents an area of country drained by a river and its tributaries. The ground rises from 300 feet above sea-level in the south-east to 1,300 feet in the extreme west. There is an isolated hill in the central part of the area which rises to slightly over 1,000 feet. The contour lines are drawn at vertical intervals of 100 feet.

Geologically, the map is simple. The strata lie horizontally and a number of the boundaries between adjacent formations outcrop along the levels of the contour lines. Other formation boundaries lie between successive contour lines at heights which can readily be estimated. From the map itself it is possible to judge the thickness of most of the beds; for example, the lower limestone whose base is at 400 feet, is about 50 feet thick, while the upper limestone with its base at 700 feet is about 130 feet thick.

The perspective drawing of a three-dimensional model of this map is shown as figure 200. The vertical succession of strata is indicated along the edges of the model and the surface shows the effect of erosion. Each of the two limestones forms cliffed topography. The shales are soft and fail to show any strong feature.

By examining figure 199 with the aid of a cross-section—for example, along the line Y–Z—the geologist should be able to reconstruct in his mind's eye the solid form of the country as represented by figure 200. This is the fundamental principle of geological maps; the geologist must be able to visualise in a three-dimensional pattern, the data provided on a two-dimensional surface. With the aid of maps and sections some of the principal geological structures will be illustrated in the following pages.

Figure **204** consists of a succession of strata, from A at the base to G at the top. The beds are horizontal, but they have been interrupted by a fault which has a vertical downthrow of about 900 feet to the east. The downthrow side is indicated on the map by short lines drawn at intervals, at right angles to the fault. On the west side of the fault, the bed D occupies the highest ground, but the downthrow of the fault has lowered this bed—so that in the eastern part of the map it crops out in the valleys while a younger bed, G forms the highest ground.

Young faults, those along which movement occurred in Tertiary times, generally betray their presence in the field by a cliff or fault scarp. Older faults, which have not moved since Mesozoic or Palaeozoic times, are more difficult to trace in an area of poor exposures, on account of the lack of a topographical feature; the upthrown side will have been eroded and the scarp therefore eliminated. Sometimes, as in the centre of figure **204**, there may be a slight depression to indicate the position of the fault line.

Figure **205** shows a group of beds, in decreasing age from A to F, dipping uniformly in direction and amount towards the west. The angle of dip is about 13 degrees. The contour lines, at intervals of 100 feet, are indicated in green and the strike lines are shown in red. The arrows indicate the direction of true dip.

Consider first the top of bed D on the map. To the west of its outcrop the dip carries the top of D below the surface, whereas to the east the beds are rising and D crops out over higher ground. In fact, along the strike line 3–4, the top of bed D lies at a height of 400 feet. Along this same strike line, as the map indicates, the base of bed D lies at a height of 300 feet. Therefore the vertical distance between the base and the top of D is 100 feet, which means, since the beds are tilted, that its thickness is rather less than 100 feet. This is illustrated in the accompanying section.

The top of D falls by an amount of 100 feet across the interval between strike lines 3–4 and 1–2. Moreover, the dip has the same direction and value in every part of the map and therefore a series of parallel strike lines may be drawn, equidistant, across the whole map. Each line can be used to provide information, in terms of hundreds of feet, about the heights of the top of D; these are given for this particular horizon, at the foot of the map. Thus, along the most westerly strike line, top D is 300 feet below sea-level, and therefore the base is at -400 feet O.D. Similarly the level of any other bed can be obtained. For example, since the base of F intersects the 500-foot contour at outcrop, the 100-foot strike line for the top of bed D is also the 500-foot strike line for the base of bed F. This can be seen on the accompanying cross-section.

Now consider again the outcrop of the top of bed D. Note how it swings east and west across its 300-foot strike line. The rule is simple: along this strike line, top D is at a height of exactly 300 feet; to the west the dip carries it below 300 feet and therefore it can outcrop only over ground below that level (i.e. between the 300- and 200-foot contours in two of the valleys), as indicated on the map by the contour lines. To the east it can only outcrop over ground above 300 feet (i.e. between the 300- and 400-foot contours), eventually reaching 400 feet where the strike line and the contour line for 400 feet intersect.

In constructing a section Y–Z across the map, the horizontal scale of 1:12,000 should be used for the vertical scale also. The topographical profile is first drawn, then the geological boundaries are inserted. On the map, the strike lines for the base and top of D have been projected down from the map itself to intersect the contour lines for the corresponding heights as they appear across the section. These intersections give the position of the base and top of D in the section. The same method is used to determine the position of the other beds in completing the cross-section.

Figure **206** is less complicated than it may appear. The strata A to I have been folded into a slightly asymmetrical anticline and syncline, each with a horizontal axis—a structure similar to that illustrated (fig. **201b**). If, instead of being deeply dissected by erosion, the ground had been perfectly flat at the 800-foot level, then the pattern of surface outcrop would have appeared as on figure **207**. In figure **206** the pattern with its isolated outcrops of young beds surrounded by older ones (OUTLIERS) and older beds surrounded by younger ones (INLIERS) is due to the combination of geological structure and topography.

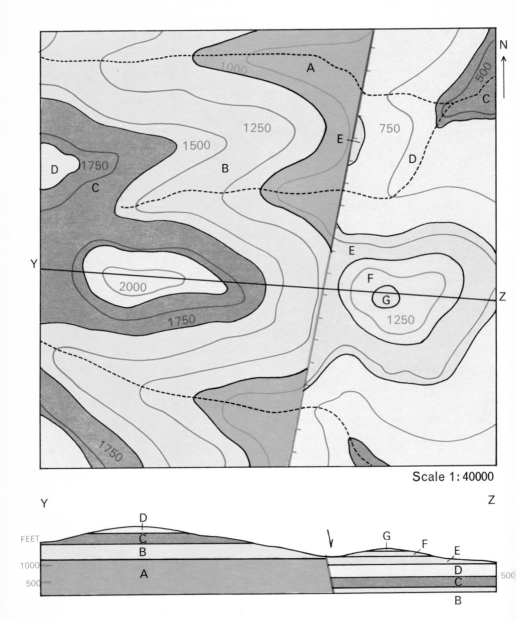

Scale 1:40000

204 Geological map and section illustrating normal faulting in horizontal strata.

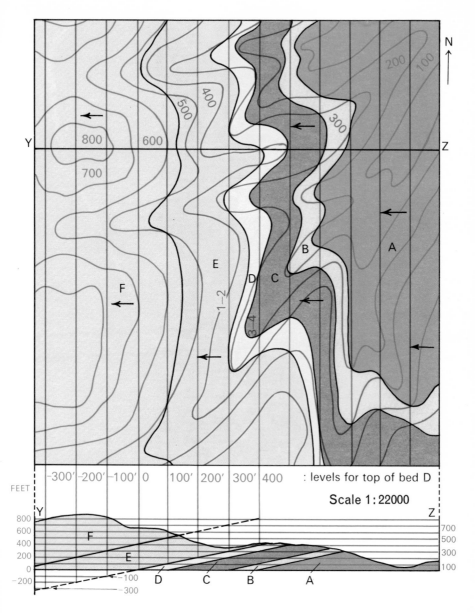

205 Geological map and section illustrating tilted strata outcropping over undulating countryside.

If figure **206** is studied, using the strike lines for a guide as in figure **205**, the reasons for the pattern should become clear. For example, the base of bed *C* reaches its highest point on the crest of the anticline where it is almost met by the 1,200-foot contour. The westerly dip carries it down to 1,100, 1,000 and then to 900 feet near the western boundary of the map. In the north-east, the same horizon is brought down to a level of 200 feet. The accompanying section shows how, by projecting strike lines, the base of bed *C* can be plotted below the surface across the map.

In figure **211** the bed *F* lies unconformably upon the older series of strata, namely, beds *A–E*. These older beds have been folded into an anticline with an axis running north–south. The beds *F* and *G*, above the unconformity, dip gently towards the north-north-west. There are also associated dykes.

The geometry of the map is a repetition of the preceding maps, but in addition, in this case there is a sequence of geological events which may be described as follows: after beds *A–E* were laid down, they were folded by earth-movements and eroded. (Before or during the period of erosion, a dolerite dyke had been intruded into the strata; this dyke was subsequently revealed at the surface by further erosion to a horizontal plane.) Subsidence then occurred and a new series of rocks, *F* and *G*, was laid down upon the horizontal surface of the older group. A gentle upward tilting of the earth's crust in the east of the area then imparted a low dip to the beds *F* and *G*. Finally, a felsite* dyke was intruded and subsequent erosion caused it, too, to appear at the surface and to give the area its present topographical configuration.

The evidence for this sequence should be clear from a reading of the map; beds *F* and *G* were laid down upon a horizontal surface because the uncon-formable junction is a plane surface with a dip identical in direction and amount with the dip of *F* and *G*. The dolerite dyke was intruded before the deposition of bed *F* because the latter overlies it and is not penetrated by it. The felsite dyke on the other hand was intruded after the deposition of the beds above the unconformity because it cuts the beds *F* and *G* as well as the dolerite dyke. Furthermore, the earlier dyke is not affected by the movements which folded beds *A–E* and was therefore intruded after this folding movement.

Figure **212** introduces the pattern of a pitching fold. The strata have been folded into an anticline and a syncline whose axes tilt towards the north. The structure is illustrated in figure **203** (page 153); the regular surface pattern in that figure is somewhat distorted on figure **212** by the topography, though the bending of the outcrop round the axis is well seen in the south of the map, as shown by the top of bed *A* and the base of bed *E*.

In contrast to the previous map, the strike lines on figure **212** converge towards the axis, following the pattern of outcrop on a horizontal surface as indicated on figure **203b**. The dip directions change with the strike lines

*FELSITE: an acid, igneous rock, very fine-grained, the product of rapid cooling. It occurs as a lava flow or a narrow dyke.

as the latter reach the axis; the dips across the section Y–Z are therefore apparent dips.

The geometrical maps which have just been described are highly artificial because it is extremely rare to find the rocks of the earth's crust behaving in regular geometrical fashion. In nature, dips frequently change in direction and value; folds flatten, or they increase in amplitude until they become faulted; an individual bed may become thicker or it may thin out as a lens shape.

Nevertheless, the purpose of the geometrical map is to teach familiarity with the three-dimensional picture which is essential to a study of geology. When this familiarity has been achieved, the geometrical map can be put on one side and the genuine map—constructed in the field on the evidence of all the surface detail available (and sometimes augmented by bore-hole evidence)—can then be profitably studied. There are geological maps covering Britain which are published on the scale of one inch to the mile, by the Institute of Geological Sciences (formerly the Geological Survey of Great Britain). They vary in geological complexity from the gently dipping rocks of Mesozoic age in eastern England to the highly involved succession of the North-west Highlands of Scotland (fig. 260).

MAJOR EARTH-MOVEMENTS

Earth-movements may be classified broadly as follows:

1. Those in which horizontal movement has been dominant—OROGENESIS.
2. Those in which vertical movement has been dominant—EPEIROGENESIS.

From earliest geological times, the crust of the earth has been subjected to these stresses, the origins of which are as yet little understood. Today, their manifestation can be seen in earthquake shocks and in volcanic activity. In the past, the movements which they produced have been permanently imprinted, as folds and faults, upon even the most ancient rocks of the crust. This aspect of the study of the earth sciences is known as TECTONICS or STRUCTURAL GEOLOGY.

Orogenesis. According to the well-established classical view of mountain building, or OROGENESIS, all the mountain chains of the world have been formed by long and continued horizontal stress acting across certain belts of the crust. Examination of the rocks within these belts shows that the formation of a mountain chain marks the culmination of a cycle of events which had been initiated many millions of years earlier.

This cycle began with the development of a GEOSYNCLINE, a large, shallow trough-like depression, occupied by a pre-historic ocean, which may have been several hundred miles wide and several thousand miles long. Rivers from the adjoining land-masses poured their loads of sand and mud into this geosyncline. The arenaceous material was deposited along the shore, while the argillaceous deposits were spread out far from the shoreline. Organisms flourished in the

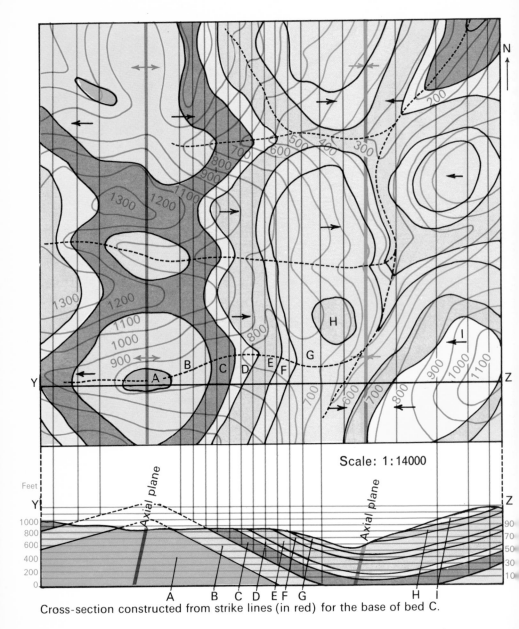

Cross-section constructed from strike lines (in red) for the base of bed C.

206 Geological map and section illustrating asymmetrical folds outcropping over undulating countryside.

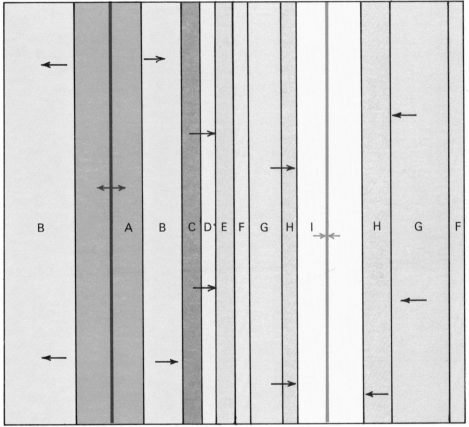

B   A   B   C D E F G H I   H   G   F

Map 206 as it would appear if the ground were level at a height of 800 feet O.D.

Scale: 1:14000

207 Geological map illustrating the folds shown in fig. 206, but outcropping on a flat surface.

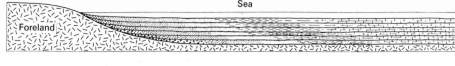

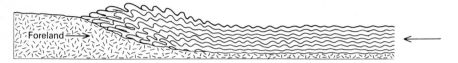

208a, b Diagrammatic sections across the foreland of a geosyncline, illustrating the formation of a mountain chain.

shallows wherever they were free from muddy and sandy deposits (fig. 2). Layer upon layer of sediment was laid down, keeping pace with the slow sinking of the floor of the geosyncline. After an elapse of perhaps 200 million years, the land on either flank became reduced to a peneplain, and by this time some 30,000 feet of shallow-water sediment may have accumulated in the geosyncline. However, along the edge of the continents, the sediments pinched out to only a fraction of this enormous thickness.

The gradual transfer of vast quantities of material from land to geosynclinal trough upsets the isostatic balance of the earth's crust (page 180). This imbalance, aided by earth shrinkage (as it used to be thought) or, in the more modern view, by movements deep inside the globe, causes the adjacent land-masses, the FORELANDS, to draw together. This movement begins to wrinkle the thin, newly formed sediments which overlie the foreland areas, and eventually two great parallel chains of contorted overthrust strata are produced which fringe the geosyncline. Away from the forelands, the rocks are folded with decreasing intensity, and those which are laid down near the centre of the geosyncline may be only slightly disturbed (fig. 208). During this folding process, which may last many millions of years, widespread igneous activity occurs, generally in the form of intrusion of granite stocks and in the extrusion of andesitic lavas.

Whereas this picture for long remained the total and complete explanation for the formation of mountain chains, it is generally conceded by modern workers that there are other factors which augment the concept of horizontal compression. Of these, the most widely accepted is that of gravity-sliding. According to this view, it is believed that many of the highly complex folds within the mountain chains of the world are produced by uplift and tilting within the zone of compression; that instability has caused the folded rocks to glide down under the force of gravity and to develop the complicated patterns known as nappe structure.

The formation of a mountain chain causes a great change in the distribution of land and sea over the whole region. The folded sedimentary rocks of the geosyncline now form high land, and small isolated basins are created, which on occasion may be below sea-level. The rocks of the mountain chain begin to be

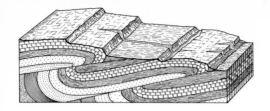

209 Block diagram illustrating the pattern of thrusting in a mountain chain.

eroded and the complex nature of the folding becomes revealed (fig. 209). Torrent streams and rivers descend on to the adjacent plains and the new strata formed by this erosive process are invariably very coarse-grained and conglomeratic, forming a succession described on the European continent as MOLASSE.

The effects of horizontal stress extend far beyond the zone of intense folding and may be seen in the development of transcurrent faults, where one block of country is pushed past another. These faults lie at an angle of generally less than 45 degrees to the direction of maximum horizontal stress. Often they develop in pairs and are described as CONJUGATE. The Craven, Dent and Pennine faults, in the north of England, may be of this type (fig. **214**).

Epeirogenesis. An entirely different tectonic pattern is provided in regions where the maximum stress is vertical, and is illustrated most dramatically in the development of RIFT VALLEYS. A rift valley consists essentially of a narrow, elongated block, known as a GRABEN, flanked on either hand by upfaulted stable blocks tilting outwards. The faults themselves are normal, having a high angle of dip. Often they form a complicated pattern in that a single fault may branch into a number of parallel faults, sharing the total throw between them (fig. 210). Locally, along the course of a rift valley, two adjacent faults may lie with a central, upthrown block between them; the latter is then described as a HORST. In the Egyptian sector of the African rift, movement along certain faults has been renewed (REJUVENATION) after a period of deposition. In cases where this movement has been insufficiently intense to fracture the newer, more plastic deposits, they have become bent to form asymmetrical anticlines.

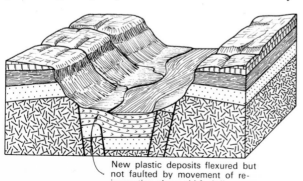

210 Block diagram illustrating the pattern of faultine in a rift valley.

New plastic deposits flexured but not faulted by movement of rejuvenation along old fault line.

163

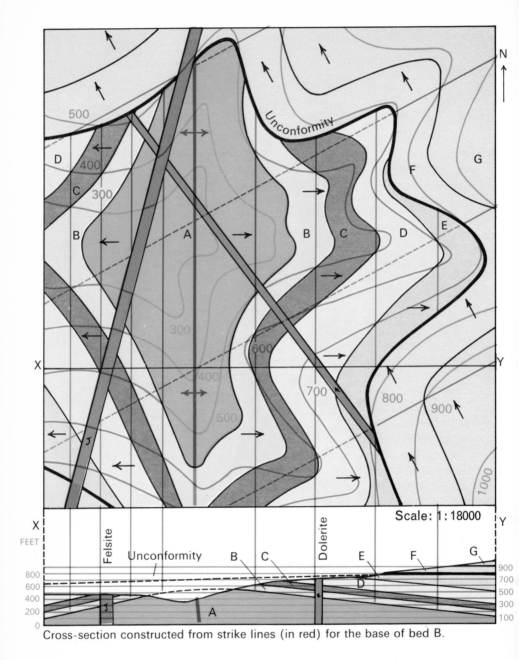

Cross-section constructed from strike lines (in red) for the base of bed B.

211 Geological map and section illustrating the interpretation of a sequence
of events.

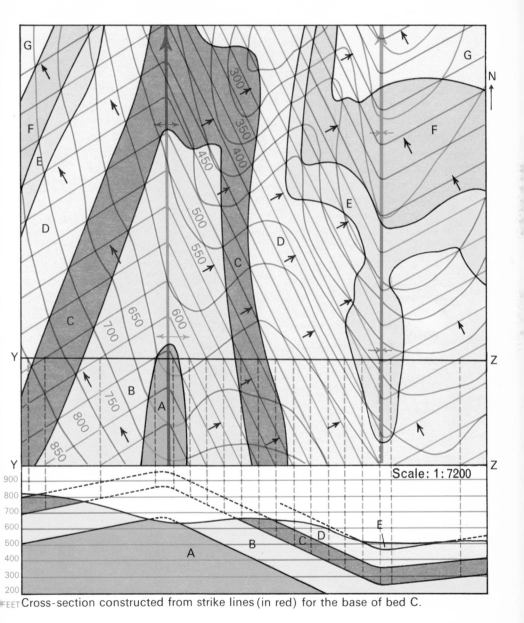

Cross-section constructed from strike lines (in red) for the base of bed C.

212 Geological map and section illustrating a pitching fold.

SEA LEVELS AND CORAL GROWTH

As is described in a later chapter (page 194), corals are mainly colonial organisms which secrete a hard, limy shell. These calcareous skeletons or corallites possess a tube-like shape surrounding and protecting the soft-bodied animal, or polyp, within. The corallites grow upwards at a rate which varies between half an inch and one and a half inches each year. Often the individual corallites are closely packed together, but some forms grow in a loose framework. Other lime-precipitating organisms, the algae, are often found in association with the corals. They provide a calcareous cement which occupies the spaces between the corallites, the whole forming a compact structure known as coral limestone.

Coral organisms grow only under marine conditions: they are sensitive to temperature change and cannot flourish below about 23°C. Furthermore, they require sunlight and therefore they can grow neither in water which is clouded by mud nor at depths (beyond about 100 feet) to which sunlight cannot easily penetrate. Living coral is never found above the level of the tide since it can only survive brief periods of exposure to the air. In short, growing coral is found only in the shallow, warm and sediment-free salt waters of the world.

Coral grows as a reef fringing the land and also as the sole land material of remote islands of the Pacific. Darwin was the first investigator to offer a scientific explanation for the origin of these coral structures. He found that coral reefs often fringe shorelines of submergence and that therefore the coral, by its rapid growth, must have been able to keep pace with the rate of subsidence of the reef, building itself up on its own earlier deposits—a response to epeirogenic movement.

Darwin extended the hypothesis of subsidence to account for coral islands or ATOLLS in the Pacific, arguing that these islands were originally volcanic cones protruding above sea-level, upon which coral reefs had developed; that slow subsidence of the islands allowed the growing coral to maintain its level. For many years, Darwin's theory remained unproven; bores were sunk into the atolls without encountering material other than coral. However, a more recent boring through one of the atolls in the Bikini area reached basalt at a depth of over 4,000 feet, whilst seismic evidence (page 174) has demonstrated that the igneous core of some atolls lies as deep as 8,000 feet below present sea-level.

There was, however, one aspect of the atoll structure for which Darwin failed to provide a satisfactory explanation, namely, the surprisingly uniform depths

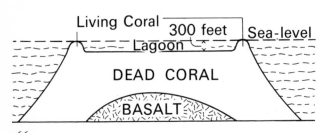

213 Diagram illustrating the structure of a coral atoll.

of the lagoons which occupy the centre of each atoll (fig. 213). These lagoons are invariably a little less than 300 feet deep, floored by dead coral and protected from the ocean waves by a ring of growing coral rising almost to sea-level. There was little difficulty in accounting for the outer ring of living coral, which is continually washed by the oxygen-rich waters of the ocean, unlike the oxygen-starved coral of the lagoon which is shielded from the ocean waters by the outer ring itself. But though this explained the existence of the lagoons it did not account for their regular depths.

In the early years of this century, the American geologist R. A. Daly offered an explanation which related lagoon-depth to the oscillations of ocean levels during the Ice Age. Daly maintained that as the water was drawn from the oceans to provide the snowfall for the vast ice sheets during the Ice Age, there must have been a lowering of ocean-levels throughout the world. Therefore the coral islands, rising above sea-level, would gradually become eroded down by the waves until they formed a flat coral platform at about sea-level.

Then came the time when the ice began to melt, accompanied by a slow rise in the ocean-level. Coral would once more begin to grow round the edges of these platforms, keeping pace with the rise of the sea and at the same time forming an effective barrier against the intrusion of fresh water into the lagoons. Thus, no additional growth of coral was added to the floor of the lagoons, which remain today at the level to which the oceans fell during the period of maximum glaciation—namely, about 300 feet below their present level.

EARTHQUAKES

When an earthquake occurs, the surface of the earth in its vicinity vibrates as though from giant hammer-blows. Cracks appear in the ground, avalanches of rock are set in motion on mountain slopes, and if the area should be densely populated, cities are destroyed. As buildings collapse, thousands are maimed and killed. A quarter of a million people lost their lives in the Tokyo earthquake; twenty-five thousand in Lisbon.

Of the damage caused by earthquakes in cities, that by fire is the most severe. Service mains are wrenched apart and escaping gas ignites and explodes. Water-pipes are broken and the supply is cut off. The sewage system is interrupted and disease adds to the toll of death. Within minutes the whole of the ordered processes of city living are brought to a halt and the survivors cluster in tents beyond the circle of destruction, dependent upon the soup kitchens of voluntary societies and of the United Nations relief agencies.

Among the almost instantaneous after-effects of the violent earthquake is the generation of the tidal-wave or TSUNAMI. Even with the most violent earth-movements on land, the actual displacement of the ground is never more than a few feet, either vertically or horizontally, along a fault-line. Yet tsunami up to 200 feet high have been recorded; the Lisbon earthquake, in the eighteenth

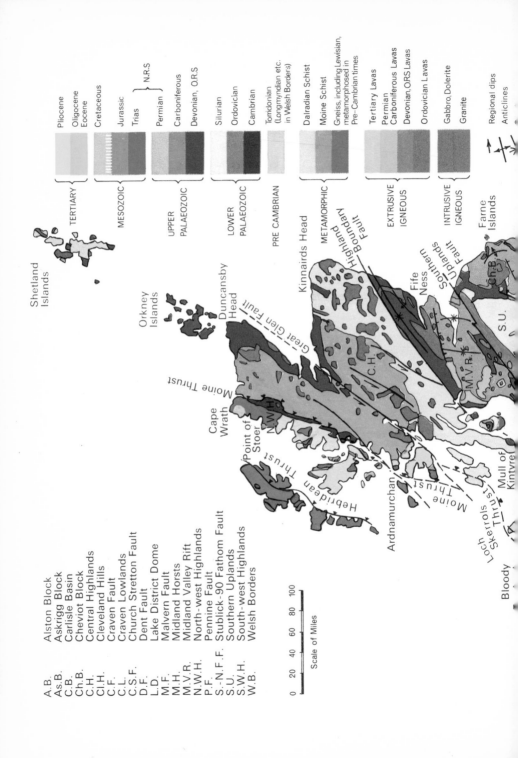

Legend (stratigraphic column):

TERTIARY
- Pliocene
- Oligocene / Eocene
- Cretaceous

MESOZOIC
- Jurassic
- Trias } N.R.S

UPPER PALAEOZOIC
- Permian
- Carboniferous
- Devonian, O.R.S

LOWER PALAEOZOIC
- Silurian
- Ordovician
- Cambrian

PRE CAMBRIAN
- Torridonian (Longmyndian etc. in Welsh Borders)

METAMORPHIC
- Dalradian Schist
- Moine Schist
- Gneiss, including Lewisian, metamorphosed in Pre-Cambrian times

EXTRUSIVE IGNEOUS
- Tertiary Lavas
- Permian Carboniferous Lavas
- Devonian, O.R.S Lavas
- Ordovician Lavas

INTRUSIVE IGNEOUS
- Gabbro, Dolerite
- Granite

Regional dips
Anticlines

Map labels:

Shetland Islands
Orkney Islands
Duncansby Head
Kinnairds Head
Fife Ness
Great Glen Fault
Moine Thrust
Cape Wrath
Point of Stoer
N.W.H.
Hebridean Thrust
Ardnamurchan
Moine Thrust
Loch Skerrols Thrust
Mull of Kintyre
Bloody
C.H.
Highland Boundary Fault
Southern Uplands Fault
M.V.R.
S.U.
Ch.B.
Farne Islands

Abbreviations:

A.B.   Alston Block
As.B.   Askrigg Block
C.B.   Carlisle Basin
Ch.B.   Cheviot Block
C.H.   Central Highlands
Cl.H.   Cleveland Hills
C.F.   Craven Fault
C.L.   Craven Lowlands
C.S.F.   Church Stretton Fault
D.F.   Dent Fault
L.D.   Lake District Dome
M.F.   Malvern Fault
M.H.   Midland Horsts
M.V.R.   Midland Valley Rift
N.W.H.   North-west Highlands
P.F.   Pennine Fault
S.-N.F.F.   Stublick-90 Fathom Fault
S.U.   Southern Uplands
S.W.H.   South-west Highlands
W.B.   Welsh Borders

Scale of Miles
0   20   40   60   80   100

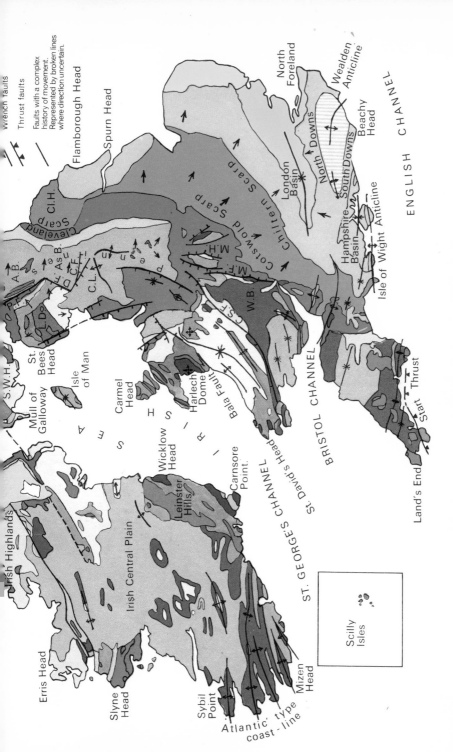

214 Geological map of the British Isles and the Republic of Ireland.

215 The ruins of Agadir after the 1960 earthquake.

century, was followed by a withdrawal of the sea and then by enormous waves which engulfed part of the city. The movement of such great volumes of water can only be explained by the sudden large-scale displacement of the sea-bed, a displacement generally far greater than that produced in the course of the earth-movement itself. It has therefore been suggested that a violent earthquake may have the effect of starting away great avalanches of rock down submarine slopes, and that it is these which, involving perhaps millions of tons of material, could be largely responsible for the tsunami.

The earthquake, even more than the volcano (the activities of the latter being more predictable) has always brought terror and bewilderment to those of its

216 The seismograph.

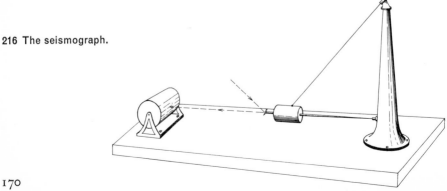

victims who escape sudden death. And as in modern times more and more people have moved into cities, so has the destruction increased. From Lisbon (Portugal) in the year 1755, to San Francisco (California) 1906, Messina (Italy) 1908, Tokyo (Japan) 1923, Napier (New Zealand) 1931, Agadir (Morocco) 1960 and Anchorage (Alaska) 1964, the swift and violent movements of the earth's surface at a single stroke have brought annihilation and chaos (fig. 215).

The causes of earthquakes have for long excited the curiosity of mankind. Even as early as the second century the Chinese had invented a mechanical device to record earth tremors. But as with many branches of scientific enquiry, it is only during the last 100 years that accurate records have been made. Towards the end of last century the Italian, Mercalli, introduced a scale by means of which the intensity of earthquakes could be assessed. It is used to this day, with certain modifications, and runs as follows:

1. Felt by only very few people.
2. Felt by a few people on upper floors.
3. Noticeable vibrations.
4. Doors, windows, shaken.
5. Felt by most people. Objects moved.
6. Felt by all. Heavy articles moved.
7. Slight damage to buildings. Chimneys dislodged.
8. Considerable damage to buildings. Monuments overturned.
9. Considerable damage to well-constructed buildings. Underground pipes broken.
10. Buildings destroyed. Landslides.
11. Underground pipes completely destroyed. Railway lines bent.
12. Total destruction. Objects thrown upwards.

Most modern knowledge of earthquakes has been gained through the detection of earth tremors by delicate instruments, especially by means of the SEISMO-GRAPH. This instrument is based upon the principle of inertia, as exemplified by the pendulum. If a heavy weight is suspended vertically by a cord from a point of attachment which can be oscillated violently in a horizontal plane, the suspended weight, because of its own inertia, will remain stationary. Similarly, a weight attached to the end of a horizontal boom and supported by a cord tied to a vertical column will remain stationary even though the latter vibrates (fig. 216). If such an instrument has a firm foundation, an earth tremor will cause everything to vibrate except the pendulum bob itself. A combination of three such instruments, with suitable devices for magnifying the movements, will enable vibrations in any plane to be recorded. Pendulum seismographs have, in fact, such a degree of sensitivity that not only can earth tremors originating on the opposite side of the globe be detected, but within the record itself several distinct types of vibrations can be recognised. The analysis of these vibrations will be discussed in the following chapter.

217 Horizontal calcareous Miocene beds, Somalia.

218 Silurian slates and greywackes folded into a steep syncline on the shore of Galloway, Scotland.

219 Silurian slates and greywackes steeply dipping on the shore of Galloway, Scotland.

220 In the Somalia desert the gently dipping Jurassic succession lies with strong unconformity upon the peneplaned, vertical strata of Pre-Cambrian. The junction between the two formations can be clearly seen.

VII. Some facts about the Earth as a Planet

THE ANALYSIS OF EARTHQUAKES

The interpretation of seismograph records has profoundly influenced man's knowledge about the nature of the interior of the earth. A typical sequence of events as recorded on a seismograph is illustrated in figure 223. First, a series of vibrations is recorded which dies out fairly rapidly; these are the so-called P (or pressure) WAVES. After an interval, a second series appears, known as the S (or shear) WAVES. Finally, a very distinct series of greater disturbances, the L (or long) WAVES, vibrate the instrument. These last are the waves which cause the damage on the earth's surface.

At an early stage in the study of earthquake shocks it was found that the various groups of waves which vibrated the seismograph differed not only in kind but also in velocity. In the case of the P waves, the tremor is propagated by a series of rapid movements of compression and extension, that is, by vibrations parallel to the direction of transmission. The velocity of these waves varies between 5 and 8 miles per second. The S waves, on the other hand, are transmitted by vibrations at right angles to the direction of propagation. Their velocity varies between $2\frac{1}{2}$ and $4\frac{1}{2}$ miles per second. The L waves travel both across the surface of the earth and within the layers of rock near the surface. They consist of vibrations which are developed at right angles to the direction of propagation. Their velocity is about 2 miles per second. The velocity of the P and S waves increases with depth below the surface, indicating a great increase in density of the rocks towards the centre of the earth. Since the L waves occur only in the surface rocks, their velocity remains constant (fig. 221).

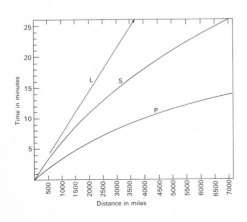

221 Graph showing the constant velocity of the L waves and the increase of velocity with depth, of P and S waves.

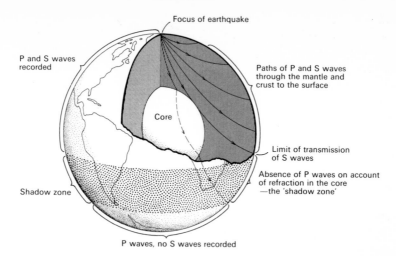

Focus of earthquake

P and S waves recorded

Paths of P and S waves through the mantle and crust to the surface

Core

Limit of transmission of S waves

Absence of P waves on account of refraction in the core —the 'shadow zone'

Shadow zone

P waves, no S waves recorded

222 Diagram of the earth, with a section removed to show the passage of the P and S waves through the mantle and of the P waves through the core.

One of the early discoveries made in the recording of earthquake shocks by means of the seismograph, was the fact that S waves cease to be transmitted through the earth below a certain depth. Now S waves are shear movements which are cut off on entering a liquid. It was therefore concluded that deep down beneath the surface, these waves must pass through rock which is in a fluid condition. This centre part of the earth is described as its LIQUID CORE; its outer margin has been judged, on the evidence provided by the cessation of the S waves, to lie at a depth below the surface of a little under 1,800 miles. The core itself has a diameter of about 4,200 miles, and recent research indicates that it may be composed of successive shells of differing composition.

Analysis of seismograph records shows that, for any particular earthquake, there is a particular zone on the earth's surface across which the P waves are absent. This EARTHQUAKE SHADOW ZONE, as it is called, is about 3,000 miles wide, and begins at the boundary along which the S waves cease—that is, about 6,900 miles from the FOCUS, the origin of the disturbance. This shadow zone is caused by the bending or refraction of the P waves as they pass into the liquid core (fig. 222). Beyond the shadow zone the P waves reappear but, of course, unaccompanied by the S waves.

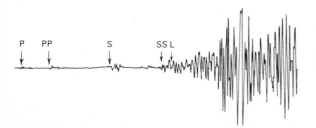

P   PP   S   SS L

223 The P, S and L disturbances as recorded by the seismograph.

224 A text-book example of glacial erosion, as seen on the Matterhorn, Swiss Alps. The sharp *aretes* are shown culminating in the spitz or horn. In the foreground, the recently glaciated landscape.

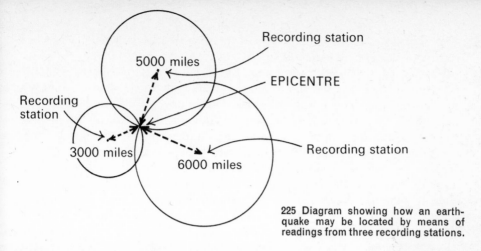

225 Diagram showing how an earthquake may be located by means of readings from three recording stations.

The relative times taken by P, S and L waves to reach various points along the surface is shown on the accompanying diagram (fig. 221). The time-interval between the arrival of the P and S waves increases with distance, since they travel at different velocities; therefore the distance between the surface station and the EPICENTRE can be calculated. (The epicentre is the point on the surface lying vertically above the focus.) With the evidence from three widely spaced stations, the actual position of the epicentre can be plotted (fig. 225).

The seismologist, Mohorovičić, noticed as early as 1909 that in the records of vibrations from near-earthquakes, two sets of P and S waves appeared, each separated by a short interval of time. He demonstrated that this was due to the refraction of these waves along a layer at about 20 miles below the surface of the continents, which marked a change in the composition of the rock. This boundary, now universally accepted by geologists, has become known as the MOHOROVIČIĆ DISCONTINUITY or MOHO; it separates the outer, lighter material of the crust from the underlying, heavier MANTLE whose composition is considered to be that of the ultrabasic rocks.

In the development of seismic surveying, in which artificially produced shocks are used, the seismograph has been replaced by the more sensitive GEOPHONE. In the design of this instrument, use is made of the fact that the electrical resistance of a crystal undergoes changes during the passage of vibrations through it. The result has been that much new information has been obtained about the nature of the crust. A discontinuity within the crust itself, first recognised by Conrad a generation ago (the CONRAD DISCONTINUITY) has been widely traced round the globe, revealing an upper and a lower layer. The velocity of transmission of vibrations through the lower layer is close to that obtained by laboratory experiment with rocks having the density of basalt, while that of the upper layer is indicative of granite. The two layers are therefore known respectively as SIMA (silica, iron and magnesium) and SIAL (silica and alumina). A further discontinuity has even been recorded within the sial itself.

This is considered to mark the floor of the very thin layer of sediments which rests upon the granite basement.

Further light has been thrown upon the nature of the crust by the establishment of the fact that the sial forms the continents but is almost completely absent below the oceans, where the crust is composed of the more dense sima. Beneath the continents (as recognised by Mohorovičić) the crust is about 20 miles thick, though beneath the oceans this figure is no more than 7 miles. The composition of the fragments of rock which have on many occasions been dredged from the deep waters is consistent with the view that the ocean floor is basaltic. A recent project, the 'Mohole', has been embarked upon with the object of drilling into the ocean-bed in order to obtain a sequence of samples from the sima.

Most earthquakes have a shallow origin, with foci lying at depths not exceeding 30 miles. Some, however, originate at depths of 60 miles or more, and a few are initiated well down in the mantle, as much as 400 miles below the surface. These are the so-called DEEP-FOCUS EARTHQUAKES, and they produce widespread tremors. SHALLOW-FOCUS EARTHQUAKES cause much more violent shocks in the region of the epicentre, but beyond a radius of some tens of miles they can be detected only by means of instruments.

P and S waves are generated from deep- and shallow-focus earthquakes alike. L waves, on the other hand, being initiated only as the P and S waves reach the surface, are the product mainly of the shallow-focus disturbance. In fact, after transmission from a deep focus, much of the energy of the P and S waves has been dissipated by the time they reach the surface, and only faint L waves are produced. Since it is the L waves which cause the havoc in areas of high population, the deep-focus earthquakes are less to be feared.

The velocity-pattern of the P and S waves illustrates not only that the mantle increases in density from its circumference towards the core, but also that this increase is remarkably uniform around the globe. This suggests that there is a considerable degree of homogeneity in the rocks of the mantle. Furthermore, since the record of the seismograph has shown that all earthquake shocks, from whatever depth, produce the same kind of compression-stretch (P) waves, it follows that the same kind of mechanism must be responsible for all shocks, whether their origin be shallow or deep.

Recent research on the nature of this mechanism has indicated that earthquakes are caused by the build-up of earth stresses which are eventually triggered-off along some major fault-line, like, for example, the San Andreas fault which passes by San Francisco. The P waves produced by this movement are, as described above, compression-stretch impulses running parallel to the direction of propagation. However, it has been found that the initial impulse may be one either of compression or of rarefaction. This is an important fact, for it helps to distinguish the earthquake shock from the explosion, whose initial P impulse is always one of compression. The reason for this difference seems to be that an earthquake shock is generated, not at a point, but along a linear zone; it will depend upon the location of the recording instrument, in relation to that zone, whether the initial impulse is one of compression or rarefaction. This evidence suggests that earthquakes are of tectonic origin (that is, they develop along tectonic zones) and are not, as has been suggested, due to volcanic explosions.

It may well be that the invention of sensitive instruments which can distinguish between the tremors produced by natural earthquakes (of which there are many thousands, of varying intensity, each year) and the man-made, underground nuclear explosion, may prove to be an important step towards the reducing of suspicion and the establishment of better relations between the Nuclear Powers of the world. An advance in this direction was made when the U.S.A., the U.S.S.R. and Britain signed the Partial Test Ban Treaty in 1963. The three Powers were able to agree to the banning of surface and atmospheric explosions because they could readily be detected as explosions distinct from earthquake shocks. However, doubt still remains (1967) about the ability of even the most sensitive instruments to distinguish between certain earthquake shocks and underground test explosions of low intensity. The signing of a Comprehensive Test Ban Treaty therefore awaits the time when the world's political leaders become convinced that scientists can identify the origin of every possible tremor which may shake the face of the earth.

THE STRUCTURE OF MOUNTAIN RANGES

Long before the nature and thickness of the earth's crust came to be known through the interpretation of vibrations from earthquakes, two workers in the middle of the nineteenth century had produced evidence which laid the foundations of the modern discipline of GEOPHYSICS. They were J. H. Pratt, an archdeacon of the Church of England, and G. B. Airey, the British Astronomer Royal of that time.

Pratt's interest in the earth's gravity field had been aroused by the consistent anomalies which Sir George Everest (after whom the world's highest mountain is named) discovered during his survey of northern India. Everest found that at stations near to the Himalayan range, on the Indo-Gangetic plain, the determination of the vertical by means of the sensitive plumb-line gave results which failed to coincide with astronomical observations. The plumb was, in fact, deflected towards the mountains.

Pratt suggested that this deflection was caused by the gravitational attraction exerted by the mass of the Himalayas, in obedience to the law discovered by Sir Isaac Newton one and a half centuries earlier. Newton had formulated the law of gravitation which stated that every particle exerts an attractive force (F) on every other particle, a force which, considering two particular particles, is proportional to the product of their masses (M_1 and M_2), and is inversely proportional to the square of the distance (D) between them, measured from the centre of each. Expressed mathematically, this reads:

$$F \propto (M_1 \times M_2)/D^2.$$

An example of Newton's law is afforded by the consideration of the mass of a body in relation to the earth. If the body is on the earth's surface it will be 4,000 miles from its centre and the force (F) exerted between the two would be proportional to $(m \times M)/(4,000)^2$, where m and M represent the masses of the body and the earth respectively. However, if the same body could be suspended at a point in outer space, say 12,000 miles above the earth's surface, then the force (F_1) between the two would be proportional to $(m \times M)/(16,000)^2$. Therefore

$$\frac{F_1}{F} = (m \times M)/(16,000)^2 \div (m \times M)/(4,000)^2 \quad \text{or} \quad F_1 = \frac{F}{16}.$$

In other words, a body with a mass of 1 lb at the surface of the earth would weigh 1 oz at a height above the earth of 12,000 miles—a situation approaching weightlessness.

The law of gravity is universal and must operate, therefore, between a mountain and a pendulum bob suspended near it. By estimating the density and volume of the Himalayas, Pratt was able to calculate their mass; he was then able to determine the force of attraction which should have been exerted between the mountain mass and the pendulum or plumb-line suspended at a given distance from it. He obtained the figure for the amount by which the plumb should have been deflected—just over 15 seconds of arc. But these theoretical calculations proved to be about three times as large as the field observations recorded by Everest.

Pratt came to the conclusion that the Himalaya was composed of slightly less dense material than that underlying the neighbouring plains, and that this lighter

226 Diagram illustrating Pratt's theory of the constitution of the earth's crust, as a series of columns of rock of different densities floating upon a denser substratum.

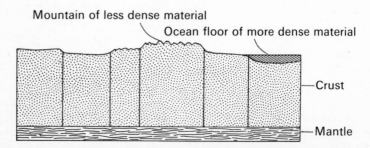

Mountain of less dense material

Ocean floor of more dense material

—Crust

—Mantle

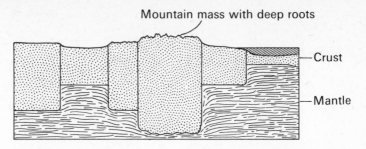

227 Diagram illustrating Airey's theory of mountain roots, showing columns of rock of equal density floating on a denser substratum, but extending downwards to differing depths.

material extended down into the earth's crust. He accounted for variations in elevation of the land by postulating columns of rock of different densities, each column extending to the same depth and floating on a denser medium as would masses of ice, wood, etc., in water (fig. 226).

Stimulated, no doubt, by Pratt's hypothesis, Airey developed ideas similar to those of the archdeacon, from whom, however, he differed by maintaining that mountains and plains have the same density. He introduced the concept of mountain ROOTS, arguing that (like icebergs) the bases of the mountains extend down into the heavier sima; that as the mountains are worn down by erosion, they rise in the more dense substratum in order to maintain balance or ISOSTA-TIC EQUILIBRIUM—a term later coined by the American, Dutton (fig. 227). In short, Airey claimed that while it is true that a plumb-line is deflected towards a mountain mass, the degree of deflection is less than would be expected, not because the mountain mass is less dense than the surrounding sial, but because it displaces the crustal sima and part of the upper mantle sima. The roots therefore exert a smaller force of attraction on the plumb than the more dense material which they have displaced. Nevertheless, this reduced force is over-compensated by the mass of the mountain which protrudes above the surrounding plain.

Subsequent research in this field, with the most delicate instruments available to modern science, has demonstrated the truth of Airey's theory. In fact, evidence from seismic shocks has shown that beneath the mountains of the earth there are roots of sial extending down 90 miles into the crustal and mantle sima, and that the Moho takes a steep downward curve in these regions.

THE MASS OF THE EARTH

Newton's law was also used by the early investigators to determine the mass of the earth. Cavendish, in the eighteenth century, tackled the problem by recording the deflection of a pendulum bob when a heavy mass was brought near to it.

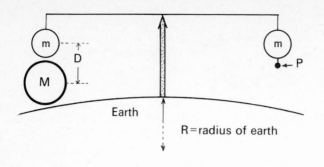

Earth

R=radius of earth

228 Diagram illustrating von Jolly's method of weighing the earth.

He compared the force of attraction exerted by the known heavy mass with that exerted by the earth on the bob, and he obtained a figure for the mass of the latter. In the nineteenth century, von Jolly used the simple method of two globular containers filled with mercury, poised on either arm of a chemical balance and having exactly the same mass, m. A heavy lead sphere of mass M was then placed immediately below one of the containers and the delicate balance was upset. A very small sphere of mercury, exerting a force P and attached to the opposite container, was sufficient to restore the balance (fig. 228).

Then, according to Newton's law, the force P acting between the lead sphere and the mercury-filled container, with centres D cm apart, is proportional to $(M \times m)/D^2$. Moreover, the force F acting between the earth and the mercury-filled container is proportional to $(E \times m)/R^2$, where E is the mass of the earth and R its radius. Hence, $P/F = (M \times m)/D^2 \div (E \times m)/R^2$, or $P/F = MR^2/ED^2$. Thus, $E = MR^2F/D^2P$. Since F is the weight of the mercury-filled container of mass m, and P is the weight of the mercury-filled sphere, all the symbols in the formula are known and E can be calculated. The figure obtained for the mass of the earth, divided by the volume of the latter gave, according to von Jolly, a density for the whole earth of 5·69 grams per c.c. More recent calculations of 5·527 grams per c.c. show how remarkably close were the earlier results.

The figure of 5·527 grams per c.c. for the average density of the whole earth is very much higher than the average density, namely, 2·67 grams per c.c., of the rocks which form the earth's crust. However, as already mentioned, the velocity of earthquake tremors through the interior of the globe indicates that the density of the rocks in the depths is much higher than at the surface. These higher densities must in part be due to the enormous pressures within the earth, as well as to the much denser materials of which the interior is composed. K. E. Bullen has pointed out that seismic evidence suggests that the mantle increases in density, from its boundary with the crust to its boundary with the core, from 3·6 grams per c.c. to 9·5 grams per c.c. He further considers that the outer 1,200 miles of the core averages about 10 grams per c.c. while for the central part the figure may be between 11·5 and 17 grams per c.c.

THE ORIGIN OF THE EARTH

Knowledge about the composition of the earth's interior, which has been gained from the application of Newton's law and from the recording of earth tremors, has been used by the astronomers in their speculations on the origin of the earth. One of the earliest ideas postulated that the sun threw off matter from its equator, to form the planets. However, mathematicians were unable to accept this hypothesis on theoretical grounds, and it was superseded at the end of last century by the concept of PLANETESIMALS, or aggregated fragments within the solar system. These fragments, according to this view, were drawn from the sun by the gravitational attraction exerted by a passing star. Yet another theory envisages the formation of planetesimals from interstellar dust and gas; that these gradually grew by accumulation to form the planets; that the meteorites of today are the remains of those of the planetesimals which failed to aggregate with the larger bodies.

Though there is still uncertainty about the origin of the earth, there seems little doubt that at an early stage in its history, it was in a molten condition surrounded by gaseous clouds. The evidence already discussed in the earlier paragraphs of this chapter suggests that the core of the globe is so dense that nickel and iron must be its predominant constituents. It seems, therefore, that these heavy elements must have sunk down by gravitation towards the centre, and that the mantle, now solid but molten in the early days of earth-history, was enriched by the heavier compounds as they were pulled down from the periphery of the globe. These compounds, containing a limited supply of silicates, evidently gave to the mantle the average composition of an ultrabasic rock, peridotite. Thus, the surface layers, impoverished by the gravitational sinking of the heavy ferromagnesian compounds, were left as light silicates, consolidating as granite: while the immediate underlying layers, only partially drained of their ferro-magnesian material, became basaltic.

THE AGE OF THE EARTH

The story of the way in which the age of the earth has come to be determined well illustrates the dependence of one branch of science upon another. In the early years of last century, the truth about the span of geological time had not yet been grasped. For example, Cuvier, the French investigator who was one of the earliest students in the identification and classification of fossils (page 186), estimated that living things had inhabited the earth for only 40,000 years. Moreover, belonging to the catastrophic school, he was influenced by the tale of Noah's Flood and believed that life on earth had previously been completely wiped out. Indeed, he came to the conclusion—based on a wrong interpretation of evidence from the Paris basin—that on four occasions since life first began on earth, all living things had been utterly destroyed; the latest of these catastrophes was considered by Cuvier to have been that recorded in Genesis. It is of interest to note that archaeologists have confirmed the existence of a devastating, but local flood in biblical times, over the site of the ancient city of Ur, in Mesopotamia, the region from where the Flood story is considered to have originated.

The catastrophists in geology were finally discredited by, among others, Sir Charles Lyell, who in his text-book published in 1830, popularised the principle of Uniformitarianism (page 12), which had been introduced by James Hutton 45 years earlier. According to this principle, it was maintained that even among the most ancient sedimentary rocks the processes causing their accumulation were precisely those which cause modern deposits to be laid down. Hutton's principle has for long been universally accepted by geologists, and is enshrined in the phrase: 'The present is the key to the past.'

As the evidence from geological mapping accumulated, it came to be realised how enormous was the total thickness of deposits which form the sedimentary succession. In the latter half of last century, Samuel Haughton found that the thickness of sedimentary rocks (taking the maximum thickness for each system) added up to nearly half a million feet. He argued that the thickness of strata was proportional to time of deposition. There was, however, a great element of guesswork in these figures, since a 6-inch bed of sandstone may be laid down during a single flood, while for a similar thickness of limestone, the period for its deposition may run into thousands of years. Nevertheless, though Haughton was wildly astray in his age-calculations, this same principle was later applied with considerable success to a local problem in Scandinavia by de Geer, in his measurement of varved clays (page 246).

Joly* approached the problem in another, and ingenious way, by attempting to estimate the age of the oceans. He assumed that the seas were originally fresh water; that salts within the rocks on land had gradually been dissolved out and had been carried into the oceans by the rivers. He calculated the volume of the oceans and the weight of dissolved salts which they contain. He then determined the weight of salts which must have been brought down annually in solution by the rivers of the world. This figure, divided by the weight of the salts in the oceans, gave a time of just under 100 million years for the age of the latter.

The Scottish physicist, Kelvin, had already grappled with the problem of the earth's age on the basis of heat loss. His theory relied upon the fact that the earth is steadily losing heat to the atmosphere, at a rate that can be calculated, and that this heat loss is not entirely compensated by the heat gained from the sun. Therefore there was a time when the earth must have been molten. Calculating the annual rate of heat loss, Kelvin finally arrived at the conclusion that the time which had elapsed since the whole globe was molten was not more than 40 million years.

But the real breakthrough in the quest for a figure which would accurately represent the age of the earth came in the early years of this century. Becquerel

* An Irish investigator of the last century: not to be confused with von Jolly.

discovered radioactivity, and one of the fundamental facts which soon emerged was that certain radioactive elements are constantly decaying, or changing into other elements, together with the evolution of heat. Here was a hitherto undiscovered source of heat which revealed the flaw in Kelvin's argument. Uranium, for example, is constantly changing into lead and helium; potassium into argon; rubidium into strontium.

The rate of spontaneous disintegration, or decay, varies enormously for different substances. It is expressed in terms of the half-life, which simply means that one gram of an element will have been reduced to half a gram at the end of its half-life, to one-quarter of a gram at the end of the half of its second half-life period, to one-eighth by the end of the next, and so on. Uranium 238 has a half-life of 4,500 million years, while that of carbon is under 6,000 years.

Many of the more rare minerals contain small amounts of uranium. The amount of uranium which must have been present at the time of crystallisation can be calculated. Therefore if, for example, it is found that in a crystal the original weight of uranium has been reduced by half, then that crystal must have been formed 4,500 million years ago. As a matter of fact, this is just about the figure which has been established for the age of certain meteorites that have recently been analysed.

Many possible errors arise in the attempts at estimation of age by radiation methods. Since the weight of uranium can be reduced not only by radioactive decay but also by chemical alteration, it is essential that only chemically unaltered rocks should be used in age determinations. Again, uranium contains the isotopes 235 and 238; these each break down to different isotopes of lead at different rates. The analyst must be able to distinguish between the two products of this breakdown process. In fact, this line of investigation is as yet in its early stages, and only by carrying out large numbers of analyses can an accurate picture be obtained. However, there is now a sufficiently large number of consistent results to give fairly accurate values for the ages of the geological systems (fig. 1). In some cases, the ages of ancient igneous rocks have been established to within an accuracy of 2 million years.

A promising line of approach in determining the age of rocks of the earth's crust lies in the analysis of feldspars and micas, both of which contain potassium, the substance which breaks down radioactively to argon. The age of many igneous rocks has been established by this means, and thus the age of the rocks into which they have been intruded can be roughly assessed. The oldest rocks containing the remains of identifiable organisms, the earliest Cambrian, are considered, on latest estimates, to have been formed about 570 million years ago, while the earliest figure for the most ancient rocks of the crust is 3,500 million years.

VIII. The Study of Fossils

HISTORICAL

The significance of the fossil remains which are found embedded in the rocks of the earth's crust was not understood by the early investigators. Among the Ancient Greeks Empedocles (fifth century B.C.), noting the bones of extinct mammals in the rocks of Sicily, concluded that a race of human giants once lived there. Herodotus (fifth century B.C.), studying the area around the Great Pyramid of Gizeh, in Egypt, was quite off-beam in his deductions about the origin of the Nummulites littering the desert floor (page 8). Aristotle (fourth century B.C.), the tutor to the young Alexander and a prince among Greek thinkers, makes no mention of fossils in his classic description of rocks. Nor does his pupil, Theophrastus, whose treatise on minerals was a valuable source of knowledge right up to the beginning of the modern age of science.

From the time of the Ancient Greeks until the end of the Dark Ages the spirit of enquiry and speculation lay dormant. Only in the seventeenth century did writers begin to refer to the mystifying 'figured stones' which occurred in certain rocks. Gradually it became established that they were the remains of once-living organisms, and by the end of the eighteenth century the way lay open for Cuvier (1769–1832), the French statesman-geologist of Swiss descent, to make the contribution which laid the foundations of PALAEONTOLOGY, the scientific study of fossils.

Cuvier was a highly skilled observer who produced numerous papers on the fossil remains in the strata around Paris; he was also a Counsellor of State at the French Court, appointed by Napoleon. His chief geological interest lay in the collection and description of fossil bones, and his studies led him to the conclusion that, repeatedly at certain times during the earth's history, all living things had been suddenly destroyed and that new forms had, each time, been created to take their place. This theory of 'CATASTROPHISM', being in line with the story of Noah's Flood, was welcomed by the Church of his day.

However, Lamarck (1744–1829), Cuvier's contemporary, was at the same time investigating the fossil shells in the rocks of the Paris region. He found evidence which suggested that the organisms whose remains were preserved in the upper beds had evolved, step by step, from those entombed in the lower, older strata. At about the same time, in England, the canal engineer William Smith (1769–1839, for long revered as the Father of English Geology) reached the same conclusion as Lamarck, and became the first to demonstrate, by recognising slight differences in form, that fossils could be used to zone the strata (see below). The researches of Charles Darwin (1809–82) and Alfred

Russel Wallace (1823–1913), through the middle of the nineteenth century, finally consolidated the truth of Lamarck's view of the continuity of life. Over the past hundred years the science of palaeontology has grown to embrace an enormous variety of fossil forms, gathered from all parts of the earth, and world-wide agreement upon their general classification has for long been established.

USES

The evidence from the vast world collection of fossil FAUNA (animals) and FLORA (plants) obtained from the sedimentary rocks has shown that any fossil-bearing succession can be zoned or sub-divided by means of the fossils which it contains. For example, much of the Jurassic can be zoned on the basis of the genera and species of Ammonoidea which it contains. Each ZONE is characterised by the presence of a particular form which, apart from a certain degree of over-lapping, is absent from the underlying as well as from the overlying strata. This is a most important principle in the analysis of the sedimentary succession (STRATIGRAPHY), and it enables the geologist to determine the relative ages of sedimentary rocks in any part of the world (their absolute age can, however, only be determined by radioactive data). The strata from the chalk cliffs of the Plateau of the Wandering in Sinai and those of Dover can be CORRELATED with one another because they contain the same fossil shells. In the Coal Measures of Britain delicate plant remains are to be found which are similar to those in the coal seams of Australia. On the other hand, though in the hand specimen the lime-stones from the Silurian in South-west England appear similar to those from the much later Devonian, careful examination confirms that their faunal assemblage is different.

Nevertheless, in comparing the organic remains from two different successions of the same age, the environment of growth (the study of which is described as ECOLOGY) must be taken into account. Corals flourish in tropical and sub-tropical seas of today and may lead eventually to the formation of reef limestones; but in a temperate or polar ocean, limestones are being formed from the skeletons of quite different organisms because, unlike the corals, they are adapted to cold environments. What is true for today was also true in past geological times.

Lime-secreting organisms, flourishing in clear marine waters, may suddenly be killed by the introduction of mud from the land, whereas similar organisms further from the land and beyond the influence of the mud, may continue to live. In other words, changing conditions may be quite local. It was partly because Cuvier did not grasp these facts of ecology (he thought that locally observed changes must be world-wide) that he was led to champion the cause of catastrophism (see opposite page).

The study of fossils has enabled the stratigraphy of the sedimentary rocks throughout the world to be built up into the systems and groups described later (page 220). In the economic field, knowledge of palaeontology has meant that important coal seams can be identified and mapped in underground workings as well as on the surface; that bitumen horizons in the great oil regions of the world can be located and their depths calculated. The study of fossils has also assisted in PALAEOGEOGRAPHY (the reconstruction of ancient geography) by providing a key to the climate in which organisms lived. This is an aspect of geology which is also of great importance in the search for oil.

PRESERVATION

Any organism or any part of an organism which becomes covered by sediment and subsequently preserved in the indurated rock is described as a fossil. The bodies of the hairy mammoth and the woolly rhinoceros which were trapped and kept, as in a deep freeze, in the frozen muds of Siberia, illustrate a rare type of fossilisation which is confined to Recent times. Another example of very complete preservation is that provided by amber. As resin exudes from a fracture in the bark of a conifer tree, it may incase insects, later solidifying as amber. The delicate bodies of insects have been preserved in this way from early Tertiary times.

The remains of vegetation—the bark and leaves of trees—are often preserved by the reducing process known as CARBONISATION, in which a carbon residue is left after the dispersion of the volatile constituents of the plant tissue. The fossil usually shows the venation of the leaves and the pattern of the bark in great perfection (fig. 236). PETRIFACTION is another form of fossilisation of plant material, caused by siliceous or calcareous solutions having been introduced into the cavities of the plant structure, where they were precipitated. In this way, the original pattern of the material is retained. The so-called 'petrified forests' are examples of this kind.

Another form of fossilisation is that of REPLACEMENT, in which the original calcareous substance of a shell is slowly replaced in chemical reaction with some substance such as silica or pyrite or other mineral matter. The process may be a more simple one, in which the aragonite of the shell is replaced by calcite, the other and more stable crystalline form of calcium carbonate. Often, in this process of replacement, the pattern of the shell may not, however, be preserved.

During the course of sedimentation, the calcareous or chitinous shell of an organism may have been buried in mud (CHITIN is the horny substance which also forms the skeletons of modern creatures like the crab). The mud presses upon the shell as the weight of overlying deposits increases. In time, the substance of the shell is dissolved away, leaving a cavity or MOULD which bears its imprint. The mould may subsequently become filled with some other chemical precipitate or matrix, forming a CAST. In a cast, the detailed structure and pattern of the shell may be preserved. This is a very common form of fossilisation. Fossil remains, similar to casts, may also be formed when worm and other invertebrate tracks, and vertebrate foot-marks, are imprinted on soft sand; if the imprint is buried by the next layer of sediment, it may be preserved.

The permanence of a fossil depends upon the subsequent history of the rock in which it occurs. Shelly residues may be washed into, and retained by a sand, but sandstones less frequently contain fossils because their porosity is such as to lead, subsequently, to the dissolving away of the hard parts of an organism. A limestone may undergo recrystallisation during the process of dolomitisation, or of metamorphism (page 55), and in this case the fossil remains will be lost. But an organic limestone, that is, a limestone built up by the accumulation of shelly remains, will be a rich source of fossil material so long as it has not suffered drastic diagenetic change. Shales, too, in the midst of a calcareous succession, yield abundant fossils.

CLASSIFICATION

All living organisms belong to one of two KINGDOMS, that of the animals and that of the plants. Each kingdom is divided into SUB-KINGDOMS or PHYLA and, each phylum into CLASSES. Further sub-divisions are into ORDERS, FAMILIES, GENERA and SPECIES. A species may be divided into SUB-SPECIES. It is also commonly found necessary to introduce SUB-CLASSES and SUB-ORDERS. Through the co-operation between palaeontologists and biologists the Linnean classification, as it is called (after Linnaeus, 1707–88, who introduced the modern terminology of classification), has been extended to include all fossil forms as well as the living.

The following table provides a few examples from this classification to show the relationship of a number of living species, one with the other.

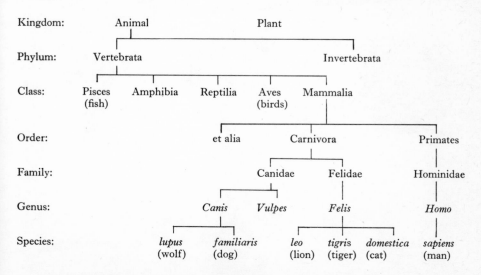

Every individual living and fossil organism bears its generic name (by convention written with a capital initial letter) followed by its specific name (written with a small initial letter). When a sub-species has been identified, a third name is added. Very often, in palaeontology, it is found to be impossible to assign a specific name to a fossil specimen; in this case it is simply known by its generic term, as is frequently seen to be the case in the descriptions which follow.

It should be noted, however, that though the above scheme of classification appears to be simple and precise, many difficulties are encountered and, as scientific knowledge increases, it becomes necessary to reassign some organisms to different or even new genera and species. For example, in the case of the Felidae, some authorities have recommended that the larger animals such as the lion, tiger and leopard are sufficiently distinct from the smaller puma, lynx and cat to warrant inclusion in separate genera. The larger group are described by these authorities as *Panthera leo*, *Panthera tigris* and *Panthera pardus* respectively; other classifiers, while using the same specific names, retain the generic term Felis (i.e. *Felis leo*, *Felis tigris* and *Felis pardus*). Moreover, the Manchurian and the Sumatran tiger are thought to be distinct enough to be placed in separate sub-species, so that they become *Panthera tigris longipilis* and *Panthera tigris sondaica* respectively. . . . Such problems of classification are continually arising.

THE INVERTEBRATE GROUPS

All living organisms are composed of tiny units or CELLS. Each cell consists of a transparent, jelly-like substance called PROTOPLASM, within which a central,

229 Some common types of Foraminifera.

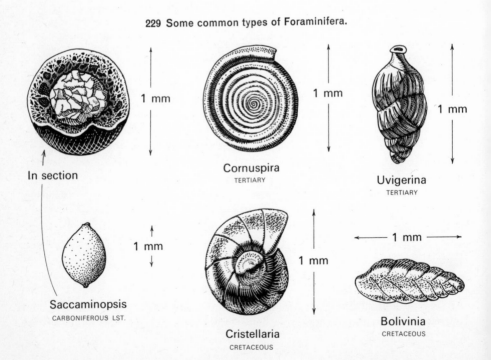

In section

Cornuspira
TERTIARY

Uvigerina
TERTIARY

Saccaminopsis
CARBONIFEROUS LST.

Cristellaria
CRETACEOUS

Bolivinia
CRETACEOUS

darker body, the NUCLEUS, resides. Within the nucleus of the cell there are numerous dark bodies which are described as CHROMOSOMES. Each chromosome consists of certain fundamental particles, some of which are the GENES. The genes contain the hereditary characters which are passed on to each generation. If the nucleus is damaged, the cell will die.

The simplest forms of life, belonging to the phylum Protozoa, are single-celled creatures. But most organisms are built up of enormous numbers of cells, specialised in various ways to perform specific functions. This is especially true of the more advanced invertebrates and the vertebrates. Thus, in the human body, the bone cells differ from those which form the muscles, the walls of the heart, the brain and so on.

In the following pages, groups of invertebrates which are important to the palaeontologist are described. They range from the simplest forms, like the Foraminifera and Radiolaria, to the most complex. The place of each group within the Linnean system of classification is indicated in the text and the distribution of each, in terms of geological time, is shown in figure 259.

Protozoa. The classification of the Protozoa is as follows:

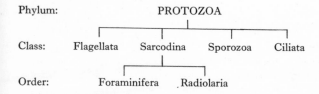

Of the four classes of the Protozoa, members of the Flagellata and the Sarcodina secrete a hard shell or TEST. Of these, the Sarcodina are especially important to the palaeontologist. There are two orders, the Foraminifera and the Radiolaria, of which the former are by far the more useful in correlation. They, with other forms, constitute what are known as the MICROFAUNA (minute animals).

The vast majority of the members of the Foraminifera are marine, mostly living on shallow sea-beds. A few float on the surface. In the simplest forms, the test is composed of a horny or chitinous substance in the shape of a hollow tube; the single cell lies within the tube but the protoplasm may stream out at either end and cover the external surface of the chitinous skeleton. Other forms of test may be globular, as in the Carboniferous genus *Saccaminopsis*, or coiled, as in the Tertiary *Cornuspira*. Such forms possess a single external opening or APERTURE.

The test in many of the groups of Foraminifera is MULTI-CHAMBERED, consisting of numerous regular, interconnecting internal spaces. The chambers may be arranged in a single (*Nodosaria*) or in a double line (*Uvigerina* and *Bolivina*), or in a flat spiral, as in *Cristellaria* or in a TROCHOID (turreted) spire.

The aperture may be a simple opening on the flat surface, as in *Bolivina*, or it may be extended as a neck-like structure as in *Uvigerina* (fig. **229**).

The substance of the test of a foraminifer may be calcareous, siliceous or arenaceous. In the case of the arenaceous type, minute grains of sand, flakes of mica or sponge spicules may be cemented to the chitinous base of the test. Those tests which are calcareous may be thin-walled and PERFORATE (that is, pene-trated by minute pores) or thick-walled and IMPERFORATE or PORCELANEOUS. Some Foraminifera, including the fusulinids, which developed during Carboni-ferous times, are notable for the fact that the test wall is composed of several distinct layers. The details of this layering can be clearly seen in thin section under the microscope.

Since the 1920s, the study of Foraminifera has grown to an enormous extent, largely because of the demands of the oil industry. Most Foraminifera are microscopic, less than the size of a pin-head (the members of the genus *Nummulites* are exceptional in attaining a diameter of almost an inch), and as such may be found in great numbers in a 3- or 4-inch core from an oil well—in these circumstances the finding of a macro-fossil is inevitably a somewhat rare occurrence. Since the Foraminifera are most abundant in Cretaceous and Tertiary formations, in which the world's oil reservoirs are chiefly concentrated, their value became apparent as the need for detailed correlation grew. Today, every large oil company employs its staff of palaeontologists trained in the recognition of the Foraminifera. Much information has also been obtained from the wide variety of Foraminifera which exist today in the seas and oceans of the world.

The Radiolaria, the other order in the class Sarcodina, are also microscopic creatures; they are wholly marine and possess siliceous tests. They are surface-floating and when the creatures die their tests, insoluble even under great water pressure, accumulate in vast numbers on the floors of the deep oceans, forming radiolarian ooze (page 24). The tests of Radiolaria occur in a great variety of shapes, often with delicate ornamentation. They have been less the subject of study than the Foraminifera and are little used as a basis for correlation.

Coelenterata. The classification of the Coelenterata is as follows:

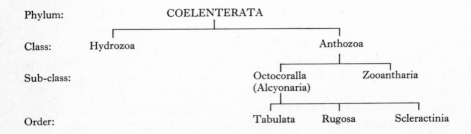

230 The glacier and *arêtes* of Mount Robson, British Colombia.

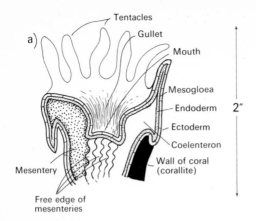

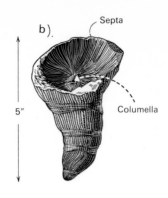

231a Section through a coral, showing relation between the soft polype and its skeleton.

231b A Carboniferous solitary coral, showing the development of septa.

The Coelenterata include all the corals, jellyfish and sea-anemones. They differ from the Protozoa in that the soft body of the organism consists not only of many cells but of two multi-cell groups, each group performing its special function. Like the Protozoa, the Coelenterata include both organisms which secrete a hard skeleton and those which possess no hard parts. The latter belong especially to the Hydrozoa, and will not be considered here.

The soft body of a coelenterate is a sac-like cavity whose walls consist of an inner group of cells constituting the ENDODERM and an outer group forming the ECTODERM (fig. 231a). Between the two layers there is a thin, non-cellular substance described as the MESOGLOEA. The body-cavity or COELENTERON opens to the exterior via the MOUTH, which is surrounded by TENTACLES. The endoderm cells perform the function of digestion while the ectoderm secretes the external skeleton or PERISARC. In the stony corals this is always present as a calcareous structure which is built upwards in the form of a tube or CORALLITE. The soft body of the organism is described as the POLYP(E). Corals may grow singly (SOLITARY) or they may be COMPOUND. In the latter case, the corallites, growing upwards, constitute the CORALLUM. Solitary corals can often be identified by the shape of the corallite and by the ornamentation on the external surface. Compound corals may also be recognised by examining the pattern of the corallites—their diameter, degree of branching, etc. However, there are more precise means of identification, as described below.

In the living coral polype, a series of vertical, radial folds of the body wall run in towards the centre of the coelenteron. They extend from the base of the gullet to the base of the polype. These folds are termed the MESENTERIES, and they are grouped in pairs. The position of each pair of mesenteries is marked across the external base of the polype by a depression. A calcareous partition or SEPTUM (fig. 231b) is secreted in the folds of the ectoderm between adjacent pairs of mesenteries and these septa are built up as the coral grows. Some of the septa join at the centre, forming a vertical calcareous rod, known as the COLUMELLA. Other septa may extend only a fraction of the way towards the centre. Vertical partitions, joining the septa, are described as DISSEPIMENTS and form a concentric pattern.

The number and arrangement of septa are both important in the identification of corals. The Scleractinia or Hexacoralla, which appeared during Trias times, possess septa in multiples of six, while the earlier Rugosa or Tetracoralla of the Palaeozoic era show a TETRAMERAL septal arrangement (in multiples of four). *Dibunophyllum* and *Lithostrotion* (fig. 235) are both common examples of the latter. These distinguishing characters can be identified by examining the polished transverse section of a coral.

In the other group of corals, namely, the Tabulata, the septal development is poor, but a continuing series of horizontal plates or TABULAE are secreted at the base of the polype as the coral grows upwards. *Halysites*, the chain coral, is a common member of the Tabulata (fig. 235).

The Rugosa and Tabulata, both Palaeozoic corals, are used as zone fossils. But both groups died out before Mezozoic times, and were replaced by the Scleractinia, which form the great coral-reefs of today.

Echinoderma. The classification of the Echinoderma is as follows:

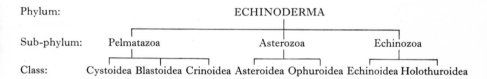

Of the seven classes given above, the Echinoidea and the Crinoidea are of chief importance to the palaeontologist. All are exclusively marine forms with an

232 View of the aboral surface of a regular echinoid (with tubercles omitted).

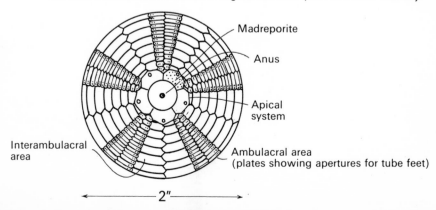

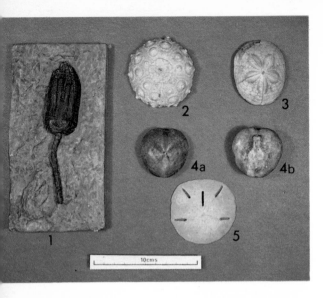

233 Representatives of the phylum Echinoderma:
1. Encrinus liliformis, a crinoid from the lower part of the Jurassic.
2. Cidaris, a regular echinoid from the Upper Jurassic.
3. Clypeaster, an irregular echinoid from the Miocene.
4. Micraster, a zone echinoid, also irregular, from the Upper Chalk: (a) shows the aboral view with the petaloid ambulacra, and (b) the oral view, showing the peristome away from the central position.
5. Mellita, a flattened, irregular, recent echinoid, showing the apertures or lunulles, and petaloid ambulacra.

234 Representatives of the phylum Mollusca:
1. Ceratites, an ammonite from the continental Muschelkalk, Trias, showing characteristic 'ceratitoid' suture pattern.
2. Gastrioceras, a goniatite from Upper Carboniferous.
3. Dactylioceras, an ammonite from the Upper Lias.
4. Pinacoceras, an ammonite from the Upper Trias, showing a complex suture pattern.
5. Microderoceras, an ammonite from the Lias.
6. Buccinum, a Recent gastropod. The break in the shell wall reveals the columella.
7. Patella, the modern limpet and a gastropod, having a non-coiled shell.
8. Euomphalus, a Carboniferous gastropod with a flattened spire and with angular shorls.
9. Aporrhais, a Recent gastropod, showing the expanded outer lip at the entrance of the coiled shell.
10. Cardium, a Recent lamellibranch, showing an internal view of the left valve.
11. Gryphaea, a lamellibranch from Lower Lias, showing incurved umbo and flattened, ill-developed right valve.

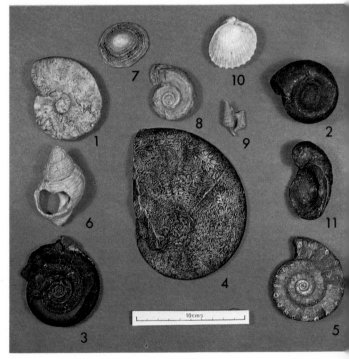

235 Representatives of the Trilobita:
1. Flexicalymene, a trilobite from the Ordovician.
2. Flexicalymene, a specimen in the rolled-up position.
3. Phacops, a trilobite from the Devonian.

Representatives of the Brachiopoda:
4. Terebratula, a brachiopod from the Tertiary.
5. Conchidium knighti, a brachiopod from the Silurian.
6. Schizophoria, a brachiopod from the Devonian.
7. Spirifernia, a brachiopod from the Carboniferous, persisting to the Jurassic.
8. Leptaena, a brachiopod from the Silurian.

Representatives of the Anthozoa:
9. Lithostrotion basaltiforme, a compound, rugose coral from the Carboniferous.
10. Dibunophyllum, in cross-section showing septal arrangement; a solitary rugose coral from the Carboniferous.
11. Lithostrotion junceum a compound rugose coral from the Carboniferous.
12. Halysites, a tabulate coral from the Silurian.

Representatives of the Graptoloidea:
13. Didymograptus, the 'tuning-fork' graptolite, from the Ordovician.
14. Monograptus, a graptolite from the Silurian.
15. Monograptus (left) and Climacograptus, graptolites from the Silurian.

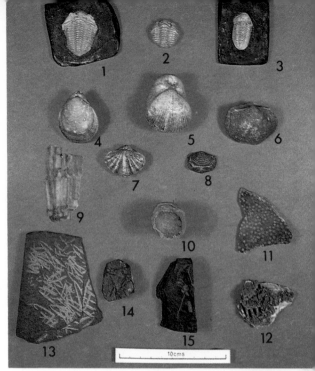

236 Coal Measure plants:
1. Calamites, showing the rounded base and the development of nodes along the length of the stem.
2. Bothrodendron, with its closely spaced pattern of leaf scars.
3. Lepidodendron, with its diamond-shaped pattern of leaf cushions.
4. Sigillaria, with its parallel arrangement of leaf cushions.
5. Stigmaria, showing scars marking points of attachment of rootlets.
6. Alethopteris ⎫
7. Sphenopteris ⎬ common examples.
8. Neuropteris ⎭

external skeleton composed of calcite plates. Of the living forms, the crinoids (sea-lilies) are attached, while the echinoids (sea-urchins) and holothuroids (sea-cucumbers) are free moving.

There are two orders in the class Echinoidea, namely, the Regularia and the Irregularia. The same fundamental architecture of the shell is shared by the two orders. The main part of the echinoid shell is termed the CORONA. In the Regularia (fig. 232) it is almost spherical and exhibits PENTAMERAL (five-fold) symmetry. It consists of five AMBULACRAL AREAS alternating with five INTERAMBULACRAL AREAS, each of which extends across the whole shell after the manner of lines of longitude. These areas, of which the interambulacrals are generally broader, each consist of two rows of calcite plates which interlock with one another in a zig-zag pattern. The junctions of the plates with those of the adjacent area, however, form a straight line. In each ambulacral plate there is a pair of small PORES. The surfaces of the plates of both areas are generally modified into the form of TUBERCLES (as in *Cidaris*, fig. **233**) to which, in life, movable spines or RADIOLES were attached. Radioles may be only a fraction of an inch in length or they may exceed six inches. They may be sharp and pointed or blade-like. The area of attachment of the radiole, known as the ACETABULUM, is concave and forms a ball-and-socket joint with the convex surface of the tubercle, called the MAMELON. In life the radioles can be swivelled about by means of very small muscles attached to them and to the tubercle.

The areas of the corona taper on the underside towards an opening which in life is covered by a membrane described as the PERISTOME. The centre of the peristome is perforated, giving the aperture known as the mouth. When the organism dies, the peristome decays, leaving the wider aperture which is loosely called the mouth. The areas of the corona also taper towards the ABORAL (opposite the mouth) pole round an area of ten plates (five large and five small) known as the APICAL SYSTEM. In life, across the apical system there is a membrane like the peristome, called the PERIPROOT, which contains a small aperture, the ANUS. The latter marks the end of the alimentary, digestive canal. One of the five larger plates of the apical system, the MADREPORITE, is a perforated structure through which water is drawn to supply the internal WATER-VASCULAR SYSTEM (fig. 232). This consists of a series of tubes which form the animal's breathing apparatus. These tubes emerge at the exterior as a host of TUBE FEET through the pores in the plates of the ambulacral areas. Each pair of tubes emerging from a plate unites on the exterior side to form a single tube foot. The tube feet in the region of the mouth are modified as suckers and enable the creature to pull itself along the sea-floor, hence the name. Inside the mouth there is a complex system of plates which forms a group of biting jaws known as ARISTOTLE'S LANTERN. The lantern is actuated by a series of muscles attached to an internal structure known as the PERIGNATHIC GIRDLE.

The second group of the Echinoids, the Irregularia, differs from the Regularia in a number of ways. The corona is bilaterally symmetrical and often heart-shaped as in *Micraster* (fig. **233**). The ambulacral areas assume a PETALOID shape and no longer extend to the peristome. The periproot becomes located in the interambulacral area which lies along the plane of symmetry of the shell, while the mouth moves forward (*Cidaris*, aboral view). The Chalk contains abundant fossils of the irregular echinoids, which are important zone fossils in this formation. The echinoids are first found in Ordovician rocks but they only become abundant in Mesozoic times, an abundance which has persisted up to the present day.

The Crinoidea are less numerous and less well preserved than the Echinoidea and are therefore of less value in correlating the rocks. The organs of the body lie within the cup or CALYX, which is supported on a STEM. The latter is composed of a large number of discs or OSSICLES, through which there runs a central canal. In life, each disc is attached to its neighbour by tissue so that a certain flexibility is imparted to the whole stem. The ROOTS, at the base of the stem, hold the organism in an upright position (fig. 237a).

The calyx consists of three rows of five plates each, named the INFRABASALS, the BASALS and the RADIALS (fig. 237b). In some crinoids, the infrabasals are fused together to form a single plate. The top of the calyx consists of five or more DELTOID plates with the mouth at the centre. The anus, in some forms raised on a short ANAL TUBE to avoid contamination of food, emerges from one of the deltoids. Apart from the position of the anus, the crinoid exhibits perfect pentameral symmetry.

The ARMS which, with the calyx, together comprise the CROWN of the organism, are each composed of a single row of large BRACHIAL plates. These plates become progressively smaller towards the free end. On the inner side of each arm the brachials bear a FOOD-GROOVE which is covered by a series of small plates or AMBULACRALS. The food-groove is equipped with fine hairs or CILIA which beat rhythmically, producing a water-current towards the mouth. In many forms the arms bear branches or PINNULES, each of which has its food-groove.

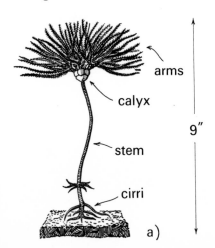

arms

calyx

9″

stem

cirri

a)

237a A living crinoid.

237b Detail of the calyx of a crinoid.

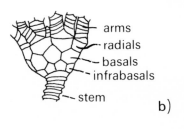

arms
radials
basals
infrabasals
stem

b)

238 The Lewisian Gneiss, of Pre-Cambrian age, forms a bare rocky landscape in north-west Scotland as is shown here beside the village of Stoer. In the photograph the overlying unconformable Torridon Sandstone can be seen beyond the bay. The Torridonian contains shaly horizons in this area, and forms a mellow landscape contrasting sharply with that of the Lewisian.

239 The Torridon Sandstone of Pre-Cambrian age is a well-indurated rock which forms many towering crags in north-west Scotland. The photograph shows the cliffs above Loch Broom, with individual beds forming traceable features or benches along the hillside.

240 The Highland Schists at Morar, on the road to the Isles, north of Fort William. They consist of sediments metamorphosed during the Caledonian orogeny which outcrop over much of central and northern Scotland.

241 Highland glaciated topography seen from Goatfell, Isle of Arran.

The preservation of a complete crinoid is rather rare, though figure **233** shows an almost perfectly preserved *Encrinus*; isolated plates can frequently be identified in the rocks, and ossicles are generally preserved in lengths of several inches. Crinoids are first recorded in rocks of late Cambrian age and were most abundant during Silurian to Caboniferous times. They continued through late Palaeozoic and early Mesozoic rocks, and they became moderately abundant during the latter part of that era. They have survived through Tertiary times up to the present day.

Brachipods. The classification of the Brachiopoda is as follows:

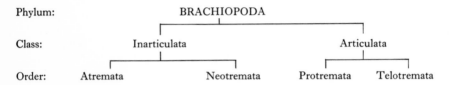

Phylum:		BRACHIOPODA		
Class:	Inarticulata		Articulata	
Order:	Atremata	Neotremata	Protremata	Telotremata

The Brachiopoda are marine shelled organisms. Some forms have been able to survive in brackish waters and others in water of high salinity. But no freshwater forms are known. The Brachiopoda are most abundant in the shallow seas at depths varying from 100 to 600 feet. In the larval stage, the brachiopod is free-swimming, but when adult it becomes fixed to the sea-floor and remains there for the rest of its life.

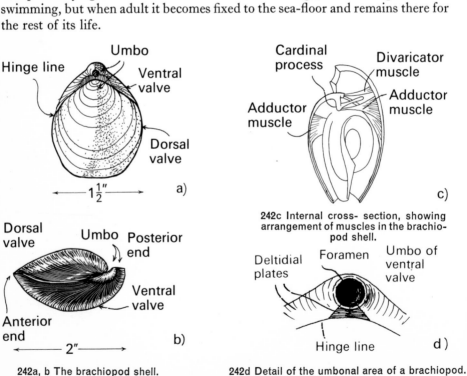

242a, b The brachiopod shell.

242c Internal cross- section, showing arrangement of muscles in the brachiopod shell.

242d Detail of the umbonal area of a brachiopod.

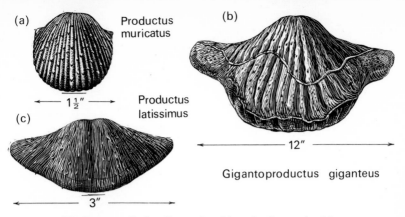

(a) Productus muricatus

(b)

(c) Productus latissimus

1½″

12″

Gigantoproductus giganteus

3″

243 Common Carboniferous brachiopods, the productids.

The brachiopod shell (figs. 242a and b) consists of two valves, the VENTRAL (lower) VALVE and the DORSAL (upper) VALVE. The ventral valve is generally the larger of the two. Each valve has a rounded protuberance known as the BEAK or UMBO, though that of the dorsal valve is smaller and sometimes barely visible. Growth lines run concentrically from the umbo across each valve, while ridges and depressions may radiate from each umbo as in *Spiriferina* (fig. 235). In the group known as the Productidae, spines are developed upon the surface of the valves. The umbones lie at the POSTERIOR END. The shell is symmetrical about a plane through the umbones which bisects the valves. The two valves are attached to one another along the HINGE-LINE, which lies adjacent to the umbones. The valves are held together by the internal muscles (see below) and their attachment is strengthened in some groups by the development of two projections in the ventral valve in the region of the hinge-line. They are known as HINGE-TEETH and they fit into corresponding hollows, or DENTAL SOCKETS, in the dorsal valve. The length of the hinge-line determines the shape of the shell (cf. fig. 235).

The valves are opened and closed—to the widest extent in the ANTERIOR (front, beside the mouth) region—by means of internal muscles which work by contraction. These are the ADDUCTOR and DIVARICATOR muscles. They are attached to the inner side of the ventral valve and to the CARDINAL PROCESS of the dorsal valve (fig. 242c). Their areas of attachment are preserved in the fossil as MUSCLE SCARS. Between the ventral umbo and the hinge-line there is a triangular area which in some forms is occupied by two DELTIDIAL PLATES or by one plate, the DELTIDIUM. On others there is an aperture in this area described as the DELTHYRIUM (fig. 242d). A muscular stalk, known as the PEDICLE, emerges either through a FORAMEN in the ventral valve (well seen in *Terebratula*, fig. 235) or between the two valves along the hinge-line, or through the delthyrium; it serves as an anchor for the organism. Alternatively, the ventral valve may in some cases become cemented to the rock of the sea-floor or may be anchored by spines.

244 The glaciated topography, as seen from Snowdon, of the Lower Palaeozoic rocks of North Wales.

245 St. Mary's Loch in the Southern Uplands of Scotland. Rolling country composed of isoclinally folded Lower Palaeozoic rocks.

246 The Cheviot Hills, forming the border between England and Scotland, are mainly lavas, of Old Red Sandstone age.

247 Whernside, with bare Carboniferous limestone outcropping in the foreground, near Chapel-le-dale, Yorkshire.

The soft parts of the body consist essentially of the mouth, alimentary canal and anus. In some forms the canal ends blindly as it does in the Coelenterata. On the dorsal surface of the mouth (there is no head in the brachiopod) there is a group of tentacles lined with cilia. The cilia create a current of water which brings microscopic food to the mouth. The tentacles were initially thought to assist the brachiopod in locomotion; described as 'arms' or BRACHIA, they gave the animal its name. They are supported by a calcareous skeleton which is an internal extension of the ventral valve known as the BRACHIAL LOOP. The whole body is enveloped by a fleshy mantle which secretes the shell.

Of the two classes of brachiopod, the Inarticulata lack hinge-teeth, and the alimentary canal ends via the anus. Of the two orders within this class the Atremata, of which *Lingula* is a notable member, possess a pedicle which passes out through an opening shared by both valves at the umbones. There is no deltidial structure. In the Neotremata, the pedicle emerges from the ventral valve. The members of the class Articulata possess hinge-teeth and the alimentary canal ends blindly. In the order Protremata the pedicle emerges through the delthyrium while in the Telotremata the pedicle opening is confined to the ventral valve and deltidial plates are developed. There are, of course, other important structures by means of which brachiopods are classified, but their description lies beyond the scope of this book.

The brachiopods are present as fossils in the earliest Cambrian rocks onwards and are still today represented by well over 100 living forms. Many groups have evolved and died out while others have persisted with little change. Of these, the most remarkable is the inarticulate brachiopod, *Lingula* which, living in the shallow-water muds of today's seas, is almost identical with the Cambrian form *Lingulella*—an example of an astonishingly conservative stock.

Mollusca. The classification of the Mollusca is as follows:

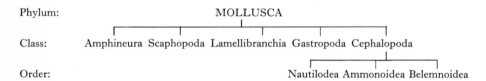

Phylum: MOLLUSCA

Class: Amphineura Scaphopoda Lamellibranchia Gastropoda Cephalopoda

Order: Nautilodea Ammonoidea Belemnoidea

The Lamellibranchia, the Gastropoda and the Cephalopoda are important. Of these, the Lamellibranchia (also referred to as Pelecypoda), like the Brachiopoda, are bi-valved shells and superficially the two may sometimes be confused. There are, however, very fundamental differences between the two groups both in the structure of the shells and in the anatomy of the organisms. Though most forms are marine, there are also some fresh-water lamellibranchs.

The two valves of the lamellibranch shell are, with certain exceptions, mirror-images of one another and are termed the LEFT and RIGHT VALVES. The umbo

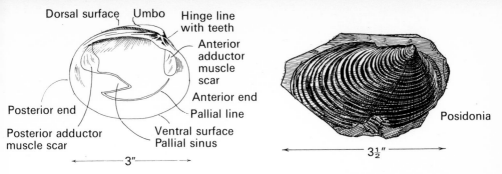

Dorsal surface Umbo Hinge line with teeth

Anterior adductor muscle scar

Anterior end

Pallial line

Posterior end

Posterior adductor muscle scar

Ventral surface

Pallial sinus

3"

Posidonia

3½"

248 The lamellibranch shell; an internal view of the left valve.

249 Posidonia.

of each valve, lying on the dorsal surface, generally points towards and is nearer to, the anterior end (figs. **234** and 248). The valves open at the ventral surface. They are united along the hinge-line by the so-called ELASTIC LIGAMENT, which is an elastic tissue lying partly internally and partly externally. This ligament keeps the valves open unless the adductor muscles are actively operating, since these muscles work by contracting. When there is only a single adductor muscle its point of attachment lies near the posterior end. Along the hinge-line of either valve there are numerous projections and depressions which, alternating with one another, provide articulation for the movements of the valves. These are known as the TEETH and SOCKETS. There are many variations in the pattern of the teeth, which are much more developed than in the brachiopods, and they play an important part in the classification of lamellibranchs.

The body of the lamellibranch is enclosed by the mantle and the lamella-like gills lie immediately within the mantle. Within the mantle-cavity there is a strong muscular organ, the FOOT. This can be thrust through at the margin of the two lobes of the mantle and is used for burrowing or even for propelling the shell forward in a series of rapid jumping movements. In a few forms the animal cements itself to the sea-floor. Along the posterior margin of the mantle there are two openings into one of which a current of water flows (created by the cilia action of the gills); through the other the water is expelled. This mechanism is incorporated into two adjacent tubes in some lamellibranchs, described as the BRANCHIAL SIPHON. The margin of the mantle is attached by muscles to the internal wall of each valve, and these muscles leave a depression, often preserved in the fossil specimen, which runs parallel with its margin. This depression is known as the PALLIAL LINE. The pallial line loops back in those forms which possess a branchial siphon, forming the PALLIAL SINUS (fig. 248).

The classification of the lamellibranchs is not easy. Some authorities make use of the pattern of the teeth, others the presence of one or more adductor muscles, while others regard the structure of the gills as an essential basis. Yet others consider the difference between free-moving and fixed forms as fundamental. Certainly the fixed form leads to the marked inequality of the valves and to the development of unusual types. In *Ostrea*, for example, the left valve is cemented

207

250 Successive lava flows forming features on the steep slopes above Glencoe; of Old Red Sandstone age.

to the sea-floor and it becomes thickened and rounded while the right valve degenerates to a mere lid (fig. **234**). This inequality is most marked in the Mesozoic rudistids, especially *Hippurites*, in which the right valve is fixed and grows upwards like a coral.

Lamellibranchs occur in Cambrian strata and numerous groups evolved during Palaeozoic times. In Mesozoic and Tertiary rocks they become abundant. Of the few fresh-water forms *Archanodon*, from the Old Red Sandstone, was probably the earliest. In the Coal Measures, *Carbonicola*, *Anthraconaia* and *Naiadites* among others are used as zone-fossils. They are fresh-water forms, as are some lamellibranchs found in Tertiary and Recent deposits.

Gastropoda. The Gastropoda are uni-valved organisms, for the shell consists of a single, usually expanding tube. The tube is open at one end and tapers at the other; in its simplest form it is represented by the hollow cone of *Patella* (fig. **234**). Generally, however, the tube is coiled in a spiral, with each coil or WHORL in contact with its neighbour (fig. 251a). The line of contact is described as the SUTURE. The tapering end of the shell is the APEX, while that part of the open end furthest from the apex is the BASE. The whorls together constitute the SPIRE. With the base pointing towards the viewer, the coiling is DEXTRAL; only rare forms show sinistral coiling. When the inner sectors of the whorls coalesce, they form a solid axis known as the COLUMELLA (this can be seen through the broken wall of *Buccinum*, fig. **234**) and the shell is described as IMPERFORATE; when a space is left at the centre between adjacent whorls, this is called the UMBILICUS and the shell is described as PERFORATE. This space may be filled with foreign material. The aperture of the gastropod shell may be circular, oval or slit-like. The outer and inner margins of the aperture are termed the OUTER LIP and INNER LIP respectively. The spire may be long and tapering or it may be short and stumpy, depending upon the rate of growth. In the former case, the SPIRAL ANGLE will be acute (*Turritella*); in the latter, obtuse (*Natica*, fig. 251b). Rarely, as in *Bellerophon*, the tube is coiled in a flat spiral. Ornamentation on the surface of the shell is common; ribs are said to be SPIRAL

251 The shells of (a) Turnitella (acute spiral angle), (b) Natica (obtuse spiral angle), and (c) Murex, showing spines.

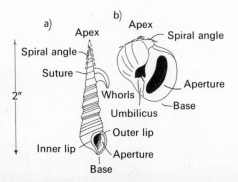

252 The living gastropod.

when parallel with the suture, and TRANSVERSE when crossing from one suture to the next. Spines are developed in some forms, as in *Murex* (fig. 251c). A flat plate, the OPERCULUM, is attached to the foot which, when the animal withdraws into the shell, almost completely closes the aperture.

The animal which occupied the gastropod shell is of more advanced form than that of the lamellibranch. It has a distinct head, at least one pair of tentacles and a pair of eyes (fig. 252). It moves by expanding and contracting its ventral surface, the foot (hence the name of the animal, 'belly-footed'), and the shell is carried on its dorsal surface. The gills are modified according as to whether the animal is aquatic or a land form like the snail. Gastropods are mainly marine but there are nevertheless numerous forms which live in fresh water, and a few which can live in both sea and river. In some forms the shell becomes degenerate and is represented by a tiny plate on the creature's dorsal surface; in others it is internal, as in the slug.

Gastropods occur right through the geological succession from the beginning of Cambrian times to the present day. For purposes of correlation they are among the less important groups. To the palaeontologist the form of the shell and the shape of the aperture are the most important features, whereas the generally accepted classification of these organisms among zoologists is based upon the structure of the soft parts of the body—of little value when dealing with extinct forms.

Cephalopoda. The extinct order, the Ammonoidea, is a key group in the zoning of the Mesozoic rocks. The members of a related order, the Nautiloidea, which has living representatives in the tropical seas of Asia, are important not so much in themselves but for the light which the study of them can throw upon the structure of the ammonoid shell.

The shell of both the Ammonoidea and the Nautiloidea consists of a tapering tube which may be either straight, or coiled in a flat spiral (fig. 253b). Only rarely is the spiral turreted or trochoid like that of the gastropods. In the coiled forms the adjacent whorls usually touch one another (though sometimes they are separated), forming a broad hollow on either side of the shell, which is described as the umbilicus. Sometimes the later whorls almost completely overlap the earlier ones as in *Pinacoceras* (fig. **234**), providing a deep and narrow umbilicus.

The tube itself is divided into CHAMBERS by a series of partitions or septa running from the ventral (outer) to the dorsal (inner) margin. The junction of each septum with the internal surface of the tube is described as the SEPTAL SUTURE, and is important in classification. The animal lives in the BODY CHAMBER, in front of the last septum. A cord passes from the body of the animal back through an aperture in each septum. This aperture is lined by a collar which is formed from a fold in the septum known as the SEPTAL NECK. The cord ends at the first chamber or PROTOCONCH. In *Nautilus* the cord, known as the SIPHUNCLE, is normally central.

Nautilus, in common with other cephalopods, is much more highly organised than either the lamellibranchs or the gastropods. There is a head with a pair of eyes and a beak-like mouth surrounded by tentacles (fig. 253a). A well-developed brain makes the cephalopod the most advanced of the invertebrate forms; it also numbers among the members of its class the giant squid—30 to 40 feet long— the largest of all the invertebrates. Records show that *Nautilus* can live in depths up to 1,800 feet. It is able to float since the chambers, filled with gas, give the necessary buoyancy.

Though the Nautiloidea attained their maximum development in the Silurian, they continued to flourish in Devonian and Carboniferous times. Comparatively few forms are found in Mesozoic rocks and only *Nautilus* itself, which first appeared in Trias times, continues in the form of several species, to the present day.

Of all the invertebrate fossil groups, the Ammonoidea are one of the most important and valuable to the palaeontologist. The structure of the shell is very similar to that of the Nautiloidea, but, during a much shorter time-span, the Ammonoidea produced a far greater variety of forms. The earliest of them appeared in the Devonian period. Of these, the most important are the goniatites (fig. 254a). These are small shells with septal sutures forming an angular pattern. This pattern, in common with all members of this group, can be clearly seen in an internal cast of the shell and is described in terms of SADDLES and LOBES; the lobes swing away from the mouth while the saddles are directed towards it. The siphuncle is generally near the ventral margin and the septal necks are

253a The living Nautilus.

253b The cephalopod shell.

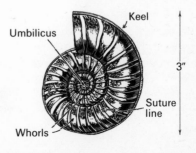

Keel

Umbilicus

3"

Suture line

Whorls

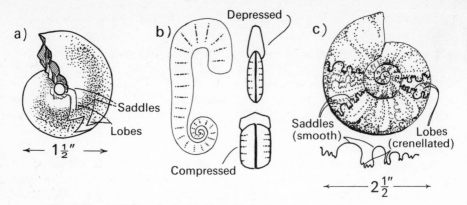

a)

Saddles

Lobes

$\longleftarrow 1\frac{1}{2}''\longrightarrow$

b)

Depressed

Compressed

c)

Saddles
(smooth)

Lobes
(crenellated)

$\longleftarrow 2\frac{1}{2}''\longrightarrow$

254 (a) The goniatite shell with its angled suture line. (b) Depressed, compressed and partially coiled forms of ammonite shell. (c) Ceratites, also showing the distinctive lobes and saddles of its suture lines.

usually directed backwards towards the protoconch. Goniatites are used as zonal fossils in the Devonian, Carboniferous and Permian.

In Trias times the so-called ceratitoid group also began to evolve, in which the septal suture develops remarkable convolutions, a character which reached its acme in the Trias form *Pinacoceras* (fig. **234**). In the ceratitoids, the saddles of the sutures are smooth while the lobes are crenellated (fig. 254c). The later groups, the Jurassic and Cretaceous ammonites, exhibit a bewildering variety of forms and, as with the ceratitoids, the variations in the pattern of the septal suture is an important diagnostic feature. In shape, the shell may be flattened (DEPRESSED), or rounded (COMPRESSED); adjacent whorls may overlap or only touch, the periphery of the shell may possess a KEEL or a MEDIAN GROOVE, while the surface of the shell may be smooth or strongly ornamented (COSTATE). Some forms, towards the end of their evolution, exhibit only partial coiling (fig. 254b).

In Britain, the Ammonoidea are important from Devonian times until the end of the Cretaceous, though they are completely absent from the non-marine Trias. Among the larger ammonite shells are those of *Perisphinctes*—2 feet in diameter —found in the Portland Stone of Dorset, in the Upper Jurassic system; while from the Continent, shells up to six feet across have been recorded. The Ammonoidea as a whole have been extensively studied and have been classified in considerable detail.

Belemnoidea. The common fossil remnant of these organisms consists of a straight, pencil-like structure, several inches in length, tapering at one end with a concave opening, or ALVEOLUS, at the other. It is described as a GUARD (fig. 255b). Sometimes within the alveolus a chambered structure, the PHRAGMOCONE (fig. 255a), is preserved. This has a pattern similar to that of the ammonite shell, but differs from it in that the siphuncle opening is along the

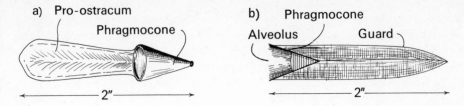

255 (a) The guard of a belemnite, and (b) the phragmocone.

ventral margin. The dorsal region of the phragmocone is extended as a spoon-shaped apparatus known as the PRO-OSTRACUM.

This skeletal apparatus of the belemnite was apparently entirely internal and the organism was related to the modern DIBRANCHIATE (two-gilled) squids and cuttle-fish. The classification of belemnite fossils relies on variations in the pattern of grooves on the guard. Belemnites first appear in early Trias and die out towards the end of the Cretaceous. They are used as zone fossils in part of the Cretaceous Chalk formation.

Trilobita. The classification of the Trilobita is as follows:

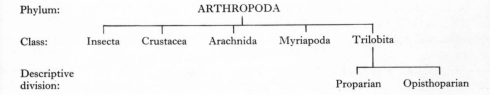

The body of the trilobite consists of three main parts, namely, the CEPHALON or head, the THORAX or body, and the PYGIDIUM or tail (fig. 256a). The head consists of a central GLABELLA and two lateral CHEEKS, the posterior angles of

256 (a) The trilobite skeleton, and two forms of Cambrian trilobite, (b) Olenus (the smaller), and (c) Paradoxides.

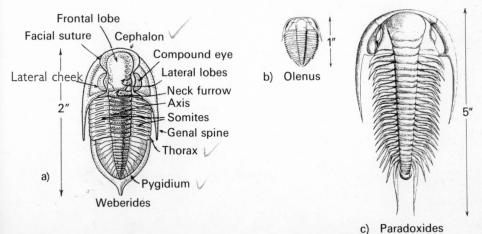

which are known as the GENAL ANGLES. The glabella is divided into a FRONTAL LOBE and several LATERAL LOBES by FURROWS and is bounded at the posterior end by the NECK FURROW. The marginal furrow borders the head both laterally and at the anterior end. An oblong plate attached to the anterior portion of the head is known as the LABRUM. The cheeks are each divided, by the FACIAL SUTURE, to form an INNER FIXED CHEEK and an OUTER FREE CHEEK. The COMPOUND EYE lies on the inner margin of the free cheek. In some forms (Paradoxides, fig. 256c) the genal angle is prolonged as a GENAL SPINE. The position of the posterior end of the facial suture is an important diagnostic feature in trilobites; when the suture joins the posterior border the organism is said to be OPISTHOPARIAN; when it terminates against the lateral border it is PROPARIAN. The cephalon was equipped with several pairs of appendages but very few specimens are preserved with them intact.

The thorax, like the cephalon, shows a three-fold division; the central raised portion is described as the AXIS and this is flanked by the two PLEURAL REGIONS. Both thorax and pygidium are divided into SOMITES or segments. There was a pair of limbs on the ventral surface of each somite of both the thorax and the pygidium. The cephalon, thorax and pygidium form the EXO-SKELETON of the trilobite; the latter, to allow movement, is thin and flexible between each somite. This is well illustrated by *Flexicalymene* in figure **235**. As the trilobite grew it regularly cast its exoskeleton, each time secreting a larger one until the adult stage was reached. This process is known as ECDYSIS or moulting.

Trilobites were bottom-living creatures and showed a remarkable degree of variation of form during their period of existence from Cambrian to Permian. Those living in deeper waters developed enormously enlarged compound eyes, or became completely blind. Others dwelling in bottom muds evolved eyes which became raised on stalks. The trilobites, of which there are a very large number of forms, are used extensively in zoning shallow-water deposits of the Lower Palaeozoic rocks. They became rare in the Carboniferous and barely survive into the Permian.

Graptoloidea. The classification of the Graptoloidea is as follows:

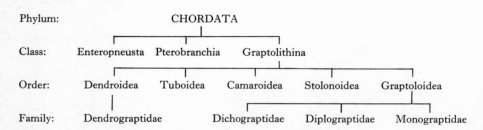

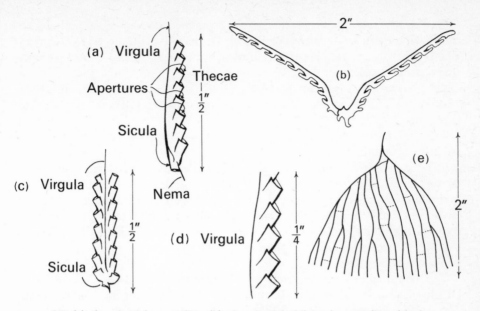

257 (a) A uniserial graptolite. (b) A uniserial, bilateral graptolite. (c) A biserial graptolite. (d) Details of a monograptid. (e) The many branched graptolite, Dictyonema.

The skeleton of the graptolite is described as the RHABDOSOME or POLY-PARY (fig. 257a). This includes the long, lath-like structure which supports the cups generally termed THECAE. Each theca opens internally into the COMMON CANAL which runs along the length of the structure. The opening or mouth of each theca varies in shape in different forms and has an important bearing upon classification, as does the actual shape of the theca itself. A rod or VIRGULA extends along the length of the structure and provided support; while at the base or PROXIMAL end of the rhabdosome there is a hollow cone described as the SICULA. In some forms a thread of NEMA projects beyond the sicula and provided a means of attachment.

There are three important families among the Graptoloidea. In the Dichograptidae the rhabdosome consists of two branches and is described as BILATERAL. Each branch, diverging from the sicula end, has its row of thecae facing inwards. In some genera, as in *Didymograptus*, the branches diverge in tuning-fork fashion and are said to be DEPENDANT (fig. **235**); in other species of this genus they extend outwards and are DEFLEXED, while in yet others they curve upwards and are RECLINED (fig. 257b).

In the family Diplograptidae the single branch possesses thecae on either side, and the rhabdosome is described as BISERIAL (fig. 257c). A well-known form is *Climacograptus rectangularis*, with characteristic square-shaped thecae. In some forms the rhabdosome divides into two branches at a certain point along its length. In others, numerous branches radiate out from a centre.

The third family, that of the Monograptidae, consists of an unbranched rhabdosome with a single row of thecae. In the genus *Monograptus* (figs. **235** and 257d) there are numerous species which can be identified according to the shape of the thecae and of the aperture.

Dictyonema (fig. 257e), in the family Dendroidea, is a multi-branched form. The branches unite at the sicula and are supported at intervals by transverse bars.

The Graptolithina were floating organisms which probably became attached to surface plankton. They are found chiefly in shales and occasionally in limestones. The chitinous substance of the skeleton was probably delicate and easily broken up. This might account for their absence in sandstones and sandy shales. As colonial organisms, the Graptolithina were for long considered to be Coelenterata, but detailed investigation has shown that they had important features in common with the Pterobranchia; they are therefore classed among the Chordata, primitive vertebrates. In this phylum, the Graptolithina are by far the most important fossil group.

The Graptoloidea extend from the Ordovician to the Devonian, while the Dendroidea appeared in late Cambrian and survived into the Carboniferous. The family Dichograptidae are confined to the Ordovician rocks while the Diplograptidae occur in the Ordovician and Silurian. The Monograptidae appeared in the Silurian and died out in the Devonian. There are a great many genera within these families and they play a most important part in the zoning of the argillaceous rocks of Lower Palaeozoic age.

THE VERTEBRATE GROUP

The study of vertebrate fossils is not usually included in a general course of geology, of which palaeontology only forms a part, and therefore only a brief reference will be made to the vertebrate group in this text.

Vertebrates play a much less important role than invertebrates in the geological succession as a whole. The earliest vertebrates, the fishes, are recorded in rocks of Ordovician age, but they became widespread only in Devonian times. The land animals, or tetrapods, represented first by the amphibians, appeared in the Upper Devonian and became firmly established in Permian times. The fossilised remains of birds occur first in rocks of Jurassic age, while mammals achieved ascendency only in Tertiary times.

However, there is a degree of continuity in the evolution of the vertebrates which appears less apparent in the invertebrate groups. The earliest of the fish, the ostracoderms, possessed an exoskeleton of hard scales. Others developed a cartilaginous internal skeleton which did not survive in the fossil state. Of the true bony fish, the Dipnoi are of importance in that they show a development in their internal structure which points towards a future replacement of gills by an air-breathing mechanism.

Some of the earliest amphibians possessed bony structures in the cranium which show links with the fishes; but these structures are absent in modern amphibians. Vestigial gill arches, too, are found in the ancient amphibians which are indicative of their fishy ancestry. Furthermore, some of the early fishes developed modifications in their limb structure which foreshadowed the amphibian limb.

The earliest reptiles, which appeared in Carboniferous Coal Measure times, shared certain features with the Amphibia; but they had already developed modifications in the arrangement of the bones of the skull which heralded true reptilian characters. The attitude of the reptilian limbs also evolved from a side-ways sprawl to a vertical position, while speed of movement was increased by the raising of the foot from a PLANTIGRADE (on the sole) to a DIGITIGRADE (on the toes) position.

During Mesozoic times a branch of the reptiles developed a flight membrane which stretched from the side of the body to the fore-limb, further supported by an enormously elongated fourth digit. This adaptation, typified in the ptero-dactyl, enabled the creature to pursue a gliding flight. *Archaeopteryx*, the first feathered vertebrate, may have been able to flap its wings, and is generally regarded as the ancestor of the birds.

The latest and most dramatic development in the evolutionary story is that embracing man himself. The remains of primitive forms of man are to be found in widely scattered deposits of Pleistocene age, that is, very young in terms of geochronology. In the reconstruction of the anatomy of primitive man and of the primitive apes, it has been shown that there are unmistakable signs of con-vergence towards a common stock from which each had sprung. The details in the search for this 'missing link' and the progress which has been made provide a fascinating story in the annals of scientific enquiry.

THE VEGETABLE KINGDOM

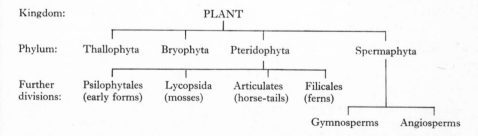

The growth of plants on land began in the Devonian period, and by Upper Carboniferous times a great variety of forms had developed (fig. **236**). Some of the Carboniferous plant groups have persisted to the present day but many have become extinct.

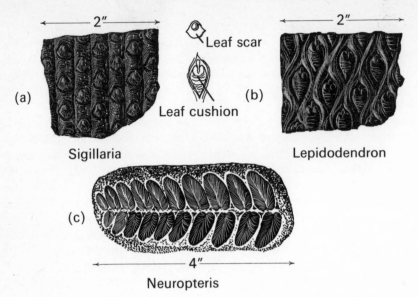

Leaf scar

Leaf cushion

(a) Sigillaria

(b) Lepidodendron

(c) Neuropteris

258 Carboniferous plants: (a) Sigillaria, (b) Lepidodendron, and (c) Neuropteris.

Among the Pteridophyta, the Lycopsida are represented in the fossil condition by three commonly occurring genera which (though they are the ancestors of the present lowly club-mosses) in Carboniferous times attained a height of 100 feet. Of these three types, *Lepidodendron* (fig. 258b) is easily recognised by the diamond-shaped pattern of its bark, provided by the shape of the LEAF CUSHIONS (each with its depression or LEAF SCAR). *Sigillaria* (fig. 258a) possesses a parallel-ribbed pattern with the leaf cushions lying alternately between the ribs. *Bothrodendron* also had a distinct bark pattern. The roots of *Lepidodendron*, named *Stigmaria*, show a spiral arrangement of scars, marking the points of attachment of the tiny rootlets.

Calamites, a tree which rose to a height of 50 feet, is the best known Carboniferous representative of the horse-tails. Its ribbed internal cast is broken by nodes and strongly resembles the pattern of the modern horse-tail.

The Pteridosperma are a group within the gymnosperms among which a number of leaf-types have been identified. These are often beautifully preserved by the process of carbonisation, so much so that the details of the venation within the leaf itself can still be seen. Among them *Neuropteris* (fig. 258c), and *Alethopteris* are characteristic (fig. **236**) as also are *Mariopteris* and *Sphenopteris*.

The Angiosperma probably began to evolve during Jurassic times and became abundant only during the Tertiary era. They include the grasses and flowering plants which dominate the modern scene. Before Tertiary times the downlands and the grasslands, as they are known especially in the world's temperate regions today, were among the features of the landscape yet to come.

259 Table showing the distribution of fossil groups throughout the geological succession.

IX. The Geological History of Britain

A man who lives for a century, with his mental faculties unimpaired, becomes a subject of interested and popular enquiry. He will recall the early years of the great railway lines, some of the first iron ships and the commercial development of electricity. He may even have conversed with Mr. Gladstone. He will have grown into manhood before the days of the popular newspaper.

Yet, in geological terms, a century is a mere moment of time. It is true that within the span of one hundred years, a few square miles of land here and there will have been submerged, by earth-movements, beneath the sea, and igneous activity will have created new volcanoes (like Paracutin) along the fringes of the great mountain chains. Certain landmarks may have slightly changed their shape; the roof of a sea-cave may have collapsed or a mountain rock-pinnacle may have fallen. But though many millions of tons of earth will have been transported from the high ground to the sea, and though the waves will have beaten constantly against the rocky headlands of the world, the changes will be barely discernible. An Old Testament poet, several thousand years ago, spoke of the everlasting hills; doubtless Mount Hermon, above the cedars of Lebanon, appears to the modern observer exactly as it did to the writer of the Psalms.

Nevertheless, over a span of 50,000 years significant changes can be shown to have occurred. Britain and the whole of northern Europe then lay hidden beneath the ice sheets; the North Sea was an ice-filled depression and the surface of the oceans lay several hundred feet below its present level. Many of today's offshore islands throughout the world were then connected to the mainland. The Mediterranean basin was probably the site of a few interconnected lakes.

However, the geologist collects data which spans more than 2,000 million years. He endeavours to assemble these data to form a coherent picture. That picture embraces the formation of mountain chains, the infilling of lakes and seas by terrigenous deposits, the development of new forms of life and the extinction of the old. Knowledge of the sequence of geological events, even in Britain after one hundred and fifty years of painstaking research, is far from complete. There are missing links not only in the evolution of life but in the known succession of the strata. Still, the broad catalogue of events over Britain (and in Europe and those parts of the world where geological exploration is sufficiently advanced) has been established, and it is the aim, in what follows, to give a brief summary of the record.

Time, in the geological sense, is sub-divided into ERAS. These eras, in order of decreasing antiquity, are the PRE-CAMBRIAN, the PALAEOZOIC, the MESOZOIC. the TERTIARY and the QUATERNARY. Each era is sub-divided into PERIODS. The succession of rocks laid down during one period of geological time comprises a SYSTEM. A system may contain a number of GROUPS or SERIES of rocks, each laid down during what is described as an EPOCH of time. The term STAGE is sometimes used to denote the sub-division of a system; it may be equivalent to a group or it may embrace several groups.

The study of the geological record indicates that in Lower Palaeozoic times, Cambrian to the end of the Silurian, Britain lay within the bounds of a great geosyncline. During the succeeding Devonian period, the great Caledonian orogenic upheavals transformed the region into a continent with intermontane basins, a continent which extended across northern Europe. The subsidence of that continent led to it being largely covered by the sea during Carboniferous times, only to emerge again during the Permian, after the onset of the Hercynian orogeny. A further marine invasion occurred early in Jurassic times and persisted almost continuously up to the end of the Cretaceous. By the early Tertiary, continental conditions had once more supervened and these conditions have prevailed, albeit with extensive and repeated changes in detail, up to the present day.

THE PRE-CAMBRIAN ERA

In regions where the rocks of the Pre-Cambrian era are well developed, it is possible to distinguish an ARCHAEOZOIC or older, and a PROTEROZOIC or newer system. The Archaeozoic rocks are generally highly disturbed and metamorphosed; those of the Proterozoic may show little or no sign of metamorphism.

There were several distinct orogenies during Pre-Cambrian times, and each was part of a great geosynclinal cycle. These cycles can be separately identified in regions where Pre-Cambrian rocks outcrop extensively, and it is clear that the processes by which the rocks of the earth's surface are being eroded today are similar to those which were active in those remote times.

The outcrops of Pre-Cambrian rocks in Britain are few and scattered; they include the LEWISIAN GNEISS and the TORRIDONIAN of North-west Scotland, possibly the schists of the Scottish Highlands and of Ireland, the schists of Anglesey and Cornwall and Devon, the igneous rocks of St. David's Peninsula in Wales, the LONGMYNDIAN and the URICONIAN of Shropshire, the CHARNIAN of the English Midlands. Of these groups of rocks, only the Torridonian, the Longmyndian and the Charnian are composed, wholly or in part, of unmetamorphosed sediments.

The Torridon Sandstone, a remarkably fine example of a very ancient, yet quite unmetamorphosed rock, is a compact, strongly indurated red or purple sandstone with well-developed current-bedding. It was deposited in shallow waters, from a source lying somewhere to the north-west. Frequently, the Torridonian contains beds of water-worn pebbles; but dreikanters have been found along certain horizons. Evidently the sandstone was laid down under water but bordered by deserts; in those days every land-mass was a desert and a further 200 million years were to pass before vegetation appeared on the earth.

The Pre-Cambrian succession differs from that of the succeeding eras in one important respect, namely, in the general absence of fossils. The abundance of life in the Palaeozoic era, and the overwhelming evidence in favour of the evolutionary process from Cambrian times onward, certainly lends credence to the view that the ancestors of the Cambrian fauna must have existed in at least Proterozoic seas, but that they lacked the hard skeletons developed by the Cambrian organisms. Indeed, impressions of worm tracks have frequently been recorded in the Pre-Cambrian rocks and these, though defying classification, point to the existence of primitive forms of life. Algal remains have been recorded from limestone rocks in North America, and coelenterates have been found in the Pre-Cambrian of southern Australia.

THE PALAEOZOIC ERA

Cambrian. The earliest deposits of Cambrian age in the North-west Highlands of Scotland are basal conglomerates, sandstones and quartzites, followed by the FUCOID BEDS and the SERPULITE GRIT, which yield the trilobite *Olenellus*. In South-east Ireland, the Cambrian is dominantly shaly, as is the upper part in North Wales where the graptolite, *Dictyonema* (fig. 257e), occurs. The lower and middle parts of the succession in North Wales are more sandy, and the latter contains the trilobite, *Paradoxides* (fig. 256c). In Shropshire and the Midlands of England, the horny brachiopod, *Lingulella*, and the trilobite, *Olenus* (fig. 256b— unknown in Scotland) occur in the Upper Cambrian.

The Cambrian sequence reaches a maximum thickness of 12,000 feet in North Wales; in the Welsh Borders it is only 1,500 feet and in the North-west Highlands, 2,000 feet thick. The Cambrian period, heralded in Scotland by conglomerates lying with strong unconformity upon the Pre-Cambrian, and represented by thick shales and greywackes in North Wales, marks the development of the Lower Palaeozoic geosyncline which was to endure for some 200 million years. The north-western shore of the geosyncline lay approximately across the line of the Outer Hebrides, while the south-eastern shore must have fringed South Wales and the Midlands (fig. **261**).

Ordovician. Ordovician times commenced in the North of Scotland with the deposition of the DURNESS LIMESTONE, a shallow-water facies which had probably already begun to be laid down in Cambrian times, since fragments of the Cambrian trilobite, *Paradoxides*, occur in it. In the upper part of this limestone, fauna of Lower Ordovician age is preserved and is similar to that in North America. In the Southern Uplands and in north-eastern Ireland, the

Ordovician succession begins with pelagic deposits similar to those of the Isle of Man. In the Lake District and in the Moffat region of the Southern Uplands, pelagic deposits persist through the whole of the Ordovician. The Moffat succession is rich in graptolites, including *Nemagraptus* and *Climacograptus* (fig. 235), while in the Lake District Didymograptidae have been recorded. In the Girvan area, however, north-west of Moffat, the Ordovician becomes progressively more neritic, and though graptolites are still found, a trilobite (*Trinucleus*) and brachipod (*Orthis*) fauna is predominant. At 5,000 feet, the Girvan Ordovician is ten times the thickness of that in the Moffat area.

There is evidence of shallow-water deposition in Anglesey where basal conglomerates are developed, and in the Wicklow region of Ireland; but graptolitic shales with Didymograptidae in the lower part and *Dicranograptus* above, are developed across most of North and South Wales. Only further east, in the Shropshire country, do shallow-water deposits occur, with the trilobite *Flexicalymene* and the brachiopods *Strophomena* and *Orthis*. The trilobite, *Neseuretus*, has also been recorded from the arenaceous Ordovician of Cornwall.

The Ordovician period differed from that of the Cambrian in the widespread volcanic activity which developed during its early history. This heralded the beginning of instability along the geosyncline which was to culminate later in the great Caledonian earth-movements. Volcanoes were particularly active in Wales, where the lavas of Snowdonia, 4,000 feet thick, were extruded, and in the Lake District, where 10,000 feet of BORROWDALE VOLCANICS today form much of the scenery for which that area is renowned. In Scotland, spilitic lavas were formed in the early Ordovician of the Ballantrae district.

The distribution of facies in the Ordovician of Britain indicates that though sedimentation continued into the Ordovician in the North-west Highlands, earth-movements produced elevation in North Scotland, so that by mid-Ordovician times the northern shore of the geosyncline lay not far north of Girvan. Furthermore, the development of neritic beds in Anglesey, and the local unconformity there below the Ordovician, suggests that earth-movement probably produced a ridge, dividing the geosyncline into a northern and a southern pelagic zone (fig. 262).

Silurian. By mid-Silurian times, there were distinct indications that the depositional phase of the Lower Palaeozoic geosyncline was drawing to a close. In the Southern Uplands the deposits had become predominantly greywackes, with monograptids of the *Monograptus priodon* type. Beds of the same age, though deposited under more pelagic conditions, were laid down in Northern Ireland. Graptolitic shales accumulated to a depth of 13,000 feet in the Lake District where they are zoned mainly by monograptids, and a similar pelagic succession was laid down in North and central Wales. In the Welsh Borderland, however, the Silurian consists of shallow-water beds, characterised especially by the limestones bearing the names of WOOLHOPE (with the trilobite *Illaenus*)

WENLOCK (with numerous species of the brachiodod, *Orthis*, and the trilobites *Flexicalymene* and *Dalmanites*) and AYMESTRY (rich in the brachiopods *Conchidium knighti* (fig. **235**), *Atrypa reticularis* and *Dayia navicula*). The shales above the Wenlock yield the lamellibranch, *Cardiola*, while at Dudley the limestone itself is rich in the trilobite *Flexicalymene*. Eurypterids, belonging to the class Arachnida, which includes spiders and scorpions, are generally represented by fragments which become abundant in the Upper Silurian. Corals, like *Halysites* (fig. **235**), become numerous.

The influence of the land to the north of Girvan was becoming increasingly apparent in the Silurian deposits of the Southern Uplands, as indicated by the presence of arenaceous material. The ridge which seems to have developed across Anglesey in Ordovician times had by now apparently extended across to northern England. Only limited areas of truly pelagic sedimentation remained—in Wales and in the southern Lake District, while the limestones of Shropshire marked the end of deposition in the south (fig. **263**).

The Caledonian Earth-movements. The onset of volcanic activity in Ordovician times, the uplift of northern Scotland and the development of elevated ridges within the geosyncline marked the beginning of the earth-movements which culminated in the mountain folding at the end of the Silurian. This was most intense in Scotland, and is described as the CALEDONIAN OROGENY.

The Lewisian Gneiss and the Torridon Sandstone of North-west Scotland formed the stable foreland against which the younger rocks on the east were compressed. The western limit of thrusting runs along a line parallel to the present west coast of Scotland, from Loch Eriboll to the Isle of Skye. The country round Assynt, where erosion has laid bare the succession of thrust masses, one overriding the other, is the classic area. It was here that Peach and Horne, the eminent Scottish field-geologists, unravelled the details of the complicated North-west Highland structures. Their results were published as a Memoir of the Geological Survey in 1907 (fig. **260**).

In the Assynt district, the three distinct areas of disturbance can be seen. First, there is the IMBRICATE zone, in which slices of Lewisian, Torridonian and Cambrian have been tilted and pushed over one another, and across the undisturbed foreland, along the plane known as the SOLE THRUST. Second, the GLENCOUL NAPPE lies upon the imbricate zone, having been thrust westwards. The BENMORE NAPPE has ridden over both. Fragments of the Benmore Nappe, known as KLIPPE, lie on the imbricate rocks, isolated from the main nappe by erosion. Both nappes are composed of readily identifiable Lewisian, Torridonian and Cambrian. Third, the MOINE NAPPE, composed of highly metamorphosed rocks—the MOINE SCHISTS—overlies the AUTOCHTHONOUS structures (structures formed of local rocks) from Eriboll to Skye, and no doubt formerly extended right across on to the undisturbed foreland. In fact, only in Assynt has erosion cut back the Moine Schists to expose the underlying thrusts.

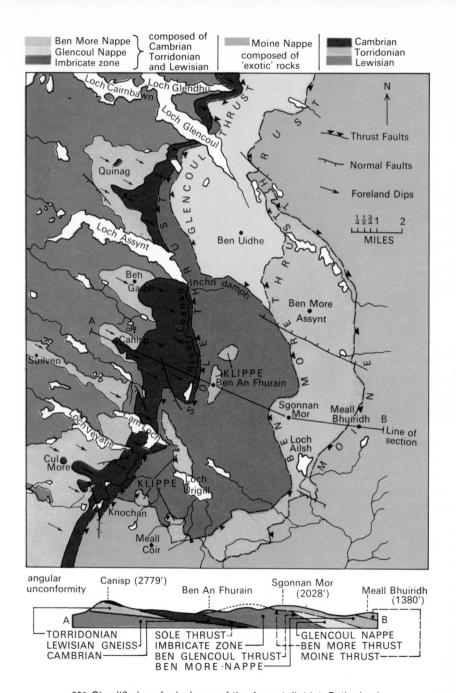

Ben More Nappe
Glencoul Nappe
Imbricate zone
} composed of Cambrian Torridonian and Lewisian

Moine Nappe composed of 'exotic' rocks

Cambrian
Torridonian
Lewisian

N

Loch Cairnbawn
Loch Glendhu
Loch Glencoul
GLENCOUL THRUST

Thrust Faults

Normal Faults

Foreland Dips

¼ ½ ¾ 1   2
MILES

Quinag

Loch Assynt

Ben Uidhe

GLENCOUL THRUST

Ben Garbh

Inchnadamph

River Loanan

SOLE THRUST

Ben More Assynt

MOINE THRUST

Canisp

Suilven

KLIPPE
Ben An Fhurain

Sgonnan Mor

Meall Bhuiridh

B
Line of section

Loch Veyatie

Cam Loch

Cul More

Loch Ailsh

MOINE THRUST

KLIPPE
Loch Urigill

Knockan

Meall Coir

A

angular unconformity   Canisp (2779′)   Ben An Fhurain   Sgonnan Mor (2028′)   Meall Bhuiridh (1380′)

A   B

TORRIDONIAN ┐
LEWISIAN GNEISS ┤
CAMBRIAN ┘

SOLE THRUST ┐
IMBRICATE ZONE ┤
BEN GLENCOUL THRUST ┘
BEN MORE NAPPE

GLENCOUL NAPPE
BEN MORE THRUST
MOINE THRUST

260 Simplified geological map of the Assynt district, Sutherland.

The Moine Schists outcrop eastwards over much of Scotland and consist of gneiss, schists and quartzites. Somewhat south of the Great Glen they are replaced by the DALRADIAN group of rather less metamorphosed rocks, including schists, phyllites quartzites and limestones. Both groups are generally thought to be Pre-Cambrian.

South of the HIGHLAND BOUNDARY FAULT (fig. **214**), the folded rocks of the Highlands are overlain by Upper Palaeozoic strata, but in the Southern Uplands the older, Lower Palaeozoic rocks outcrop. These rocks of the Southern Uplands are the shales, slates and greywackes of Lower Palaeozoic age. They exhibit faulting and folding, some of it isoclinal, and represent the zone within the geosyncline which was more remote from the foreland. Similar structures occur in the Lake District, the Isle of Man, Northern Ireland and North Wales; but in central and South Wales and in the western Midlands, the Lower Palaeozoic succession was less strongly affected by the Caledonian orogeny.

Devonian and Old Red Sandstone. These deposits mark the beginning of Upper Palaeozoic times. The strong Caledonian earth-movements transformed the geography of the British region. Where formerly there had been a low land-mass, now there was a folded mountain chain, and in place of the old geosynclinal sea there were now folded and faulted uplands. Marine conditions persisted only across what is today the south-west of England.

In Britain, there are two distinct facies belonging to the system of rocks which were laid down after the folding of the Lower Palaeozoic succession. In southern Scotland and over much of England these rocks are sandy, becoming conglo-meratic in the north near the Highland Border. In Devon and Cornwall they are marine. The northern facies is described as the Old Red Sandstone while its southern, marine equivalent is the Devonian.

The Old Red Sandstone deposits of England and Scotland were derived from the erosion of the Caledonian mountains. There were several great depressions (CUVETTES) within the mountainous region, namely, in North-east Scotland, in the Midland Valley of Scotland (which includes the Tay-Forth-Clyde region), in Northern Ireland and in the Border country. From time to time torrential deposits were swept into these mountain-girt basins, creating temporary lakes in what was generally an arid region. In Scotland, for example, im-mediately south of the Highland Border at Stonehaven, several thousand feet of conglomerates (fig. **4**) were laid down. These conglomerates are replaced by sandstones in the Midland Valley, while towards the English Border, shale intercalations become frequent. These Old Red Sandstone deposits lie with a strong angular unconformity upon the older, folded beds of Lower Palaeozoic age.

The fauna which survived under the rigorous Old Red Sandstone conditions in the north of Britain was more restricted than in the rocks of the Lower Palaeozoic; representative of the lamellibranchs is *Archanodon*, the fresh-water mussel. Marine creatures are absent, but fresh-water representatives of the eurypterids and fish occur; on the evidence of the latter, the succession in the Midland Valley and the Scottish Borders is divided into a Lower (with *Pteraspis* and *Cephalaspis lyelli*, the armoured fish) and an Upper Old Red Sandstone (with the ganoid, *Holoptychius*). This faunal change is reflected in a stratigraphical break, with an unconformity, between the Lower and Upper subdivisions. However, there is no fauna of Lower Old Red Sandstone age in the deposits of North-east Scotland, but a Middle or ORCADIAN division (containing *Coccosteus*) has been established there, followed by the Upper division.

South of the main influence of the Scottish mountains in central Britain, the retreat of the Silurian sea was marked by the formation of a series of transition beds. These beds are ascribed to the DOWNTONIAN stage, which is assigned to the earliest Devonian. They are well developed in the Welsh Borders. The LUDLOW BONE-BED marks the base of the Downtonian, and this is followed by about 200 feet of sandstones and shales containing a mixed marine and lagoonal fauna. This fauna includes the brachiopod, *Lingula*, the eurypterid *Pterygotus* and fish like *Thelodus, Birkenia* and *Cephalaspis*.

The Downtonian was followed by conditions in which a wide zone of lateral overlap existed between Old Red Sandstone and marine Devonian. For example, in South-west Ireland and in South Wales there are marine intercalations in the predominantly sandy facies, with brachiopods and corals; but the succession becomes marine in the upper part. As far south as North Devon the Old Red facies is sometimes present with the non-marine *Holoptychius*, in what was otherwise a marine environment.

The marine Devonian is present in Cornwall, Devon and West Somerset with the development of shales, limestones and some sandstones. Characteristically marine fauna, including brachiopods (*Stringocephalus, Spirifer verneuili, Rhynchonella cuboides*) and rugose corals (especially *Calceola*) occur. The Ammonites (*Agoniatites*) begin to appear in these rocks, but the graptolites (apart from the dendroids) had died out before the close of the Lower Devonian period. Trilobites, including *Phacops* (fig. **235**), were becoming less common and varied. A similar succession of marine Devonian was laid down over much of Europe. These deposits were, in fact, being deposited on the fringe of a newly developing geosyncline which extended across southern Europe into Asia. In this area, in contrast with the conditions in Scotland where the Caledonian earth-movements had folded the Lower Palaeozoic rocks, the Devonian lies conformably upon the older strata.

The main outbursts of igneous activity associated with the Caledonian movements took place during Lower Old Red Sandstone times. Lavas, which were mostly andesitic, were poured out from volcanic centres in Argyll, Ayrshire, Forfarshire, the Lothians and the Cheviots. Granite stocks were intruded into the folded schists all over northern Scotland and into the Lower Palaeozoic of South-west Scotland. The southern limit of these intrusions is marked by the

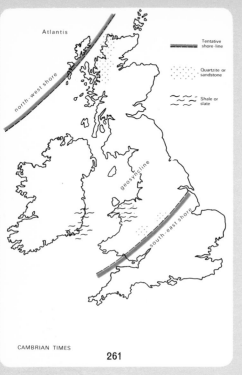

Atlantis

Tentative
shore-line

Quartzite or
sandstone

Shale or
slate

north-west shore

geosyncline

south-east shore

CAMBRIAN TIMES

261

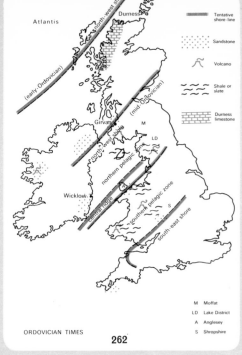

Atlantis

north-west shore

Durness

Tentative
shore-line

Sandstone

Volcano

Shale or
slate

Durness
limestone

(early Ordovician)

(mid Ordovician)

Girvan

M

LD

north-west shore

northern pelagic zone

Wicklow

central ridge

southern pelagic zone

S

south east shore

M   Moffat

LD Lake District

A   Anglesey

S   Shropshire

ORDOVICIAN TIMES

262

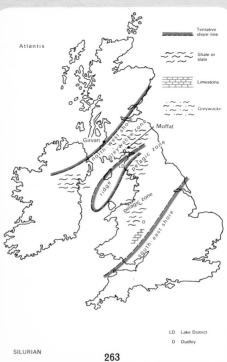

Atlantis

Tentative
shore-line

Shale or
slate

Limestone

Greywacke

Moffat

Girvan

north-west shore

greywacke zone

ridge

pelagic zone

pelagic zone

D

south east shore

LD Lake District

D   Dudley

SILURIAN

263

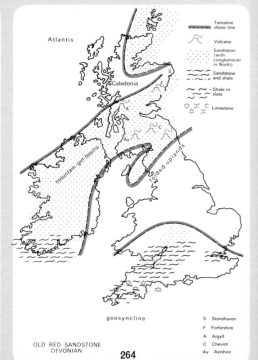

Atlantis

Caledonia

Tentative
shore-line

Volcano

Sandstone
(with
conglomerate
in North)

Sandstone
and shale

Shale or
slate

Limestone

S

F

A

C

Ay

mountain-girt basins

folded uplands

geosyncline

S   Stonehaven

F   Forfarshire

A   Argyll

C   Cheviot

Ay Ayrshire

OLD RED SANDSTONE
DEVONIAN

264

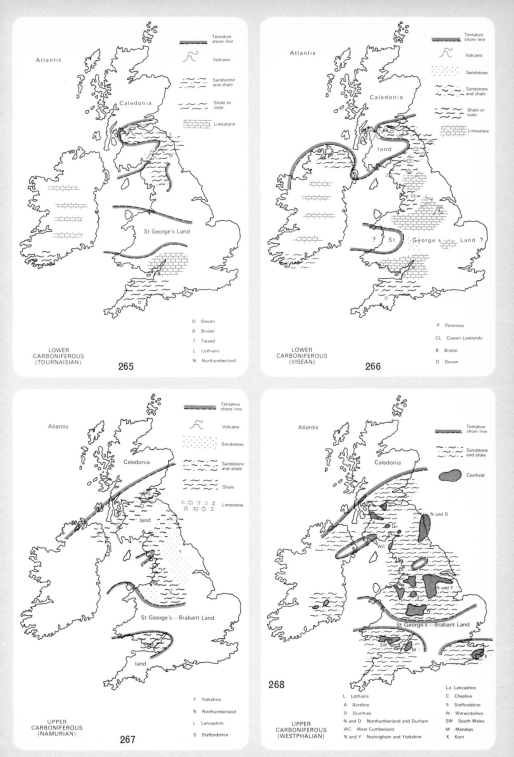

LOWER
CARBONIFEROUS
(TOURNAISIAN)

265

D Devon
B Bristol
T Tweed
L Lothians
N Northumberland

LOWER
CARBONIFEROUS
(VISÉAN)

266

P Pennines
CL Craven Lowlands
B Bristol
D Devon

UPPER
CARBONIFEROUS
(NAMURIAN)

267

Y Yorkshire
N Northumberland
L Lancashire
S Staffordshire

UPPER
CARBONIFEROUS
(WESTPHALIAN)

268

L Lothians
A Ayrshire
D Dumfries
N and D Northumberland and Durham
WC West Cumberland
N and Y Nottingham and Yorkshire

La Lancashire
C Cheshire
S Staffordshire
W Warwickshire
SW South Wales
M Mendips
K Kent

261–8 Sketchmaps illustrating the palaeogeography of Britain.

stocks at Shap, in the Cheviots and in Leinster (South-east Ireland). Widespread intrusions of dykes brought the Old Red igneous cycle to a close (figs. **214** and **264**).

Carboniferous. The Old Red Sandstone/Devonian geography—with its great land-mass extending across Scandinavia and most of Britain and with its open ocean covering the rest of Europe and beyond—underwent considerable change during early Carboniferous, marking the so-called DINANTIAN stage. A wide-spread transgression of the sea occurred and limestones, shales and sandstones were laid down in areas where formerly there had been land.

In the British area, mountain chains still extended across northern Scotland. The most northerly Carboniferous beds of Lower Dinantian, that is, of TOUR-NAISIAN age, are found in the Midland Valley where the succession includes shales and thin sandstones with occasional impure limestones. The latter, sometimes containing Algae and the brachiopod, *Syringothyris*, represent marine incursions in an otherwise lagoonal environment. These deposits extend southwards, as the CEMENTSTONE GROUP, into Northumberland. In the Tweed valley they lie conformably on the Upper Old Red Sandstone, but further west they overstep the Silurian. They are overlain throughout Northumberland by 1,000 feet of FELL SANDSTONES. These rocks, like a localised repetition of the Torridonian, are current-bedded throughout and are evidence of the continued strong influence of the northern land-mass. Fossils are very rare indeed, but the fresh-water *Archanodon* has been recorded. These sandstones are in turn overlain by a succession of shales, with occasional marine limestones, sandstones and coal seams constituting the SCREMERSTON COAL GROUP. In the Lothians of Scotland they are represented by the bituminous OIL SHALE GROUP.

In the Bristol area there is a complete succession of the Dinantian, lying con-formably upon the Devonian; it consists almost entirely of marine limestones with occasional shales. The limestones are coral-bearing, and with the brachio-pods they were used by Vaughan to zone the succession. These zones are represented by the corals *Kleistopora*, *Zaphrentis* and *Caninia*. In Devon, the succession is shaly with occasional sandstones, and is continuous with the underlying Devonian. This facies is known as the CULM and is indicative of the deposits on the edge of the geosyncline.

The Tournaisian stratigraphy indicates that the main areas of deposition lay in southern Scotland and northern England, much of Ireland, South Wales and South-west England. The Pennine region was apparently an area of uplift while a land-barrier (St. George's Land) probably extended from Wales across the Midlands (fig. **265**).

In the Scottish and Northumbrian regions the upper division of the Dinan-tian, the VISÉAN, consists of limestones and shales and sandstones with occasional coal seams. In the North Pennines, the base of the Viséan lies on Silurian and the limestones thicken southwards at the expense of the sandstones and shales.

Top of rhythm

- **Coal**
  - Current bedding
- **Sandstone**
- **Sandy shale**
- **Calcareous shale**
- **Limestone**

Base of rhythm

- **Coal**

269 Diagram illustrating a rhythmic sequence in the Carboniferous system.

Vaughan's coral zones—*Caninia, Seminula* and *Dibunophyllum*—are well represented here, together with abundant productid brachiopods (including *Gigantoproductus giganteus, Productus latissimus* and *Productus muricatus* (fig. 243), and the lamellibranch *Posidonia* (fig. 249). In the Pennines the Viséan attains a thickness of 2,000 feet, of which all but the upper 800 feet is continuous limestone. This upper division is made up of limestones, shales and sandstones, resembling the succession of the Tournaisian in Northumberland. It is described as the YOREDALE SERIES.

The Yoredalian succession demonstrates what has come to be known as a RHYTHMIC or CYCLIC sequence or CYCLOTHEM. When the sequence is complete, it consists of the following beds in ascending order: limestone, calcareous shale, sandy shale, sandstone, sandstone with current-bedding, seat earth, coal (fig. 269). The limestone indicates clear-water, marine conditions; the shale marks the approach of deltaic conditions while the current-bedded sandstone is evidence that the deposits had accumulated almost to water-level—a situation attained by the growth of vegetation and the subsequent formation of coal seams. Frequently, however, a cyclic sequence in the Yoredale type of succession is found to be incomplete, especially in the absence of one or other of the 'end-members', limestone or coal.

In the Craven Lowlands, the Viséan is represented by shales containing marine fauna, including the lamellibranch *Posidonia*, followed by the goniatite, *Eumorphoceras*, at the very top of the succession. These beds are the marine equivalents of the Yoredales.

In the South Pennines, the whole of the Viséan is predominantly limestone, as is also the case in the Bristol region. In Devon, the Viséan is represented by the culm facies.

There is little fundamental change in the Viséan geography compared with that of the Tournaisian; the Pennine ridge had now subsided so that

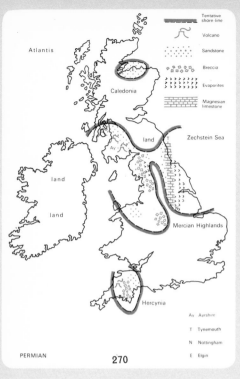
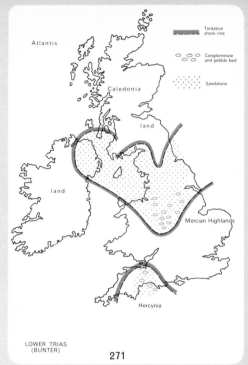
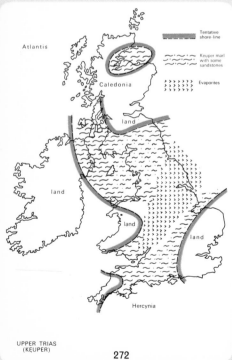

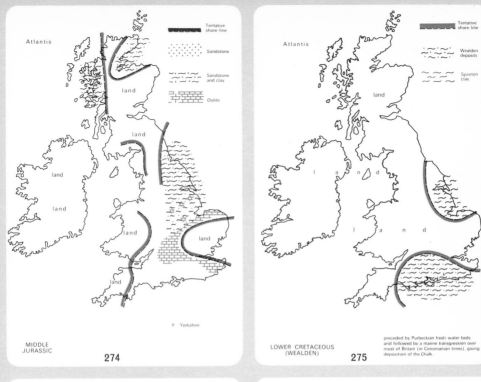

274

Atlantis

land

land

land

land

land

land

land

land

Tentative shore-line

Sandstone

Sandstone and clay

Oolite

MIDDLE JURASSIC

Y Yorkshire

Atlantis

land

l a n d

l a n d

Tentative shore-line

Wealden deposits

Speeton clay

LOWER CRETACEOUS (WEALDEN)

275

preceded by Purbeckian fresh-water beds and followed by a marine transgression over most of Britain (in Cenomanian times), giving deposition of the Chalk.

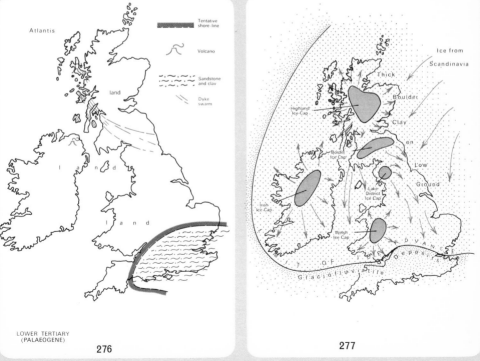

Atlantis

land

l a n d

l a n d

Tentative shore-line

Volcano

Sandstone and clay

Dyke swarm

LOWER TERTIARY (PALAEOGENE)

276

Ice from Scandinavia

Thick

Boulder

Clay

on

Low

Ground

Highland Ice-Cap

Border Ice-Cap

Lake District Ice-Cap

Irish Ice-Cap

Welsh Ice-Cap

LIMIT OF ICE ADVANCE

Glaciofluviatile Deposits

277

270–7 Sketchmaps illustrating the palaeogeography of Britain.

sedimentation took place over the whole region of Britain, except for the ridge across the western Midlands and Wales, which still persisted.

In Ireland, there appears to have been sedimentation throughout Tournaisian and Viséan times. In the extreme south, the culm series is developed; in the centre of the country there are limestones up to 3,000 feet thick with most of the fossil zones represented. In the extreme north, the succession is comparable to that in Northumberland and Scotland (fig. **266**).

The Upper Carboniferous in Britain is represented by the NAMURIAN and the WESTPHALIAN, of which the former consists largely of the MILLSTONE GRIT. Within the Millstone Grit several distinct facies occur. In Yorkshire it reaches its fullest development at over 3,000 feet and consists mainly of sandstones of the Fell and Torridon type, with current-bedding. In northern Durham and Northumberland, however, it is more a Yoredale type of deposit though with rare limestones. In Lancashire and Staffordshire it consists of dark shales and thin limestones (the BOWLAND SHALE facies) with a marine fauna of goniatites, of which the zone fossils are, in ascending order, *Eumorphoceras*, *Homoceras*, *Reticuloceras* and *Gastrioceras* (fig. **234**). In Scotland, limestone formations are developed, while in South Wales there is again marine sedimentation with goniatite shales.

Clearly the land to the north was still a dominant influence during Upper Carboniferous times and provided sediment which constitutes the arenaceous facies of the Millstone Grit. The deltaic conditions, however, were restricted and marine environments persisted at times in Scotland and across the north Midlands. The lack of sedimentation in all but the southern part of Wales suggests that St. George's Land still remained as an area above sea-level (fig. **267**).

The Westphalian consists of the COAL MEASURES, which are represented by shales, sandstones and coal seams, a typically deltaic facies. Calcareous rocks are rarely developed though marine invasions are indicated by the occurrence of beds with *Lingula*. During Coal Measure deposition, the water at times became sufficiently clear for the development of fresh-water lamellibranchs. In Britain, at least three divisions can be established by means of these lamellibranchs, which occur abundantly in certain thin shale horizons: In the Lower Coal Measures by *Carbonicola pseudorobusta*; in the Middle Measures by *Naiadites modiolaris*, and in the Upper by *Anthraconaia*. In addition there is a rich flora in the coal seams and zones with *Alethopteris*, *Neuropteris* (fig. **236**) and *Pecopteris* have been established.

The Coal Measure group may have been deposited over the whole of the north of England and of Ireland, but if so, subsequent erosion has removed much of the succession. There are working coal pits in these deposits in the Lothians of Scotland, in Ayrshire and Dumfries, while in England, the chief coal-mining areas are in Northumberland and Durham, West Cumberland, Nottingham and Yorkshire, Lancashire and Cheshire, Warwickshire and Staffordshire. In central Wales and the southern Midlands no deposits occur but in South Wales, the Mendips and Kent there are workable seams which are replaced southwards by the culm facies.

The stratigraphical evidence points to a general submergence of the land after Millstone Grit times, with the spread of deltaic conditions. Sandy material was still being brought down from the northern continent. St. George's Land still persisted across central Wales into England and beyond, to the Brabant, in Belgium, separating the southern areas of deposition from those on the north (fig. **268**).

There was considerable igneous activity during the Carboniferous period, in the form of both extrusions and minor intrusions. Basalt flows, dating from Tournaisian times, are found on either side of the border between England and Scotland and in the Midland Valley. In Viséan times there were repeated extrusions of porphyritic lavas across the Midland Valley from Edinburgh to the Isle of Arran. These lavas are mainly basaltic, many of them showing little alteration, in contrast to the andesites of Old Red Sandstone times. Volcanoes in Derbyshire were active during the Viséan, though on a much smaller scale; there the basalts and tuff are described as 'TOADSTONES'. Minor eruptions also occurred in the Isle of Man and in Somerset. Finally, in eastern Scotland, there were explosive eruptions of lava in Namurian times.

The Midland Valley of Scotland was also the centre of intrusive activity during Lower Carboniferous. Dykes and sills are chiefly dolerites. In Northumberland and Durham a group of west–east dykes was intruded during Permo-Carboniferous (fig. **19**), having the composition of quartz dolerite. They provided the material for the Great Whin Sill which outcrops across the two counties (fig. **20**).

The Hercynian Earth-movements. All through Devonian and Carboniferous times there had been a gradual accumulation of deposits in the geosynclinal trough which extended west–east through southernmost Ireland, South-west England and across Brittany into central Europe and Asia. As has been shown, the British Isles formed part of a shelf region during these times, with shallow seas and sometimes with wide areas of land. This shelf was subject to the repeated influx of arenaceous material brought down from the northern mountains of Caledonia.

However, the close of the Carboniferous period, like that of the Silurian long before it, was marked by the development of earth-movements which culminated in the growth of the HERCYNIAN orogeny and the establishment of the mountain chains of that name. This folding movement affected the rocks only across the southern fringe of the British Isles. The whole of the shelf region, with its older rocks strongly compacted by the Caledonian folding orogeny, formed part of the foreland against which the new, soft deposits of the geosyncline were compressed.

There are, therefore, two distinct patterns of disturbance in the rocks of Britain which are directly attributable to the Hercynian orogeny. First, south of a line running approximately west–east through southern Ireland and South

278 Exploitation of geology by modern technology: drilling for oil near Owerri, Eastern Nigeria.

279 Exploitation of geology by ancient craftsmen: the 'Treasury', Petra, Jordan, carved in Nubian Sandstone. The Nubian is a porous, thick-bedded sandstone which forms a cliff many hundreds of feet in height at Petra. Current-bedding can be seen on the weathered rock flanking the monument. This sandstone outcrops across Sinai and southern Egypt into the Sudan.

Wales and across the Bristol Channel, the Devonian and Carboniferous rocks are strongly folded and show low-grade metamorphism. The START THRUST, in Cornwall, is an example of the intensity of stress to which these rocks were subjected, while folding on a grander scale occurs in the same belt across Europe. Second, to the north of this line, movement of the strata was confined to gentle folding, faulting and tilting. As is usual when an old, well-fractured block of country is subjected to new earth-movements, the lines of disturbance tend to develop along the old trends. Thus, in Wales, the fault lines, especially the Stretton Fault, follow a Caledonian direction (generally described as 'CALEDONOID' to indicate direction rather than age), as do the powerful transcurrent faults, including that of the GREAT GLEN, in Scotland. The MALVERN FAULT, however, developed in a north–south direction while at Nuneaton and along the southern part of the Pennine axis, the trend lies west of north. In the northern Pennines and along the Scottish border, there is local evidence of thrusting, and possible transcurrent movements along the CRAVEN, DENT and PENNINE FAULTS (fig. 214).

Just as granitic intrusions in Scotland accompanied the Caledonian orogeny, so also the Hercynian mountain-building phase was marked by a series of major intrusions in South-west England. Including the Isles of Scilly, there are six great granite masses which are thought to be either of stock or laccolithic form. Unlike the Caledonian intrusions, there are no associated lava flows, but the Hercynian granites are cut by a series of dykes trending in an E.N.E.–W.S.W. direction. In the north-east of England doleritic intrusions, forming the west–east dykes and the Great Whin Sill, were widespread from Bamburgh southwards to Teesdale.

Permian. Before the earliest Permian beds began to be deposited, the youngest of the Coal Measure rocks, the RED BEDS of North Staffordshire, foreshadowed a change of climate. Coal seams now become rare and the succession shows that the deltaic environment was replaced by hot, arid conditions.

In the north-east of England, the earliest Permian deposits, the YELLOW SANDS, are dune-bedded sandstones with well-rounded grains. They outcrop as a narrow belt from Tynemouth to Nottingham and lie unconformably upon the tilted Coal Measures. Occasionally they are absent altogether, but in some areas they attain a thickness of 150 feet. They are completely barren of organic remains. Above them is the MARL SLATE, a shale succession rarely exceeding 30 feet in thickness, in which the scales of the fish *Palaeoniscus* are found. The Marl Slate is the British representative of the much thicker KUPFERSCHIEFER of the continent of Europe. The lower part of the Permian—the ROTHLIE-GENDE, is absent in Britain. The Marl Slate is in turn succeeded by the MAG-NESIAN LIMESTONE, 600 feet thick. Brachiopods, including *Horridonia*, and the lamellibranchs, *Schizodus* and *Bakewellia*, have been recorded from the Magnesian Limestone, together with the bryzoan, *Fenestella*. This limestone is subdivided according to its platy or brecciated nature, and is followed by up to 500 feet of anhydrite and salt deposits with marls.

In North-west England, the Permian deposits include breccia beds (fig. 5), locally known as 'BROCKRAM', and desert sandstones (the PENRITH SAND-STONES) which are nearly 1,000 feet thick. The HILTON PLANT BEDS, with their Permian flora, at 130 feet thick, belong to a higher horizon than the Marl Slate, while the Magnesian Limestone is almost entirely absent. Marls with gypsum, 250 feet thick, form the youngest Permian deposits.

Other areas of Permian deposition in Britain include North-east Scotland where, at Elgin, desert sandstones are developed, with reptilian remains. In the Midlands and South-west England, breccias and dune sandstones predominate. In Ireland there are late Permian deposits of Magnesian Limestone, while in southern Scotland sandstones occupy depressions in the Lower Palaeozoic floor.

Like the Old Red Sandstone in Scotland, the Permian succession in England was laid down in a group of inland depressions. The Pennine region separated a western from an eastern depression, and in the former the scree material from the hills probably helped to provide the material for the local brockram. Similarly, the breccias from the Midlands were derived from the high ground near by, described as the MERCIAN HIGHLANDS, while those of southernmost England came from the new continent of Hercynia. Only the eastern depression was connected to the sea, the ZECHSTEIN SEA, in which, extending across to Europe, thick limestones were formed. These limestones later became dolomitised. There were, however, times when the Zechstein Sea was cut off from its northern ocean, and intense evaporation caused the deposition of salt and anhydrite. Recent exploration for oil and gas has shown these deposits to be extensive under the North Sea (fig. 270).

Whereas the igneous intrusions of the north-east of England occurred before the deposition of the Permian, the extrusives of the Mauchline district of Ayrshire—including basaltic lavas and tuffs—were produced in early Permian times, from a large number of small vents. The only other known area of Permian igneous activity lies in the south-west of England where lava flows of widely varying chemical composition occur, known collectively as the 'EXETER TRAPS'.

THE MESOZOIC ERA

Trias. Local earth-movements at the end of Permian times led to some uplift in the Midlands and to the erosion of the youngest Permian beds before the deposition of the BUNTER PEBBLE BEDS and the succeeding BUNTER MOTTLED SANDSTONES. These arenaceous beds are widespread in the Midlands and south-west of England, and the alternation of water-laid sandstones with inter-calated conglomerates is reminiscent of the Old Red Sandstone of Scotland. In areas such as the north-west of England, the Midlands and the south-west, similar arenaceous sediments are characteristic of the Permian as well as of the

239

280 A diapiric salt dome at Tang-i-Angora, Persia. The watercourse has eroded along the line of the junction between the salt on the left and folded Eocene limestone on the right.

281 The field geologist's equipment: hammer, lens, clinometer for measuring the dip of the rocks, maps . . .

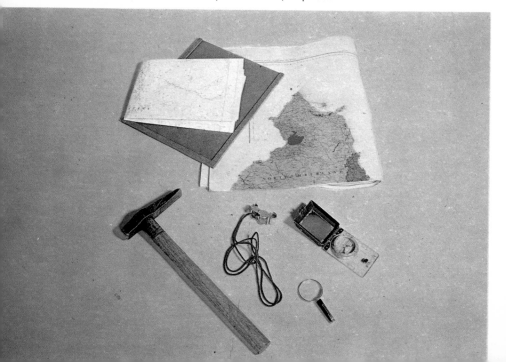

Trias, and the two formations, although belonging to different systems (indeed, to different eras) are grouped together as the New Red Sandstone.

On the continent of Europe, the Bunter beds are followed by a marine deposit known as the MUSCHELKALK. This group of rocks is unrepresented in Britain, where the KEUPER SANDSTONE lies directly upon the Bunter. The Keuper Sandstones overlap the Bunter; they are more widespread and the overlying KEUPER MARLS (which average about 1,000 feet thick), contain thick beds of rock-salt and gypsum.

Marine Trias is quite unknown in Britain. It was laid down within the TETHYS SEA across southern Europe (which was to endure throughout Mesozoic times) and yields a rich fauna. The British succession, being almost wholly continental, has a poor fauna. The bivalve crustacean, *Estheria*, occurs in the Keuper, wherein fragments of amphibian and reptilian bones have also been found. In some horizons, continental flora is represented by *Equisetites*.

The geography of the Trias period seems to have been very much a continuation of that of the Permian. The succession of water-laid sandstones and conglomerates instead of breccias and dune-bedding, indicates a higher rainfall with torrent streams pouring down from the Hercynian and Mercian Highlands on to the Trias plain. The overlap of the Keuper formations indicates an extension of the old Permian depressions, but the development of evaporite deposits in the Keuper Marls suggests that the depressions were, for the most part, landlocked. The similarity of the Trias deposits to those of the Old Red Sandstones (though the latter lack the products of intense evaporation), together with the abundance of red hematite staining, is evidence in favour of very similar geographical conditions (figs. **271** and **272**).

Jurassic. There is a very marked contrast between the deposits laid down in Trias times and those of the Jurassic across Britain. A series of dark marine shales, with limestones, marks the earliest Jurassic, known as the RHAETIC. These beds were laid down over much of England and parts of Scotland. Near the base of the Rhaetic, there is a well-known bone-bed, though its fauna is an impoverished one. A few lamellibranchs occur, such as *Pteria contorta*, *Chalmys* and *Protocardia*, which are also characteristic of the continental Rhaetic.

The Rhaetic is followed by a succession of shales with occasional limestones, often impure, which constitutes the LIAS or Lower Jurassic. This formation has an average thickness of about 500 feet, within which important bedded ironstones are developed. The Lias is subdivided into Lower, Middle and Upper. There is little variation in the lithology except in western Scotland, where some of the beds become more arenaceous. Ironstone deposits are well developed in the Middle group (fig. **273**).

In contrast to the Trias, the Lias is rich in marine fossil remains. Ammonites are especially abundant, and among them *Amaltheus*, *Dactylioceras* (fig. **234**) and *Harpoceras* are used as zone fossils. The lamellibranch, *Gryphaea incurva* (fig. **234**), is very common, as are the brachiopods *Spiriferina walcotti* (fig. **235**) and *Rhynchonella tetrahedra*. Among the few crinoids, *Pentacrinus* occurs.

The Middle Jurassic is divided into a lower, BAJOCIAN and an upper, BATHONIAN. Each group consists of a lower oolitic limestone (the INFERIOR OOLITE and the GREAT OOLITE respectively) followed by an estuarine series. The oolitic limestone, so-called from the ooliths (page 24) of which they are composed, contains shelly material while the estuarine material contains carbonaceous remains. The latter is well developed in Yorkshire where, indeed, the succession is reminiscent of that of the Carboniferous Coal Measures, except for its distinctive Jurassic flora (fig. **274**).

The abundant fauna of the Lias continues through the Middle Jurassic. Among the ammonites, *Parkinsonia* is an important zone fossil as is *Macrocephalites*. Of the lamellibranchs *Trigonia costata* and *Pholodomya* are common.

The Upper Jurassic consists of marine clays with sandy limestones (the OXFORDIAN) followed by coral and shelly limestones (the CORALLIAN). The overlying KIMMERIDGIAN is mainly shaly; this is followed by the PORTLANDIAN, which contains the well-known limestone of that name. The uppermost beds of the Jurassic in Britain are mostly fresh-water limestones, described as the PURBECKIAN.

The Upper Jurassic is notable for the development of the Scleractinia, especially in the Corallian, where *Isastrea* and *Thecosmilia* occur. The echinoids, *Hemicidaris intermedia* and *Cidaris florigemma* (fig. **233**) are common in the Corallian as are the ammonites *Perisphinctes* and *Cosmoceras*. Belemnites are also common while the Foraminifera occur throughout. The giant reptiles were evolving throughout the Jurassic, including the marine *Ichthyosaurus* and *Plesiosaurus*. In the fresh-water Purbeck Limestone the lamellibranchs *Unio* and the Gastropod *Viviparus* are present.

The end of Trias times was heralded by the transgression of an arm of the Tethys Sea over the old continental depressions. At first, during Rhaetic times, the sea was still partially landlocked, and life was consequently restricted. However, by Lias times, marine conditions had become widespread, and sluggish rivers brought down mud from the now low-lying Caledonia on the north, and Hercynia on the south. The Lias deposits are pelagic, whereas the oolites and estuarine series are neritic, indicating a shallowing of the sea. By the end of the Jurassic, much of Britain was land and the deposits, which were fresh-water, were confined to the south-east.

Cretaceous. The Cretaceous follows the Jurassic without unconformity. But the earliest deposits, of shales sandstones and lignites, known as the WEALDEN formation, are confined to the south-east of Britain. They contain plant remains, including the first of the flowering plants, the Angiosperms. A vertebrate fauna is also present, including the reptile *Iguanodon* and the fish *Lepidotus*, while the fresh-water invertebrates of the Jurassic still persist.

The Wealden deposits are followed by a rather more widespread succession of sandstone and shales, still bearing evidence of a deltaic environment, with a similar fossil assemblage. However, in Yorkshire and Lincolnshire, an entirely different facies of Lower Cretaceous is developed, known as the SPEETON CLAY. This is a marine succession which is zoned by means of its belemnite fauna (fig. 275).

The Upper Cretaceous is marked by the deposition of a marine shale, the GAULT, heralding the widespread marine transgression of the CENOMANIAN epoch. Important zone fossils include several belonging to the ammonite genus, *Hoplites* The CHALK, which is widespread and uniform in facies, was evidently laid down across most of Britain. In Northern Ireland it is preserved along the east coast while in western Scotland it is represented by a thin, sandy formation.

The main body of the Chalk, which attains an average thickness over eastern England of 2,000 feet, consists of minute fragments of shells and tests of Foraminifera amidst a fine matrix of precipitated calcium carbonate. Occasionally it becomes marly and certain horizons are rich in flint nodules. Ammonites are far less abundant than in the Jurassic and, apart from *Schloenbachia varians* at the base, zoning relies on the irregular echinoids *Micraster* (fig. 233), *Ananchytes* and *Holaster*, on the lamellibranch *Ostrea vesicularis* and on the brachiopods *Rhynchonella cuvieri* and *Terebratulina lata* and on certain belemnites. Corals are rare, but the crinoid *Marsupites* is an important fossil. The Chalk has also been zoned in detail by means of the Foraminifera.

The earliest Cretaceous rocks, confined as they are to the south-east of England, mark a continuation of the restricted area of deposition which characterised the late Jurassic. However, the deposition of the Gault and GREENSAND preceded the so-called Cenomanian transgression in which marine conditions spread westwards from the Tethys Sea, over almost the whole of Britain. Chalk is a pure form of calcium carbonate, and it is concluded that it was laid down in shallow seas free from mud, probably because of the desert areas by which they were surrounded. The Chalk is very widespread over both Europe and the Middle East.

THE TERTIARY ERA

The deposits belonging to the Tertiary era are classed as Lower or PALAEOGENE, and Upper or NEOGENE. The Palaeogene includes the EOCENE and OLIGOCENE systems, while the Neogene contains the MIOCENE and PLIOCENE. The Palaeogene rocks in Britain are confined to two basins in the south, the London and the Hampshire basins. In each, the Eocene is well developed and consists of an alternation of deltaic and marine deposits lying unconformably upon the Chalk. The marine sediments, of which the LONDON CLAY is an important member, are better developed in the east of the two basins, while the deltaic deposits like the READING BEDS, thicken towards the west. The Eocene succession is thicker and more complete in Hampshire and the Oligocene system is represented there though absent in the London basin.

There are no Miocene rocks in Britain but the Pliocene is represented in East Anglia by a series of sands rich in shells, described as 'crags', and followed by an estuarine formation—the CROMER FOREST BED—containing the remains of once-floating driftwood. This is succeeded by the morainic and boulder clay deposits laid down during the Ice Age which were spread over much of Britain and which belong to the Quaternary Era. The Ice Age is discussed below.

In addition to the sediments of the south of England, a great mass of igneous rocks of Tertiary age outcrops in Northern Ireland and in western Scotland. This igneous activity was part of the great Brito-Icelandic Province, which is still represented by volcanic eruptions in Iceland at the present time.

These igneous rocks, as has been mentioned in an earlier chapter (page 36), consist mainly of an enormous volume of plateau basalts which, at their time of extrusion, must have covered many thousands of square miles of what is now sea-bed between Ireland, Scotland and Iceland. The basalt probably reached the surface through dykes in the form of fissure eruptions; some of these dykes can clearly be seen penetrating earlier flows. Along the west coast of Scotland, many of the islands of the Inner Hebrides, including Skye, Eigg and Mull, are partly, if not largely built of the plateau basalts.

Intrusive igneous activity on a major scale also took place in these regions in Tertiary times. In Skye, for example, ultra-basic intrusions are followed by gabbros and granites. In Ardnamurchan, a complicated pattern of ring-dykes and cone-sheets was injected, while from Mull a dyke SWARM radiated out. Some of the individual dykes of this swarm reached as far as the north-east of England.

The Eocene contains a rich fauna though of a kind very different from that of the preceding Chalk. Instead of marine forms, brackish and fresh-water groups become dominant, including *Cerithium* among the gastropods and *Cardita* and *Cardium* (fig. **234**) among the lamellibranchs. Some marine forms, however, still persist, and the foraminifer, *Nummulites*, is abundant. The Pliocene of East Anglia contains many lamellibranchs and gastropods closely related to those found in the shallow and warmer seas of today.

The end of Cretaceous times was marked by a general uplift of the land and a retreat of the sea from most of Britain. Only the embayment of the great Tethys Sea to the south extended as far north as southern England, covering the London area and Hampshire. These two depressions had developed through earth-movements at the end of Cretaceous times, and the upper horizons of the Chalk had been eroded off the flanks of these depressions, so that Eocene beds were laid down upon them unconformably (fig. **276**).

However, it was during Miocene times that the great ALPINE orogeny developed well to the south of Britain, involving the thick Mesozoic deposits which had been laid down in the Tethys geosyncline. The trend of these folds lay broadly in an east–west direction. Several of them were initiated across southern England, including the Isle of Wight anticline, the Wealden anticline and the London and Hampshire synclines (fig. **214**). They mark the northern limit of the Alpine folds, and are of minor importance compared with the great nappe structures of the same age in the European Alps. In the north of England, movement was confined to the rejuvenation, sometimes extensive, along certain old fault lines, and to the outpouring of the basalts of the west of Scotland and Northern Ireland, as already described.

THE ICE AGE

In the long geological history of the earth, the present times are exceptional. Only rarely have ice sheets, ice caps or mountain glaciers developed upon the earth's surface. There are records of former ice ages—several in Pre-Cambrian times (including one just prior to the Cambrian period) and one during the Carboniferous period. The latest, whose initiation marks the beginning of the Pleistocene period, is often referred to as the Quaternary Ice Age. The Quaternary also includes the succeeding Holocene (or Recent) periods.

Geological dating by the most sophisticated methods indicates that the Ice Age began about two million years ago. There is no certainty about the reasons for its oncome. Some theories require the influence of extra-terrestrial factors—such as changes in the condition of the sun or in the concentrations of atmospheric dust—perhaps causing the known cooling of the oceans since Cretaceous times. Other theories indicate that the explanation may lie in movements of the earth's crust—the elevation of the Tertiary mountain chains, which would have lowered the land temperatures; or the emergence above sea-level of new landmasses with the consequent deflection of ocean currents; or even polar wandering. This last theory postulates a redistribution of land and sea in relation to the poles which may have led to more favourable conditions for precipitation and the isolation of cold air in those regions.

Though the reasons for the oncome of the Ice Age are speculative, the fact of the former existence of ice-fields over northern Europe and North America—and of glaciation in the mountainous regions of the world—is beyond dispute. The evidence shows that, over Britain, great glaciers from the highlands of Scotland spread south and were joined in their course by smaller glaciers which were nourished in the uplands of Cheviot, the Pennines, the Lake District and in the mountains of Wales. Moreover, the occurrence of erratics of larvikite (a well-known Norwegian syenite) in the glacial till of the Durham/Yorkshire coast is proof that a vast field of ice must have moved south-westwards from Norway, crossed the North Sea and linked up with the glaciers travelling down the east side of Britain (fig. **277**).

There were times during the Ice Age when the climate became more temperate and the ice retreated, only to be succeeded by a further onset of freezing conditions. These milder times constitute the INTERGLACIAL STAGES, of which four have for long been identified in Europe, namely, in decreasing age GUNZ, RISS, MINDEL, WÜRM. Recent research, however, has shown that even within each of these stages there have been intervals of time marked by the occurrence of glacial conditions—GLACIAL PHASES, followed by retreat of the ice—INTERSTADIALS.

The date of the 'ending' of the Ice Age was calculated early in the century by the Swede, De Geer, by means of sequences of VARVED CLAYS. He noted that during each summer melting, streams entering the Baltic marginal lake had deposited a layer of coarse sand followed by mud. Much of the latter was deposited slowly from suspension during the winter months, when frozen streams halted transport of further sandy material. Each season, therefore, was marked by a clearly recognisable pair of deposits, generally not exceeding $\frac{1}{2}$ inch in thickness—a light-coloured sand and a dark clay—constituting a varve. By counting up these varves and correlating them northwards towards the present ice-front, De Geer estimated that about 8,700 years had elapsed since the ice occupying Scandinavia had separated into two distinct ice-caps. This seemed a suitable point in time to mark the ending of the latest glacial phase.

More precise data has, however, been presented by W. D. Urry and his colleagues. He discovered that the proportions of certain isotopes of oxygen in a shell of calcium carbonate depends on the temperature of the water in which the organism secreted its shell. Therefore the temperature of that water can be calculated. Furthermore, the same shell substance may be tested for age by the RADIO-CARBON or CARBON-14 method. This method depends upon the knowledge that living organisms absorb from the atmosphere a certain amount of the isotope 'carbon 14'. Knowing the rate of decay of C^{14}, it is possible to determine the age of the shell substance. These two tests, taken together, have established that there was a significant rise in temperature of the oceans, of $4°C$ (from $6°$ to $10°C$), about 11,000 years ago. By this means, de Geer's original figure has been modified and the date of the end of the Pleistocene has been more precisely established.

The radio-carbon test can be successfully applied to deposits not exceeding 70,000 years old. Therefore it cannot be used to determine the date which would mark the beginning of the Pleistocene period, and the onset of the Ice Age. However, recent work on the dating of Pleistocene volcanics by means of potassium and argon isotopes within biotite and feldspar minerals, suggests that this period began at least two million years ago. As new techniques develop, no doubt the dating of the other great climatic changes within the Ice Age will become established.

However, it is not yet possible to predict future climatic changes, and the last chapter in the history of the Ice Age has still to be written. If the ice over the poles and in the mountainous regions of the world should finally melt away, the configuration of the coastlines would be altered beyond recognition. The level of the oceans and the seas of the world would, it has been estimated, rise about

100 feet through the addition of melt-waters from the ice-fields. For example, without allowing for further isostatic readjustment (which would certainly occur) the sea would encroach over much of the lowland area of Britain and many of the coastal centres of population would be engulfed. If, on the other hand, the full rigour of the Ice Age should once more come upon the world, much, if not the whole of Britain might once more be scraped clean of the works of man, of forests and grassland, of the fertile soil upon which so much of man's activities depends.

The evidence discussed in this chapter indicates that climatic changes do not come about rapidly. Such changes are measured, not in terms of a man's life-span, but in thousands of years. It may be, as some experts maintain, that if a series of thermo-nuclear bombs were exploded in the Arctic with the object of breaking up the ice, the ocean would be partly freed of ice. But this could lead to unexpected consequences; more of the sun's heat would be absorbed by the water, evaporation would increase and heavy precipitation, in the form of snow, might herald the formation of snowfields over Siberia and northern Canada. The consequences are as yet too uncertain for man to attempt to change the climate of the world.

THE BRITISH SCENE AND ITS ROCK FOUNDATION

The topographical map of the British Isles broadly reflects the geology. Either metamorphic or igneous rocks dominate the scene in the central and northern highlands of Scotland, in northern and south-eastern Ireland, in parts of the north-west and south-west of England and in western Wales. In all these regions the land is high, the soil poor and the ground uncultivated. On the other hand, sedimentary rocks occur over the whole of eastern and southern England, the Welsh borderlands, the Midlands, parts of northern England and across Ireland. In these regions the land is low, the soil rich and much of the ground is extensively cultivated (fig. 214).

The North-west Highlands of Scotland provide the most barren country in the whole of the kingdom. Here the intensely metamorphosed Lewisian Gneiss forms a poor base for the development of soil. A similar terrain, though far more mountainous, is that of the Torridon Sandstone which overlies the Lewisian and forms bare rocky crags rising to a height of 3,000 feet. The Torridonian generally consists of an unbroken succession of sandstone, but across the Stoer peninsula there is a development of a shaly facies which provides a comparatively rich soil. This forms gently undulating grassland in marked contrast to the rocky Lewisian near by (figs. 238 and 239).

The Moine and Dalradian highlands are also notable for their rugged topography, but the rocks are mainly overfolded schists and though bare crags are common, the soil cover is superior to that of the Lewisian. Deep fault depressions running north-east to south-west (page 238) each with its long narrow loch, dissect the highlands. It is a land of heather and moss, deer and sheep, with extensive views from its many mountain peaks (figs. **240** and **241**).

The Southern Uplands of Scotland are remarkable for their high grassy hills composed of strongly folded Lower Palaeozoic slates and greywackes. They extend in a broad belt, 50 miles wide, from North Berwick to the Mull of Galloway. Natural exposures of rock are few and the region is devoted almost entirely to sheep-rearing (fig. **245**). The topography is more rounded than that of the Highlands of Scotland, a reflection of the lower grade of metamorphism to which these rocks of the Southern Uplands have been subjected, and thus their poorer resistance to the forces of erosion. They form a similar type of scenery in the northern and southern areas of the English Lake District, in eastern Ireland and in northern Wales (fig. **244**). The Borrowdale volcanics of Ordovician age, in the central part of the Lake District, provide scenery more characteristic of the Scottish Highlands.

The Old Red Sandstone deposits in southern Scotland and the New Red Sandstones of central England provide rich, cultivated farmland, broken by occasional high ridges which mark the occurrence of thick interbedded sandstone formations. In the south of England and in South-west Ireland, where the Old Red or Devonian is strongly folded, the country becomes more hilly; while the extensive areas of lavas of Old Red Sandstone age which occur in the Cheviot Hills of northern England and in the Ochils and Sidlaws of the Midlands Valley of Scotland, are characterised by rounded grass-covered, but heather-free hills not unlike those of the Southern Uplands (fig. **246**).

Certain horizons of the Carboniferous system are dominated by thick sandstones; this is especially true of the Lower Carboniferous of Northumberland where the Fell Sandstones occur, and of the Upper Carboniferous of Yorkshire, where the Millstone Grit is widespread. These sandstones form uncultivated areas of heather and bracken, dominated by scars and dip slopes. The thick limestone formations, on the other hand, provide the grass-covered hills of the southern Pennines, with their extensive outcrops of well-jointed karst (fig. **247**). The Coal Measures contain a high proportion of shale which forms the low, uninteresting topography of much of the industrial areas of Britain.

The Magnesian Limestone of Permian age forms a westerly facing scarp across Durham county, while the oolitic limestones and the Chalk, of Jurassic and Cretaceous age respectively, each provide a prominent series of escarpments across eastern England. The downland of the thick Chalk succession, especially of the Chilterns and of the North and South Downs, provides a type of rolling, undulating topography unique to this formation.

The areas of Tertiary deposits are restricted to the sediments of the London and Hampshire basins and to the plateau basalts of Northern Ireland and the Inner Hebrides. The former deposits provide low, rich farmland, except where smothered by the London conurbation, while the plateau basalts, especially of Antrim, have created a rough countryside of heather-clad scarps and dip slopes.

The effects deriving from the Ice Age are confined in Britain to an area lying north of a line between the Severn and the Wash. The high ground, including the Highlands of Scotland, the Lake District and North Wales, has been eroded after the manner of mountain glaciation, and all the characteristic landforms derived from these processes may be recognised in these areas. However, the lower country was blanketed by ice during this time and much of the solid rock is covered by a thick deposit of boulder clay which completely masks the pre-glacial topography. In yet other areas, where the covering of boulder clay is no more than a few feet thick, the pre-glacial, angular scarps are reflected in the smooth-surfaced, asymmetrical ridges of boulder clay.

This is but a brief survey of the British scene, viewed through the geologist's eye. There is not space to discuss the great North-west Highland thrusts, revealed through vegetation and topographical changes; the sudden and dramatic contrast of the desolate Cross Fell moorlands with the adjacent downthrown, lush Eden vale; the granite tor-country of Dartmoor and the soft Mesozoic grasslands to the east. The geology of the countryside throughout the world, be it moorland, desert or jungle, can be analysed in all its detail; every hill, every depression, indeed every change of slope tells its story. But this is not an arm-chair study; it is a task for the hillside and mountain-top, where, given fair weather, the physical effort fully earns its reward.

X. Applied Geology

WATER SUPPLY

The conservation and distribution of water, both above and below the surface of the ground, is technically described under the term HYDROLOGY. Hydrology is becoming of increasing concern in the world's economy. The demands of industry in the developed countries of the world require ever-increasing supplies of water—demands which some authorities think will only be satisfied by the, as yet, highly expensive process of desalination of sea water. On the other hand, the poverty of the world's developing nations is at least in part due to their lack of knowledge of methods of water-finding and water-conservation. An important aspect of the work of U.N.E.S.C.O., one of the Specialised Agencies of the United Nations, is that which is concerned with hydrology. Trained hydrologists are employed by the Agency to advise governments of the newly independent countries on methods of increasing water-supply. With the co-operation of the engineer and the agriculturalist, a country with an inadequate or ill-conserved rainfall can have its economy transformed and the standard of living of its nationals raised to a level never before enjoyed.

Rainfall upon the face of the earth is dispersed either as FLOOD FLOW over the surface, by EVAPORATION back into the atmosphere or by PERCOLATION into the underlying rock. The degree of evaporation varies enormously according to climate. In hot regions of the world it may account for most of the total disposal, where rainfall is low; at the poles it is virtually nil; in Britain it is extremely low in winter months but rises considerably during summer. Dispersion is dependent, too, upon vegetation. Forests absorb rainfall and retain much of what would otherwise drain into streams or percolate into the underlying rock. Flood flow has been dealt with in an earlier chapter (page 129); the present discussion is concerned with the distribution of rain-water underground.

Rainfall which sinks into the rocks of the earth's crust is called GROUND-WATER. The presence of ground-water depends upon the texture of the rock.

282 Diagram of a block of sandstone, highly magnified, with the grains (a) poorly cemented, and (b) well cemented.

(a)

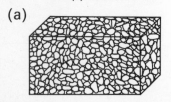

(b)

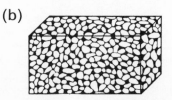

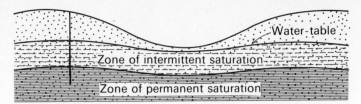

283 The water-table.

A sandstone, for example, may be highly PO RO US, and as such will act as a good reservoir rock or AQUIFER. The degree of porosity depends upon the packing of the grains, their absolute size as well as their variation in size, and upon the extent of cementation. A loosely packed sandstone, free from cementing material, may be 25 per cent porous. A sandstone whose grains are tightly packed has its porosity reduced thereby, while with variation in size, the smaller grains may partially occupy the pore spaces between the larger individuals. Cementation may reduce porosity to zero (fig. 282).

In a porous silt, the spaces between the grains are so minute that the forces of surface tension prevent water from entering the pore spaces. Therefore a silt, and likewise a clay, though it be porous, will be lacking in PERMEABILITY.

Other rocks, like limestones, are certainly non-porous, since their constituent grains interlock one with the other. But limestones are often extensively fissured and this inter-communicating network may support an ample supply of water (fig 287). Evaporite deposits are likewise non-porous and because they remain plastic they do not undergo fissuring. Again, all igneous rocks are non-porous, but if they too are fissured, they may act as aquifers, or they may be so deeply weathered as to become porous.

Water entering a thick formation of rock of uniform texture will fill it up to a certain level known as the WATER-TABLE. The water-table reflects approximately the undulations of the surface topography. Its level varies according to the season. In Britain it is high in winter, since lack of evaporation increases downward percolation. The ZONE OF NON-SATURATION lies above the water-table; the ZONE OF INTERMITTENT SATURATION is that between summer and winter levels of the water-table, while the ZONE OF PERMANENT SATURATION lies below the summer level. In order to ensure a constant supply of water, a well must be drilled into the zone of permanent saturation (fig. 283).

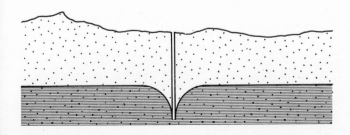

284 The cone of depression

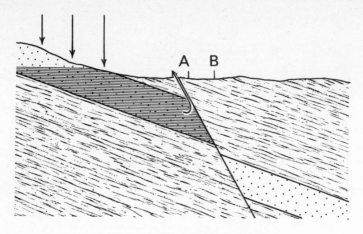

285 Water supply provided by faulting.

A water well will collect ground-water only from the immediate neighbour-hood of that well. Over-zealous pumping will pull the water-table down to form a CONE OF DEPRESSION, and the well will run dry (fig. 284). The water will slowly regain its level and pumping can then be renewed. But each time the rate of withdrawal exceeds the rate at which percolation can replace supply, the well will become exhausted.

Geological conditions—variations both in the composition of the rock and in its structure—generally complicate the simple picture described above. A sandstone aquifer, underlain by shale, may outcrop in an area above the level of the surrounding country. The dip of the sandstone may carry it far below the surface to a position where a fault brings it abruptly against an impervious layer

286 An aquifer insufficiently displaced to provide a water supply.

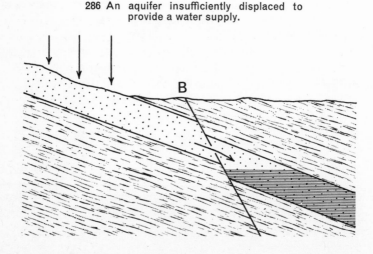

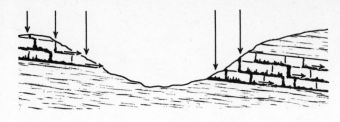

287 Escape of water from a limestone aquifer outcropping on a hillside.

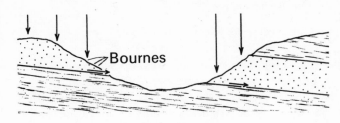

Bournes

288 Escape of water from a sandstone aquifer outcropping on a hillside.

of shale. Rain-water percolating downwards from outcrop will be halted on reaching the shale and may accumulate in the sandstone so that the head of water rises above the level of the surrounding lower ground. If the fault plane is not tight, water may rise up it and form a SPRING, or a line of springs, at the surface. In an attempt to increase the supply by drilling, it would be necessary to know the dip of the fault plane, since a well drilled at A would penetrate the aquifer, whereas one drilled at B would reach only the adjacent shale (fig. 285).

When a tilted aquifer, underlain by shale, outcrops on a hillside, water will escape from its base as a spring or series of springs. A thick sandstone with a wide catchment outcrop is often the source of a large and constant supply of water. After heavy rain, the water-table may rise above the level of a valley floor; a series of intermittent springs will then develop, known as BOURNES (figs. 287 and 288).

The siting of reservoirs is dependent upon the nature of the country-rock. If the rock which forms the floor of a proposed reservoir is an aquifer which outcrops down-dip in an adjacent valley, there will be constant leakage unless the aquifer is grouted with cement. Regions of igneous or metamorphic rock are chosen as the sites for the great reservoirs of the world, both because of the strength of the rock and because there is less likelihood of leakage. Yet even in the case of igneous and metamorphic rocks, jointing and fissuring may allow water to escape.

Under certain conditions, wells driven into an aquifer will produce not only a constant but also a free-flowing supply of water. Such a source is said to be ARTESIAN. Artesian supply is generally associated with a large-scale geological structure, like that in Australia, but technically any free-flowing supply, such

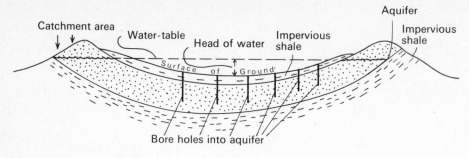

289 The conditions essential for an artesian supply.

as that described above (fig. 285) is artesian. In Australia, permeable rocks outcrop in the high mountainous region along the east of the continent, where rainfall is abundant. The rain-water percolates westwards down-dip into what is structurally part of a great basin, whose western lip outcrops above the level of the central desert. The permeable rocks are both underlain and overlain by impervious shales. In the centre of the basin the land surface is well below the level of the water which has accumulated within the aquifer. Therefore wells driven into the aquifer in this region provide an artesian supply. Several thousand wells in central Australia supply the needs of cattle in an area where there is little or no rainfall.

A similar geological structure in the Sahara involves the Nubian Sandstone (fig. **279**), a highly porous rock which overlies a basement of Pre-Cambrian granite and metamorphic rocks. The Nubian Sandstone outcrops in the southern part of the Sudan over which the monsoon rains fall. The rain-water percolates into the Nubian, which dips steadily towards the north. Above it lies Cretaceous shale. Beneath the arid Sahara, up to a thousand miles north of its outcrop, the Nubian Sandstone is involved in a series of anticlinal structures, some of which bring it to the surface. Therefore across each fold with outcropping Nubian there is a constant water supply—the essential conditions for a desert oasis (fig. 147).

A third example of an artesian supply comes from the London basin where fissured Chalk underlies London Clay but separated by the arenaceous Reading Beds. The Chalk forms the Chiltern Hills north of the London basin, while on the south it outcrops as the North Downs. Rain-water from these catchment areas percolates through the fissured Chalk and collects as an artesian supply. For many years artesian wells in the centre of London provided that city's water supply, and today many of these wells are still used as a reserve or emergency source. But the water requirements of London, or any of the world's industrial cities, have for long been beyond the capacity of ground-water accumulations to satisfy. Whereas a village or small town may still flourish on water from a local well, that for a city must be calculated in terms of bigger and better reservoirs, usually with heavy reliance also upon the nearest river.

The requirements for an artesian supply of water may be summarised as follows (fig. 289):

1. There must be adequate rainfall in the catchment area of outcrop of the aquifer.
2. There must be a suitable geological synclinal structure.
3. The outcrop of the aquifer must be above the level of the ground below which artesian supply is required (i.e. there must be a suitable head of water).
4. There must be impervious strata above and below the aquifer.
5. There must be no means of escape for the water other than through wells or, as in the Sahara, through an anticlinal fold.

OIL

The world's first oil-producing well was drilled in the year 1859, but the commercial demand for petroleum products began to grow only by the beginning of this century, following the invention of the internal combustion engine. Crude petroleum varies greatly in chemical composition from one oilfield to another, and almost invariably it has to be refined before its products are suitable for delivery to the world's markets.

The refined products include high-grade aviation fuels, the lower-grade 'petrols' suitable for the motor-car engine, the paraffins for diesel machines and jet engines, and the tars for road-surfacing. In addition, there is a large range of by-products from the refining of crude petroleum, from which articles like soap, dye-stuffs and plastics are produced. In recent years the manufacture of by-products has become an increasingly important part of the petroleum industry.

Like ground-water, petroleum is found in the pore-spaces of permeable sandstones or in the joints and cavities of dolomites and limestones; occasionally it occurs in the weathered margins of an igneous rock. Unlike ground-water, petroleum exhibits an almost universal tendency to rise or MIGRATE to the highest part of the so-called RESERVOIR ROCK. Therefore it is essential that the reservoir rock should be overlain by some impervious strata. In practice, it is found that either clay, or non-brittle shale or an evaporite deposit provides the most suitable CAP ROCK. Gas, representing the lightest fraction, is generally found associated with deposits of crude petroleum. It rises above the oil while the latter is usually underlain by salt water.

Many accumulations of commercially valuable oil deposits must have been dispersed and lost during geological time, because a lack of suitable trapping conditions allowed the oil to migrate to ground surface. Other reasons for the loss of oil may be that deep erosion eventually exposed the reservoir at the surface, or that intense folding of the rocks caused metamorphism and dispersion.

There must have been not only a suitable reservoir rock and a cap rock but also a structural oil trap to ensure that there has been a commercial accumulation

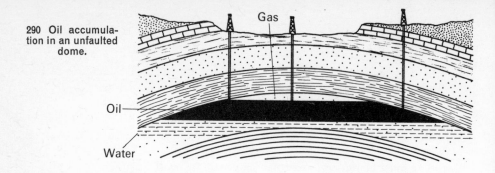

290 Oil accumulation in an unfaulted dome.

Gas

Oil

Water

of oil. Various types of geological structures provide suitable trapping conditions. The ideal structure is an unfaulted dome with the strata dipping away gently and symmetrically from the highest point or CULMINATION (fig. 290). An elongated dome or PERICLINE is also suitable as is any anticlinal structure which, perhaps with faulting, forms a trap against the further migration of oil. Other structures include those provided by faulting alone (fig. 291), by a buried unconformity (fig. 292) or by a salt dome (fig. 293). Deeply buried formations of salt are often forced upwards by the weight of overburden. They either arch up the overlying rocks or cut through them to the surface, where they appear as diapirs (fig. **280**). The size of area covered by a single oilfield therefore depends upon the nature of the geological structure; that of a pericline with steeply dipping flanks may be long and narrow while that of a dome of gently dipping strata may extend beneath many square miles of country. The volume of trapped oil depends not only upon the dimensions of the structure but also upon the permeability of the reservoir rock and the effectiveness of the cap rock.

During the past century, many theories have been evolved to account for the enormous deposits of petroleum which have accumulated within the earth's crust. In the early days of oil exploration some authorities considered that petroleum was formed through the heating of coal seams by igneous intrusions; others have maintained that the slow process of chemical change within a coal seam, without the assistance of igneous heat, could alone lead to the formation of liquid petroleum. However, it is now generally agreed that oil is derived from the decay and burial of the soft parts of organisms in an environment of rapidly forming marine muds. The fact is that all the world's great oil-fields are situated

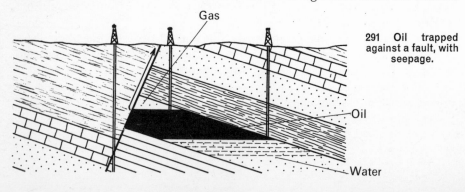

Gas

291 Oil trapped against a fault, with seepage.

Oil

Water

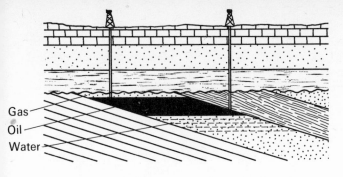

Gas
Oil
Water

292 Oil trapped beneath an unconformity.

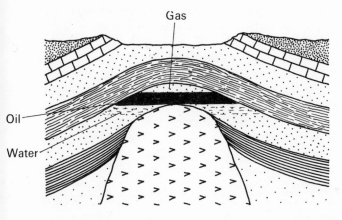

Gas

Oil

Water

293 Oil trapped in fold produced by a salt dome.

in regions where there is a thick geosynclinal development of marine shales, —generally dating back not earlier than the Mesozoic era. This is certainly true of the great oilfields of the Middle East, Burma, Assam, Indonesia, western Canada and the United States, and western South America. However, the precise chemical processes as a result of which the soft bodies of marine creatures have become transformed into crude petroleum is by no means yet understood.

The world's consumption of oil has multiplied several times in the past twenty years, and is likely to continue increasing even more rapidly in the future. On the other hand, the world's proven reserves are greater now than ever before and it is calculated that there would be sufficient crude petroleum to provide for the world's requirements until the beginning of the twenty-first century. Furthermore, new and more elaborate techniques are continuously being evolved for the recovery of oil from ever-increasing depths—20,000 feet is now by no means exceptional for an oil-well—and vast areas for exploration have been opened up since the introduction of offshore drilling.

The most remote parts of the earth are now accessible to the aeroplane with its cameras, and it has become routine practice for an oil company to produce a reconnaissance geological map of jungle or desert entirely by means of the laboratory study of air photographs. Use is also made of changes in the strength of the earth's magnetic and gravity fields; such changes can be recorded by sensitive geophysical instruments and may point to the presence of a geological structure in which oil may be trapped. The seismic method of exploration—in which vibrations from small explosive charges on the earth's surface are reflected from a recognisable geological horizon and are used to map it—is now in general use. It was by this technique that the gas-yielding structures under the North Sea have been located.

COAL

Over the past two generations, oil has become the chief source of power among the developed nations of the world, and in relation to oil the consumption of coal has declined. Oil is a product of marine conditions; coal is produced from the decay of vegetable material in a deltaic swamp. Coal seams, formed in layers like other sedimentary rocks, are easy to locate but much more difficult and costly to exploit, especially if the seams are thin. Oil, on the other hand, is extremely difficult and costly to find but very easy and cheap to exploit. The search for oil is beyond the resources of all but the most wealthy countries of the world; the location and estimation of size of a coal-field depends merely upon the existence of a reliable geological map. It is therefore not surprising that among the developing countries of the world, the exploitation of coal is rising.

As described elsewhere (page 231) a coal seam in situ represents the end member of a cyclothem. Its thickness depends upon the length of time during which the vegetation accumulated before subsidence of the land and its consequent burial under new deposits. It may be an inch thick or over six feet. Coal seams with a thickness of no more than 18 inches are mined. Seams which outcrop at the surface are gleaned by drift mining, in which an adit is cut down the dip slope, the coal being removed along the major joint planes. Deeper seams are exploited by sinking vertical shafts from which adits are cut down-dip or along the strike if the dip is high. Whereas coal was traditionally won by pick and shovel, much of the work in modern mines is mechanised and therefore productivity (quantity mined per man) has greatly increased.

In Britain, the need for increased supplies of coal during the second world war led to the establishment of open-cast working, where the coal was quarried rather than mined. This method proved economical in areas where there were a number of workable seams in a succession. Machinery was developed which could cut a cliff several hundred feet deep into the Measures, lifting off the overlying shales and sandstones before removing the coal.

Though coal and oil deposits seldom occur in juxtaposition, and have different origins, the occurrence of large quantities of gas beneath the North Sea and in North-west Germany and Holland is now thought to have been derived from coal. The gas is trapped in the Permian and in the Carboniferous Coal Measure sandstones, and it is suggested that the pressure and heat consequent upon deep burial of the coal has stimulated the evolution of gas. If this should prove to be the case, then gas-fields throughout the world in suitable geological structures, adjacent to buried coal-fields, may be more common than has hitherto been suspected.

ORE DEPOSITS

Over 99% of the weight of the earth's crust is made up of a very small number of commonly occurring elements. These elements, with their percentage proportions by weight as they occur in igneous rocks of the crust, are as follows:

	%		%
Oxygen	46	Sodium	3
Silicon	28	Potassium	2·5
Aluminium	8	Magnesium	2
Iron	5	Titanium	0·5
Calcium	4	All others: less than	1

They combine with one another to build the rock-forming minerals (pages 49 and 50).

Apart from the few metals in this list, those used in industry occur in the earth's crust in only minute proportions. Tin, for example, is one thousand times, and gold ten million times more rare than iron.

Most igneous rocks are therefore valueless as a source of metals of economic importance. However, natural processes within igneous magmas do sometimes produce a concentration of metalliferous minerals. When such concentrations are sufficiently high to make their exploitation economically worthwhile, they are described as ORES. Ores also occur in sedimentary rocks, due not only to sedimentary processes like evaporation and mechanical sorting, but also to chemical interaction between igneous and sedimentary material.

There have been a number of different bases of classification of ore deposits. One of the earliest of these depended upon the external form of the deposit—whether it was in beds, in veins or in irregular masses. All the later classifications, however, have been GENETIC, that is, based upon mode of origin; of these, one in common use divides ore deposits into those which are EPIGENETIC and those which are SYNGENETIC. Epigenetic ores include all those which occur in deposits older than themselves, while syngenetic deposits are those which were formed at or about the same time as the rock in which they themselves are found.

Epigenetic Deposits. When a magmatic intrusion is approaching final consolidation, gases rich in chemicals and under great pressure may force their way upwards into fissures in the adjacent rock. These gases generally contain compounds of boron, fluorine and silica, and they produce deposits or VEINS (sometimes referred to as LODES) within rock fissures. This is described as a PNEUMATOLYTIC process. In Cornwall, as has often been the case elsewhere, ascending gases reacted with granite, and veins of quartz, mica and topaz were deposited in an association described as GREISEN. When tourmaline predominates in such a reaction, the vein is described as the product of TOUR-MALINISATION. In addition to these GANGUE, or economically worthless minerals, metalliferous compounds including those of tin (cassiterite) and manganese (wolfram) may also be formed, as in Cornwall. A further reaction took place in that region, for hot gases attacked the feldspars in the granite with the result that they were reduced to kaolin or china clay, a process known as KAOLINISATION.

Another end-process in the consolidation of a magma involves the production of hot, watery solutions which force their way into fissures in much the same manner as the gases described above; they, too, may impregnate and react with the rock. The species of ore which are formed by these processes are known as HYDROTHERMAL deposits; they seem to vary according to the temperature of the waters. They include ores of copper, lead, mercury, silver, zinc. Certain tin-tungsten deposits are also thought to be derived from hydrothermal action (including perhaps some of those in Cornwall) for among a few minerals there is doubt about origin; it may be either hydrothermal or pneumatolytic. There is a close similarity in the pattern of deposits considered to be due to past hydrothermal activity with those associated with modern hot springs and geysers (fig. **40**).

The term METASOMATISM is used to describe those processes in which the country-rock has been partially or completely replaced through the chemical action of circulating solutions or gases, whether METEORIC (from the surface) or hydrothermal. PYROMETASOMATISM, which by definition excludes meteoric influences, is most apparent in regions close to igneous intrusions, especially at contacts between granite and limestone. Ore minerals which are particularly associated with this process include magnetite and hematite, pyrite and copper pyrite, blende, galena and cassiterite.

The SUPERGENE (also referred to as REPLACEMENT) deposits are formed by the action of descending (meteoric) waters. The outcrop of a mineral vein may be so badly weathered by oxidation as to form a crumbly mass known as GOSSAN

294 The enriching of an ore vein through leaching.

Gossan (mainly limonite)

Leached zone

Oxidised zone (malachite, native copper)

Water Table

Zone of secondary enrichment (chalcopyrite, etc.)

Primary ore (chalcopyrite, pyrite, etc.)

(fig. **139**). Leaching may occur below the gossan, leading to the concentration of ores at the level of the water-table, and known as the zone of SECONDARY ENRICHMENT (fig. 294). This zone is of great economic importance.

Another type of supergene deposit is formed when enriched surface waters react with the strata below. In West Cumberland, for example, the iron-charged waters from the New Red Sandstone have percolated down into the underlying Carboniferous limestone, where, in the form of hematite, the iron has replaced calcium carbonate. There are many examples of this kind of supergene deposit throughout the world.

Syngenetic Deposits. Among these deposits, the minerals concentrated in the lower layers of an igneous intrusion by gravitational differentiation (see page 50), otherwise MAGMATIC SEGREGATION, may be very important economically if metalliferous compounds are involved. Concentrations of chromite in the Bushveld gabbros of South Africa are considered to have been formed in this way.

In the period before a granite intrusion reaches final crystallisation, RESIDUAL LIQUORS are sometimes present; they are rich in volatile material. These mobile liquids deposit their material in veins which run through the body of the intrusion itself, and are classified as syngenetic. Sometimes they spread beyond the bounds of the intrusion, into the country-rock; they then become, technically, epigenetic deposits. The contents of these veins, which are notable because of the size of the crystals in them, are predominantly quartz, feldspar and mica. However, there may also be sufficient concentration of metalliferous compounds to form an ore. Of these, there are two varieties: pegmatites and aplites (page 53).

Most of the syngenetic deposits are those which have been formed by sedimentary processes. Evaporite deposits which owe their origin to chemical precipitation in inland lakes (page 25), are rich in calcium, magnesium, potassium and sodium salts. ALLUVIAL or PLACER deposits are often rich in those chemically stable ore minerals which have been weathered out from a decaying igneous mass, and then transported and deposited by water. Because of their density they have become concentrated in the beds of streams or in beach sands. They include the diamond deposits along the beaches of South-west Africa, the chromite sands of Oregon and the sands of Travancore, India, which contain monazite, ilmenite and zircon.

Sedimentary iron ores occur in association with the succession of the Coal Measures of Britain in the form of clay-ironstones, mainly as siderite (a carbonate). Formerly these deposits were extensively used in the smelting industry before means of transport enabled the use of richer, but more distant deposits. The Cleveland and Northamptonshire ironstones, of Lower and Middle Jurassic age respectively, are both oolitic, in the form of siderite and chamosite, a hydrated iron silicate. Bog-iron ore, or limonite, also occurs in these deposits. Pyrite is also a common ironstone deposit (fig. **114**).

295 Quarrying the Portland Stone. Blocks of stone are removed after wedging apart the rock along the joint planes. (From a photograph in Holmes' *Principles of Physical Geology*)

BUILDING MATERIALS IN BRITAIN

In the past, of all the rocks used for building, sandstones have been the most important. The best sandstones (or FREESTONES, as they are often called) are well cemented, for they should be impervious to water and to the action of frost. They must be non-micaceous, otherwise they would readily split and crumble away.

Pure-quality sandstones, containing very little clay, described as GANISTERS, are used as refractory bricks in steel furnaces. Extremely pure sandstones, with a composition of 99% silica, are used in the manufacture of glass.

Among the limestones, the white Portland stone and the oolitic limestones, both from the Jurassic (page 242 and fig. 10) are among the best-known building-stones in Britain. Limestones, especially the Permian Magnesian Limestone, is also used extensively in agriculture. Igneous rocks are less often used as building materials, except locally where granite stocks outcrop, as at Aberdeen and Dalbeattie in Scotland, and in South-west England. Brick has long since become a universal building material and its ingredients are quarried especially in the clay pits of the Jurassic and from many deposits of glacial till.

Old farm buildings in Britain still have their heavy stone-flagged roofs, but where the modern artificial tile is not in use, the blue Welsh slates from the Lower Palaeozoics (page 57) and the thicker green, ashy slate, from the Ordovician Borrowdale volcanics of the Lake District, may still be employed.

River gravel and sand throughout the country is collected extensively for concrete manufacture. Igneous dykes, sills and occasionally lava flows are used as a source of chips for road metal. Granite and dolerite curb-stones have mostly been replaced by the inferior cement slabs, while the Caithness flag has long since been superseded by the ubiquitous cement square.

FURTHER READING

INTRODUCTION. *The Birth and Development of the Geological Sciences* by F. D. Adams—Baillière, Tindall and Cox, 1938.

The Nature of the Physical World by A. S. Eddington—Everyman's Library (Dent), 1935.

Science, Faith and Society by M. Polanyi—Riddell Memorial Lectures, University of Durham. O.U.P., 1946.

CHAPTER I. *Sedimentary Rocks* by F. J. Pettijohn—Harper and Bros., 1957.

CHAPTER II. *Petrology for Students* by A. Harker, revised by C. E. Tilley, S. R. Nockolds and M. Black—Cambridge University Press, 5th ed., 1954.

CHAPTER III. *Metamorphism* by A. Harker—Methuen, 3rd ed., 1950.

CHAPTER IV. *An Introduction to Crystallography* by F. C. Phillips—Longmans, Green and Co., 2nd ed., 1956

Rutley's Elements of Mineralogy by H. H. Read—Thomas Murby, 25th ed., 1962.

Minerals and the Microscope by H. G. Smith, revised by M. K. Wells—Thomas Murby, 4th ed., 1956.

CHAPTER V. *Principles of Physical Geology* by A. Holmes—Nelson, 1965.

The Face of the Earth by G. Dury—Pelican Books, 1959.

CHAPTER VI. *Outlines of Structural Geology* by E. S. Hills—Methuen, 3rd ed., 1953

CHAPTER VII. *Principles of Physical Geology* by A. Holmes—Nelson, 1965.

CHAPTER VIII. *Introduction to Palaeontology* by A. Morley Davies, revised by C. J. Stubblefield—George Allen and Unwin, 3rd ed., 1961.

Palaeontology Invertebrate by Henry Woods—Cambridge University Press, 8th ed., 1963.

Fossils in Colour by J. F. Kirkaldy—Blandford Press, 1967.

FURTHER READING—*continued*

CHAPTER IX. *The Physiographical Evolution of Britain* by L. J. Wills—Arnold, 1929.

Palaeogeographical Atlas by L. J. Wills—Blackie, 1951.
Stratigraphic Geology by Maurice Gignoux—Freeman, 1955.
The Stratigraphy of the British Isles by D. H. Raynor—Cambridge University Press, 1967.

Geology and Scenery in England and Wales by A. E. Trueman—Pelican Books, 1949.

CHAPTER X. *Principles of Physical Geology* by A. Holmes—Nelson, 1965.

Index

(Names of stratigraphical divisions in italic)

266